The Employment Impac
China's WTO Accession

GW01418736

The book explores the macroeconomic (trade and investment liberalization) and sectoral employment (in agriculture, industry and services) implications, of China's accession to the World Trade Organization. It argues that short-run employment losses may occur due to global competition, the phasing out of protection under WTO rules and the restructuring of state-owned enterprises. It discusses three possible measures to protect employment against competition: devaluation, non-compliance and a production shift from tradeables to non-tradeables. The book argues that the first two measures are unlikely while the third is feasible in a large country like China. In the longer term China will be able to generate additional employment particularly in the tertiary sectors. It will also be able to maintain its comparative advantage in labour-intensive exports by relocating production from the high-cost coastal areas to the labour-abundant, lower-cost hinterland.

A.S. Bhalla is an Economic Consultant based in Geneva. He was formerly Fellow of Sidney Sussex College, University of Cambridge, and Special Adviser to the President of IDRC (Canada). He has held academic positions at the universities of Manchester, Oxford and Yale. His fields of specialization include comparative economic development, poverty alleviation, and globalization.

Shufang Qiu is an Economic and Business Consultant based in Cambridge, UK. He has worked for the Chinese Government on economic reforms. His research interests include poverty alleviation, the World Trade Organization and economic transition in China.

Also by A.S. Bhalla

Blending of New and Traditional Technologies (co-editor)

Economic Transition in Hunan and Southern China

Environment, Employment and Development (editor) (also in Portuguese)

Facing the Technological Challenge

Globalization, Growth and Marginalization (editor) (also in French)

Market or Government Failures? An Asian Perspective

New Technologies and Development (co-editor)

Poverty and Exclusion in a Global World (co-author)

Regional Blocs: Building Blocks or Stumbling Blocks?

Small and Medium Enterprises: Technology Policies and Options (editor)

Technological Transformation of Rural India (co-editor)

Technology and Employment in Industry (editor) (also in Spanish)

Towards Global Action for Appropriate Technology (editor)

Uneven Development in the Third World

RoutledgeCurzon studies on the Chinese economy
Series editors
Peter Nolan
University of Cambridge
Dong Fureng
Beijing University

The aim of this series is to publish original, high-quality, research-level work by both new and established scholars in the West and the East, on all aspects of the Chinese economy, including studies of business and economic history.

The Employment Impact of China's WTO Accession

A.S. Bhalla and Shufang Qiu

Routledge
Taylor & Francis Group

LONDON AND NEW YORK

To our wives Praveen and Hazel

First published 2004 by Routledge

2 Park Square, Milton Park, Abingdon, Oxfordshire OX14 4RN
711 Third Avenue, New York, NY 10017

Routledge is an imprint of the Taylor & Francis Group, an informa business

First issued in paperback 2018

Typeset in Times by LaserScript Ltd, Mitcham, Surrey

British Library Cataloguing in Publication Data
A catalogue record for this book is available from the British Library

Library of Congress Cataloging in Publication Data
A catalog record for this book has been requested

ISBN 978-0-415-30839-7 (hbk)
ISBN 978-1-138-37124-8 (pbk)

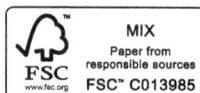

MIX
Paper from
responsible sources
FSC
www.fsc.org   FSC™ C013985

Printed in the United Kingdom
by Henry Ling Limited

Contents

Figures

Tables

Preface

In this book we are concerned mainly with trade liberalization as required under the WTO rules, competition and its impact on employment in the Chinese economy with particular reference to the industrial sector and State-owned Enterprises (SOEs). It is often claimed that WTO membership will benefit China by increasing exports and employment and forcing domestic firms to improve efficiency through competition, and that benefits will accrue through improved resource allocation and greater economic efficiency resulting from trade liberalization and greater global competition. We argue that *net* overall benefits will accrue only in the long run. In the short term, some sectors will benefit from competition but others will suffer a great deal. Tariff reductions agreed under the WTO Protocol of Accession could force some weak domestic firms to close, thereby contributing to unemployment. Although trade will expand after accession, this will be less important for a large-sized country like China with its huge domestic market than it is for smaller economies. At any rate, depending on the particular sectors exports will expand with a time lag due to capacity and other constraints. During the transition period China will face enormous problems related to the restructuring of SOEs, and banking, insurance and financial services, entailing loss of employment.

Western and Chinese literature has thus far neglected an analysis of such social effects of accession as unemployment and income inequalities, which, we believe will present a major challenge to Chinese politicians and policy-makers. This book is a modest attempt to overcome this lacuna.

The book addresses three sets of related issues: (i) the employment impact of China's accession to the WTO; (ii) the applicability of a 'flying-geese model' of trade and development within China whereby low labour costs in the hinterland would help maintain its comparative advantage and global competitiveness; (iii) China's possible response to global competition which might aggravate the serious unemployment problem especially resulting from the closure of inefficient SOEs. Some observers believe that social hardships resulting from accession may trigger a drastic response by China. We study three possible scenarios here: (i) non-compliance of the WTO Agreement, (ii) devaluation to protect inefficient industries, and (iii) a shift from the global to rapidly growing domestic market. We examine whether the benefits of WTO entry (such as increased market access and trade, greater efficiency, lower costs and wider consumer choice) will outweigh the costs involved in terms of an expected increase in unemployment and social hardship.

The book's main focus is on the impact of China's accession to the WTO in terms of employment opportunities created or suppressed. Forecasts of the possible gains and losses in employment in different sectors vary widely depending on the assumptions made. To assess the employment impact, we need to examine (a) the current unemployment situation and its causes; and (b) inter-sectoral employment trends over time.

China has been experiencing rapid growth in unemployment since 1949, particularly urban unemployment which has become a serious problem. Rural redundant labour will also continue to increase. The actual unemployment rate on the eve of the WTO accession (2001) is much higher than the official estimates. This situation will worsen as a result of layoffs in SOEs. We examine whether a reduction in employment in the state sector will be compensated by an increase in employment in the non-state sector, especially the private sector.

Currently China's regions, particularly the eastern coastal areas, where most exports are produced, do not have a comparative advantage in terms of low labour cost compared to India, Indonesia and other developing countries. We pose the question whether the 'flying-geese' theory of trade and development postulated for Southeast Asia applies also to China within its territory. According to this theory, the more industrially advanced countries with higher value-added and capital-intensive industries pass on the older (mature) labour-intensive industries to less developed and more labour-abundant countries where labour costs are much lower. Will the forces of global competition after WTO accession lead to a relocation of production within China to the lower labour cost, non-coastal areas? China's inland regions and provinces, which supply a large proportion of materials, still enjoy a relatively abundant, low-cost labour supply. Will a combination of natural resources and cheap labour in the middle and western regions and a sharing of funds, technologies, marketing channels and experiences between coastal and non-coastal enterprises (a government policy for developing the hinterland), enable China to continue to enjoy a comparative advantage in its trade with the rest of the world after accession? These are some of the questions addressed in Chapter 7.

The book contains both conceptual/analytical and empirical studies. Chapters 1 to 3 develop an analytical framework which provides the basis for Chapters 4 to 8. Chapters 4 to 6 are devoted to sectoral output, export and employment issues. Chapter 7 deals with the flying-geese theory and its relevance to China. The final chapter summarizes the main conclusions and discusses different scenarios for China in the context of the challenge of increasing global competition arising from its WTO membership.

Research for this book was undertaken within the framework of the Sino-Indian Project of Sidney Sussex College of the University of Cambridge where, one of the authors, A.S. Bhalla, was a Fellow from 1997 to 2001. We have benefited from discussions with several people, notably Dr Xiaming Liu of

Aston University; Professor Shujie Yao of Middlesex University; Dr Guy Liu of Brunel University, London; Professor Peter Nolan and Dr Ha-Joon Chang of the University of Cambridge, Professor Thomas Rawski of the University of Pittsburgh; Professor Yasheng Huang of Harvard Business School, Harvard University; Professor John Gilbert of the Department of Economics, Utah State University; Professor Nicholas Lardy of the Brookings Institution, Washington DC; Dr Wang Zhi of the US Department of Agriculture; Professor Justin Yifu Lin of Peking University and University of Science and Technology, Hong Kong; Professor Changjun Yue of the Department of Education, Peking University; Professor Cai Fang of the Institute of Population Studies, Chinese Academy of Social Sciences (CASS); Professor Hu Angang of Qinghua University, Beijing; Professor Wu Jinglian of the Development Research Centre (DRC) of the State Council of the People's Republic of China; Mr Wang Shouhai, Secretary of the Guizhou Provincial Government; Dr Guo Shuqing, Deputy Governor of the People's Bank of China; Mr Yuebin Lu, Alstom China Ltd; Dr Yongzhuang Bian, Oxford-Cambridge International Limited, Beijing; Dr Wang Shou Wen and Ms Sun Licheng of MOFTEC, Beijing; Dr Yilmar Akyüz and Dr Mehdi Shafaeddin of the United Nations Conference on Trade and Development (UNCTAD). We are also grateful to the participants for their useful comments and suggestions at the 13th Annual Conference of the Chinese Economic Association of the UK (25–26 March 2002, London) on 'China's Economic Development and the WTO', at which we presented a paper on the Employment Effects of China's WTO Accession.

We are grateful to Ms Jane Kwiatkowska-del Pozo of the Accessions Division of WTO and Mr Arunas Butkevicius of UNCTAD, Geneva, for assistance with tariffs and trade statistics. Thanks are also due to Mr Charles Aylmer, Head of the Chinese Department in the University Library at the University of Cambridge; to the staff of the Marshall Library of Economics at the University of Cambridge, in particular, to Ms Hazel Zheng and Ms Silva Ule; and to Mr R.F. Morarjee of the WTO Library in Geneva for excellent and willing assistance in the preparation of the book; to Arman Bhalla for the processing of data and preparation of graphs, and to Praveen Bhalla for skilful editing of the manuscript.

A.S. Bhalla
Commugny, Switzerland
Shufang Qiu
Cambridge, England

Acknowledgements

The authors and publishers gratefully acknowledge the following institutions for permission to use material from the following publications:

1. The United Nations Conference on Trade and Development (UNCTAD) for the use of material in the following paper, China's WTO Accession: Its Impact on Chinese Employment, *UNCTAD Discussion Paper* No. 163 (November 2002).
2. *China Economic Review* and Elsevier for using data from Tables 1 and 5 of the following article: Changjun Yue and Ping Hua (2002) 'Does Comparative Advantage Explain Export Patterns in China?' 13, 2 and 3.

Abbreviations

ABC	Agricultural Bank of China
ADB	Asian Development Bank
AIG	American International Group (of insurance companies)
ANU	Australian National University
ASEAN	Association of South-East Asian Nations
BOC	Bank of China
CAC	Capital Account Convertibility
CAPS	Centre for Asia Pacific Studies (Lingnan University, Hong Kong, China)
CASS	Chinese Academy of Social Sciences
CCB	China Construction Bank
CCI	Current Competitiveness Index
CD	Compact Disc
CERDI	Centre d'Etudes et de Recherches sur le Développement International (France)
CFTI	Chinese Federation of Textile Industry
CGE	Computable General Equilibrium
CGPRT	Regional Coordination Centre for Research and Development of Coarse Grains, Pulses, Roots and Tuber Crops in the Humid Tropics (Indonesia)
CNN	Cable News Network
COE	Collectively-owned Enterprise
COMTRADE	Commodity Trade Statistics Database (United Nations)
DIJ	German Institute for Japan Studies
DRER	Domestic Real Exchange Rate
DRC	Development Research Centre
DSM	Dispute Settlement Mechanism
DVD	Digital Versatile Disc
EAI	East Asia Institute (Singapore University)
EU	European Union
FBIS	Foreign Broadcast Information Service
FDI	Foreign Direct Investment
FFE	Foreign Funded Enterprise

FRI	Fijitsu Research Institute
GATS	General Agreement on Trade in Services
GATT	General Agreement on Tariffs and Trade
GCI	Growth Competitiveness Index
GTAP	Global Trade Analysis Project
ICBC	Industrial and Commercial Bank of China
ICITO	Interim Commission for the International Trade Organization (UN)
IIT	Intra-industry Trade
ILO	International Labour Organization
IMF	International Monetary Fund
IP	Internet Protocol
ITA	Information Technology Agreement
ITO	International Trade Organization
MFA	Multi-Fibre Arrangement
MFN	Most Favoured Nation
MII	Ministry of Information Industry
MLSS	Ministry of Labour and Social Security
MOFTEC	Ministry of Foreign Trade and Economic Cooperation
MPT	Ministry of Posts and Telecommunications
NAFTA	North American Free Trade Agreement
NATO	North Atlantic Treaty Organization
NBS	National Bureau of Statistics
NER	Nominal Exchange Rate
NIC	Newly Industrializing Country
NIE	Newly Industrializing Economy
NTB	Non-Tariff Barrier
NTR	Normal Trade Relations
OCP	Open Coastal Province
OECD	Organization for Economic Cooperation and Development
OEM	Original Equipment Manufacture
PICC	People Insurance Company of China
RCA	Revealed Comparative Advantage
RCRE	Research Centre for Rural Economy (China)
REER	Real Effective Exchange Rate
RIS	Research and Information System for the Non-aligned and other Developing Countries (India)
SAIG	Shanghai Automotive Industry Group
SAM	Social Accounting Matrix
SCRES	State Commission for Restructuring Economic Systems
SETC	State Economic and Trade Corporation
SEZ	Special Economic Zone
SITC	Standard International Trade Classification
SOAS	School of Oriental and African Studies (London University)
SOE	State-owned Enterprise

TAIG	Tianjin Automotive Industry Group
TNC	Transnational Corporation
TRIM	Trade-Related Investment Measures
TRIP	Trade-Related Intellectual Property Rights
TRQ	Tariff Rate Quota
TVE	Town and Village Enterprise
UNCTAD	United Nations Conference on Trade and Development
UNESCAP	United Nations Economic and Social Commission for Asia and the Pacific
UNSD	United Nations Statistics Division
USITC	United States International Trade Commission
VCD	Video Compact Disc
VD	Visual Disc
WDS	Western Development Strategy
WEF	World Economic Forum
WHO	World Health Organization
WTO	World Trade Organization

1   The road to WTO membership

China's bid to become signatory to the General Agreement on Tariffs and Trade (GATT, predecessor of WTO) started in July 1986 when China sought to replace the Republic of China (Taiwan) in 1950. China argued that there was only one China and that the Taiwanese seat rightly belonged to it. China sent several delegations to the GATT – China Working Party between October 1987 and February 1992 (see Lai, 2001). Taiwan applied for membership of the GATT (WTO) in 1992, which may have, *inter alia*, prompted China to accelerate the process of its own membership. China insisted all along that its own membership must precede that of Taiwan (Lardy, 2002: 16).

In this chapter, we examine the background to China's protracted negotiations for accession to the WTO. This historical perspective is essential to appreciate the circumstances in which China had to negotiate and agree to stringent concessions and obligations, which, in some cases, are quite unique (see Negotiations and China's motivation below). We show that China had been making preparations for entry to the WTO for over a decade by progressively liberalizing its trade, investment and foreign exchange regimes. These reforms prior to its WTO entry certainly soften the impact on China of the resulting global competition and opening up of its domestic market to foreign goods. The last section of the chapter discusses the implications of the WTO Agreement and Protocol of Accession especially in respect of output, exports and employment. Thus this chapter provides a background to the subsequent chapters (Chapters 3 to 6), which discuss the employment impact in more detail in both macroeconomic and sectoral terms. Chapters 7 and 8 discuss policies and measures that China may adopt to minimize the negative impact of Accession on employment.

Negotiations and China's motivation

China's attempts to join the GATT began with its (a) resuming in April 1980 its seat on the United Nations Interim Commission for the International Trade Organization (ICITO) and (b) by becoming a party to GATT's Multi-Fibre Arrangement (MFA) in 1984. Also in 1984 China signed the Arrangement Regarding International Trade in Textiles, which allowed industrialized countries to impose limits on textile imports from developing countries during periods of market disruption and urging them to gradually lower these limits (see Jacobson and Oksenberg, 1990). Through these efforts China sought to familiarize itself with GATT procedures and to facilitate exports of its textiles to industrial countries. Two years later, in 1986, China formally applied for membership of GATT (see Table 1.1 for a chronology of events leading up to its accession to the WTO in November 2001).

Many observers, both Chinese and foreign, have questioned why China felt the need to apply for GATT (WTO) membership when this entailed many costs, at least in the short run, in terms of social hardships and major restructuring. The

Table 1.1 Chronology of events leading up to China's accession to the WTO

Year	Event	Comment
April 1980	China resumed seat on the UN Interim Commission for the ITO.	ITO was never created; the Interim Commission appointed the GATT Secretariat.
Nov. 1982	China was granted observer status in the sessions of the GATT Contracting Parties.	This ministerial session determined GATT's work programme/priorities for the 1980s.
1984	China joined (a) GATT's Multi-Fibre Arrangement (MFA), and (b) arrangement regarding International Trade in Textiles.	Industrialized countries limited imports of textiles from developing countries on the grounds that they might cause market disruption.
1986	China formally submitted application for GATT membership.	
1987	(i) GATT set up a Working Party on China's membership. (ii) China established the State Council Inter-ministerial Coordination group on GATT Negotiations.	
1988	China dissolved the Inter-ministerial Coordination Group and transferred its functions to MOFTEC.	
1989	China's GATT negotiations stalled due to the events of Tiannanmen Square.	
1998	By 1998 China had negotiated bilateral trade agreements with 12 countries including Australia, Japan, New Zealand, the Republic of Korea and Singapore.	
Nov. 1999	China signed a bilateral trade agreement with the US.	
May 2000	China signed a trade agreement with the European Union.	
Nov. 2001	China's accession to the WTO and signing of the Protocol of Accession took place.	The Agreement was signed at the fourth WTO Ministerial Conference at Doha (Qatar).

Chinese leadership has certainly been aware of the possible negative social impact of accession, but it has made a calculated guess of the potential net positive benefits resulting from improved resource reallocations and subsequent increase in economic efficiency. Accession to the WTO might have been considered as a means to counter critics of rapid structural adjustment and economic reforms within the country. There are indications that SOE reforms encountered difficulties despite Premier Zhu Rongji's announcement in 1998 of the goal of achieving SOE restructuring within three years. Bureaucrats and party officials who benefited from the *status quo* also resisted further reforms (see Lai, 2001). In April 1999, at a joint Press Conference with the then President Clinton at the White House, Premier Zhu Rongji stated: 'The competition arising from the WTO membership will also promote a more rapid and more healthy development of China's national economy' (cited in Lardy, 2002: 20). Chinese critics felt that Premier Zhu had given too many concessions to the US without obtaining any concessions in return. They were further infuriated by the NATO bombing in May 1999 of the Chinese Embassy in Belgrade, which led to some cooling off of negotiations between China and the US.

The top Chinese leaders (particularly, Premier Zhu) were convinced that increased competition in China's domestic market following WTO entry would be beneficial in so far as it would put pressure on SOEs to undertake/accelerate the necessary structural reforms. (This view was echoed during our discussions with senior staff at the Ministry of Foreign Trade and Economic Cooperation (MOFTEC) in Beijing in April 2001.) WTO membership was expected to help China increase its exports and employment and force domestic firms to improve efficiency through competition. However, in principle if tariff reductions are substantial and sudden, they can force weak domestic firms to close, thereby increasing unemployment at least in the short run. As we show in Chapter 3, some sectors will benefit from competition while others will suffer a great deal especially in the short and medium term. The net overall benefits are likely to be positive but will accrue only in the long run. As we note below, China has been preparing for WTO Accession over an extended period by progressively liberalizing foreign trade through reduction of tariff and non-tariff barriers (NTBs), and reform of its investment and foreign exchange regimes. Therefore, the negative impact in the short run may not be as great as many observers predict.[1]

There were many other reasons for China's bid for GATT entry in 1986 and subsequent efforts in this direction. First, having adopted an open-door policy in the 1980s, China wanted it legitimized by the international community so as to enjoy easy access to modern technology, foreign investment and global markets. Second, China wanted most-favoured-nation (MFN) status from the United States on a permanent basis. The prevailing Jackson-Vanek amendment to the 1974 US Trade Act, called for an annual review and approval of China's MFN status in the light of its record on human rights. Third, China may have feared discriminatory treatment and the blocking of its textile exports as a result of the Jenkins Bill of 1985 which aimed at limiting textile imports from China

(Jacobson and Oksenberg, 1990).[2] Chinese textile exports also faced considerable quota restrictions from a large number of countries (see Chapter 5 for their implications on employment). As a party to GATT, China would have access to its Dispute Settlement Mechanism, enabling it to more easily ward off any protectionist actions by the industrialized countries than if it remained outside the Agreement. Bilateral negotiations are less effective than multilateral ones.

China may have assumed that it would receive developing-country status under which it would be able to retain a number of subsidy and protection measures for its industry. Article XVIII of the GATT has provisions under which a developing country can protect infant industries and provide subsidies for the development of its incipient economic activities. Similarly, a developing country can impose import restrictions to overcome its balance-of-payments problems. Also, it was believed that China could benefit from longer transition periods to meet its WTO obligations.

The US and a few other countries opposed granting of developing-country status to China. They argued that China should be treated as a middle-income developed country owing to its large size and the fact that it was already a major world trading partner and growing at a very rapid rate. However, this hurdle was finally overcome when the US withdrew its insistence and a compromise was reached which allows China to enjoy phase-in periods for reduction of tariffs and NTBs and subsidies, and it could continue state trading in sensitive products in agriculture and industry.

Lardy (2002) refers to the Taiwan factor in the protracted negotiations of China's WTO membership. It is not clear how important this factor was in China's willingness to bear the 'potentially high short-term costs' of WTO membership. It is true that China was opposed to Taiwan joining the Organization first, whereas the US argued that Taiwan's WTO membership should not be linked to that of China and that it should be judged on its own merits. It may also be true that. China did not want to be seen as a laggard in negotiations compared to Taiwan.

Pre-WTO liberalization

Trade liberalization

The impact of China's WTO accession on output, exports and employment is likely to be felt mainly through tariff reductions and elimination of non-tariff barriers. The impact – large or small and sudden or phased – depends on whether the level of trade barriers, such as tariffs, on the eve of China's accession was high or low.

China's tariff policy to date has been guided by several considerations. First, it has aimed to provide revenue for the central government. Second, it has been designed to control imports in order to provide protection to China's infant industries. Therefore, lower import duties are levied on raw material inputs than on semi-manufactured or manufactured goods. Very high rates of import duties are imposed on goods produced in China, or on those considered non-essential.

Finally, zero or low tariffs are levied on those imports which are not domestically produced, and are thus non-competing, but essential for people's livelihood.

Many observers believe that China's tariff and non-tariff barriers are still very high. While this may be true relative to developed countries, its tariffs are not particularly high compared to those of other developing countries such as the Republic of Korea (Lardy, 2002). They are half the level of tariffs in India and comparable to those in Brazil and Mexico (see Table 1.2 for tariff reductions in China up to the time of accession). Tariff revenue also (as a proportion of value of imports) is quite small: it declined to 3 per cent in 1994. Lardy (2002: 37) describes it as 'the lowest rate of tariff collection of any developing economy'. One of the reasons for this low collection was illegal smuggling of dutiable goods. The ratio increased in subsequent years with the introduction of a rigorous anti-smuggling campaign.

It is true that China's trade barriers are high for particular goods (e.g. automobiles). But even in this case tariff rates on the date of accession (November 2001) were 51.9 per cent compared to 80–100 per cent earlier (see Table 1.3). As Table 1.2 shows, on the eve of China's WTO entry the average tariff level had already declined to 15 per cent, that is, two-thirds less than the highest level in the 1980s. Furthermore, goods processed for export are exempted from import tariffs. Since 1987, all raw materials and parts and components required for the processing of final goods for export have been imported duty free. Imported capital goods by joint ventures and wholly foreign-funded enterprises have also been free of import duty. These provisions were intended as incentives for export expansion. With the rapid increase in FDI and growth of trade in processed goods, duty-free import of these goods increased significantly.

Non-tariff barriers to China's imports are more important than tariff barriers. They take several forms, namely, import licensing, quotas, and restricting trading rights to a limited number of companies, especially state trading corporations. Before the economic reforms started in 1979, China's trade was regulated and controlled by a rigid planning system, which gradually gave way to licensing and quotas as trade expanded and China adopted an open-door policy.

Thus unlike other developing countries such as India where prior to 1991 reforms the licensing system was very restrictive, in China this system represented some trade liberalization with the loosening of strong government control (Lardy, 1992 and 2002). Across-the-board controls were replaced by selective controls.

Import and export licensing served several purposes. First, as noted above import licensing enabled China to protect its incipient domestic industry. Second, it enabled China to rationalize the use of scarce foreign exchange by controlling imports. In the 1980s the Chinese policy-makers feared that the then overvalued currency would make imports cheap and could thus lead to excessive import demand. On the export side, China introduced licensing to gain monopoly rents on commodities in which it is a major world supplier and thus is not a price taker. Third, export licences enabled China to monitor the fulfilment of quotas in such exports as garments to the US and the European Union (EU)

Table 1.2 Lowering of tariff and non-tariff barriers in China (1986–2005)

Year	Tariffs and taxes	Non-tariff barriers
1986–91	Reduction of tariff rates for 81 tariff lines out of 6,300 by 30–85 per cent.	
1992	Reduction of tariff rates by an average of 7.3 per cent for 3,596 tariff lines in January and December.	Reduction in the number of export goods subject to quota-licence regulation, from 212 to 183.
	Elimination of adjustment tax on 16 classes of imports.	Elimination of import quota licence for 16 types of goods.
1993	Reduction of tariff rate on 2,898 lines by an average of 8.8 per cent.	Elimination of export licence for 9 categories of goods comprising of 283 goods.
		Import licensing restrictions applied to 53 product categories.
1994	Reduction of tariff rates on automobiles from 180–220 per cent to 110–150 per cent.	Discontinuation of mandatory plans for imports and exports.
	Stipulation of temporary tariff reduction for 282 lines.	Elimination of import licences for 195 goods.
		Elimination of import licences for 120 goods.
1995	Reduction of tariffs on 19 tariff lines including wine, liquor and tobacco, ranging from 120 to 150 per cent down to a uniform rate of 80 per cent.	Elimination of 30 per cent of remaining quotas.
1996	Reduction of tariff rates for 4,997 lines by an average rate of 35 per cent.	Reduction of import licensing requirements to 35 commodity categories.
1997	Tariff cuts on 4,874 items; reduction of general tariff level from 23 to 17 per cent.	Reduction of import licensing to 8.4 per cent of total import value.
1999	Reduction of tariffs on 1,014 tariff lines in textiles, toys and forestry, ranging between 0.2 to 11 percentage points.	Reduction of import licensing requirements to 4 per cent of the total.
2000		NTBs reduced to tariff equivalent level of 9.3 per cent, accounting for 33 per cent of imports.
2001	Reduction of tariffs on 3,462 product lines from 16.4 to 15.3 per cent.	Elimination of quota restrictions on automobiles.
2004	Reduction of average tariff on agricultural products to 17 per cent, and industrial products to 10 per cent (25 per cent on automobiles, and 10 per cent on spare parts).	
2005	Elimination of all tariff restrictions on semiconductors, computers, telecommunications equipment and paper products.	

Sources: Zhang *et al.* (1998); Liang (2000); Lardy (2002); MOFTEC (Beijing); Bhattasali and Kawai (2001); WTO (2001a).

Table 1.3 China's import tariff rate reductions by commodity (1998–2006)

Commodity/Product	Tariff rate (%) 1998–2000	Bound rate at date of accession (Nov. 2001)	Final bound rate (%)	Implementation year
Wheat		74	65	2004
Rice		74	65	2004
Maize seed		32	20	2004
Maize flour		64	40	2004
Paper and paper board		15	7.5	2004
Silk yarn		9.5	6	2003
Silk fabrics		20.2	10	2004
Woven cotton fabrics		14.5	10	2003
Woven fabrics and yarn		23.6	14	2004
Woven clothing		25	14	2005
Automobiles	80–100	51.9	25	1 July 2006
Trucks	30–50	24–40	15–25	2004/2005
Buses	50–70	41.7–55	25	2005
Automobile parts and accessories		24.6	10	2006
Colour TV	35	31.7–39	30	2002/2004
Black and white TV	20	16.7	15	2002
Washing machines	20–35	19–31.7	10–30	2002–200
Refrigerators	18–30	20	10	2005
Hair dryers	35	25	10	2004

Sources: *Protocol of China's Accession to the WTO* (November 2001). For 1998–2000 rates, *Customs Import and Export Tariff of the People's Republic of China*, 1998, 1999 and 2000.

which imposed quota restrictions. Fourth, China introduced quantitative controls to prevent possible domestic shortages of those commodities whose domestic price was lower than the world price and for which there was, therefore, an incentive to export. Such controls, through quotas, are intended to compensate for the differential between domestic and world prices.

Import licensing is the most important of NTBs – accounting for 18 per cent of imports –followed by quota restrictions and state trading (see Table 1.4). As shown in Table 1.2, NTBs have been gradually reduced in preparations for WTO membership. For example, in 1996, import licensing covered about a third of China's imports compared to more than half in 1992 (World Bank, 1997: 14). Furthermore, state trading and designated trading accounted for a little over 18 per cent of China's imports, whereas this proportion declined to only 11 per cent in 1998 (see US International Trade Commission, 1999). By 2000, NTBs represented no more than 4 per cent of the tariff lines subject to import licensing. Most

Table 1.4 Non-tariff measures affecting China's imports in 1996 (percentages)

Import	State trading	Designated trading	Import licensing	Quotas
Rice	100	0	100	0
Wheat	100	0	100	0
Coarse grains	0	0	0	0
Non-grain crops	50	22.9	0	72.9
Livestock	0	72.7	0	72.7
Meat and milk	0	0	0	0
Other food products	37.2	0	0	31.7
Natural resources	46.6	12.8	0	0
Textiles	0.3	5.7	12.7	12.7
Clothing	0	0	0	0
Light manufactures	0	9.3	0	0
Transport industries	0	0	35.8	35.8
Machinery & equipment	0	0	9.2	9.2
Basic heavy manufactures	18.7	16.2	23.5	22.7
Services	0	0	0	0
Total	11	7.3	18.5	16.3

Source: World Bank (1997: 15).

essential commodities such as rice and wheat are subject to state trading (under which trading rights are monopolized by the central government), whereas designated trading (under which a number of trading companies are designated to trade in selected goods) is more common in livestock and non-grain crops.

As a non-tariff barrier, trading rights have become less important over the years. At the time of the reforms, only twelve trading corporations were responsible for China's trade. Since then the number of trading corporations, including private trading companies (authorized in October 1998) has increased considerably, to more than 23,000 by 1998 (see Lardy, 2002: 42) and to about 35,000 by 2001 (WTO, 2001a). Although foreign-funded enterprises enjoyed the right to trade, this was restricted to the importation of raw materials and goods for production purposes. China has agreed to grant trading rights to a much larger number of domestic and foreign companies thus opening its domestic market to foreign goods. State trading in only a selected number of essential commodities (mainly in agriculture) will continue under special provisions of the WTO Agreement.

Investment liberalization

In the 1980s China adopted an open-door policy, involving *inter alia*, investment liberalization to attract not only investment but also modern technology and management skills. In 1986 China issued draft regulations on direct investment which provided for reduction in taxes and costs of certain inputs. Under these regulations enterprises enjoyed greater access to energy and transportation which are under state control. Approval and licensing procedures for foreign firms were streamlined. Investment liberalization measures included special tax concessions, liberalized leasing of land to foreign companies in coastal cities, and foreign participation in property development, port development, power generation and retailing. China also established selective joint ventures with foreign firms which were allowed to sell in the domestic market (e.g. Schindler Elevators of Switzerland and Volkswagen Santana of Germany). Foreign-funded enterprises enjoyed a tax holiday of two profit-making years and a 50 per cent reduction for a further two years. Besides these central government tax breaks, local authorities also offered incentives to foreign enterprises in the form of lower taxes on land, utilities and property. However, many of these incentives were withdrawn in 1996 in order to offer equal treatment to domestic and foreign enterprises.

Special economic zones (SEZs) were established in coastal areas to attract foreign direct investment (FDI) and technology. Municipalities and counties in the eleven open coastal provinces accounted for about 40 per cent of the gross value of industrial output and 33.4 per cent of gross domestic product (Kueh, 1996: 165). Corporate tax in SEZs was much lower (15 per cent) than for other foreign-funded enterprises (33 per cent) and Chinese enterprises (55 per cent).

China has successfully used fiscal policy instruments to channel FDI into particular regions, sectors, industries and types (e.g. contractual joint ventures, equity joint ventures, and wholly foreign-owned enterprises). Initially China preferred joint ventures to maintain control and to attract advanced technologies. Wholly foreign-owned enterprises were allowed only in SEZs until 1986 when a law was passed enabling them to set up business also in other parts of China (OECD, 2002).

As a result of new guidelines issued in 1995, such sectors as transportation and communications, insurance and other service industries were opened up for FDI. Foreign-funded legal and consultancy agencies are now being allowed to operate (Broadman and Sun, 1997) and China was revising its investment guidelines prior to its accession to the WTO (WTO, 2001a). These guidelines are intended to ensure greater transparency and better property rights for foreign and domestic investors, the lack of which had previously discouraged FDI from developed countries.

Some observers and organizations (e.g. Kueh, 1996; OECD, 2002) argue that despite some liberalization the Chinese FDI regime continues to be very restrictive in terms of entry forms, foreign ownership shares and industry scope. Wholly foreign-owned enterprises are still not allowed in 31 industries. In 32 industries (e.g. coal mining, key water projects, automobiles, production of grain, cotton and oilseeds) China still insists on joint ventures with majority shareholding by Chinese partners (OECD, 2002: 330–31). On the eve of the WTO Agreement, foreign investors were still not allowed entry into most service industries which would become open under the Agreement. Mergers and acquisitions (M&As), an important channel for FDI, are still at an experimental stage, which may partly explain why the developed-country share in China's total FDI is relatively small. Overseas Chinese investors continue to account for the bulk of the country's FDI inflows. OECD (2002: 336) notes that 'in general, foreign direct investment from developed countries tends to be inelastic with respect to short-term tax concessions'. Favourable tax concessions offer a greater incentive to overseas Chinese investors with much smaller investments and non-patented or low-level technology than is the case with developed-country multinationals.

In terms of geographical areas, in the 1980s the Chinese policy attracted FDI first to eastern (coastal) provinces. It was only a decade later that the hinterland was opened up to foreign investors. This led to uneven regional development which is now being checked through the launching of the 'Western Economic Development Strategy' under which a number of preferential measures have been introduced to attract FDI to the central and western regions.

Notwithstanding the above, the fact that China now accounts for about 40 per cent of all FDI flows to developing countries and 10 per cent of cross-border commercial debt flows and growing portfolio investment (World Bank, 1997: 21) bears testimony to its increasing financial integration into the world economy.

Foreign exchange liberalization

Prior to economic reforms, a single official exchange rate existed in which all trade and non-trade accounts were settled. This rate was kept overvalued in order to subsidize the import of capital goods. But an overvalued exchange rate inhibited export growth. Foreign exchange control was relaxed in 1979 with the introduction of a foreign exchange retention system under which exporting enterprises could retain a certain proportion of the foreign exchange they earned. This proportion rose from an average of less than 10 per cent of export earnings in 1979 to over 40 per cent by 1988 (Lardy, 1992). The foreign exchange retention system enabled exporters to finance necessary imports outside the plan. In the early 1980s a series of exchange rate reforms were introduced in order to earn foreign exchange. Under the *Regulations Concerning the Issues of Increasing Foreign Exchange Income Through the Development of External Trade* the government stipulated that from 1981 onwards an internal settlement exchange rate would be used to settle external trade accounts. This rate was linked to the domestic average cost of foreign exchange with a mark-up for profit (Lin *et al.*, 1996: 161). This rate was abolished at the end of 1984 when the official rate reached the level of the settlement rate through devaluation of the Chinese currency. In 1986, a secondary market for foreign exchange (the 'swap' market) was introduced in which the exchange rate was higher and more favourable to exporters. Firms producing export goods could sell their retained foreign exchange earnings in the swap market in order to purchase domestic currency.

In 1994, the dual-track exchange system, the official rate and the market rate were merged to introduce a unified exchange rate so as to better reflect the supply of and demand for foreign exchange. Besides moving from a planned to a market-based economy, this unified rate was one of the conditions for China's rejoining the GATT (and thereafter WTO). The Chinese currency is pegged against the US dollar, with the result that it has no flexibility to respond to internal and external shocks or to changes in the value of the US dollar or other currencies such as the Japanese yen. During the Asian financial crisis China maintained a fixed exchange rate parity with the dollar fearing that any devaluation on its part would further lead to declines in the value of other Asian currencies (see Chapter 8).

During the 1980s and 1990s China considerably relaxed foreign exchange controls; since 1996 the currency has been convertible on current account although not on capital account. China exercises central control on banks and corporations, which are not allowed to borrow or lend capital abroad without government approval. A compulsory foreign exchange settlement system operates under which domestic enterprises must sell their foreign exchange earnings to authorized foreign exchange banks. The government allows these enterprises to purchase foreign exchange if their commercial contracts involve payments in foreign exchange. Such foreign exchange controls make the economy less vulnerable to external shocks or speculative attacks and changes in investor sentiments.

In China's negotiations on WTO entry, some members of the WTO Working Party on Accession expressed concern that foreign exchange controls were being used to regulate the level and composition of trade in goods and services (WTO, 2001a). In response, the Chinese Representative pointed out that many measures had already been taken to rationalize and liberalize the foreign exchange market. The practice of multiple exchange rates in swap centres has been abolished. China has also unified the official *renminbi* (RMB) exchange rate with the market rates with a view to expanding the role of market forces. Domestic and foreign enterprises can purchase foreign exchange at market rates from designated banks.

Implications of the WTO Agreement

The Protocol of China's Accession to the WTO signed in November 2001 in Doha (Qatar) contains articles and clauses which can be grouped into four major categories, namely, (a) economic issues, (b) trade issues, (c) legal issues and (d) institutional and administrative issues. China's commitments and obligations under each are briefly discussed below:

Economic: (i) Price controls will be gradually reduced or eliminated. Prices will be determined by market forces, and multi-tier pricing will be abolished; (ii) China will eliminate most export taxes and charges. China will not maintain or introduce any export subsidies on agricultural products; (iii) China shall eliminate subsidy programmes. Subsidies to SOEs are considered specific (see UNCTAD 2002); (iv) China shall eliminate local content and export or performance requirements; and (v) Distribution of import licences, quotas, and tariff rate quotas (TRQs) will not be conditional on the availability of domestic suppliers, local content or technology transfer requirements, export performance or undertaking of R&D in China.

Trade: (i) China will eliminate special trade arrangements such as barter trade, which do not conform to the WTO Agreement; (ii) Within three years of Accession (i.e. in 2004) all enterprises will enjoy the right to trade (import or export goods) in all goods except those permitted under state trading; (iii) Import purchasing procedures of state trading enterprises will be made fully transparent; (iv) China will provide full information on the pricing mechanisms for exported goods adopted by these enterprises; (v) China shall phase out non-tariff barriers including those in agriculture; and (vi) In compliance with the trade-related investment measures (TRIMs) Agreement China shall eliminate trade and foreign exchange balancing requirements, and local content and export performance requirements.

Legal: (i) China will establish or maintain tribunals and procedures for the prompt review of administrative actions relating to the implementation of laws and regulations under Article X:1 of the GATT 1994, Article VI of the General Agreement on Trade in Services (GATS) and the relevant provisions of the Trade-Related Intellectual Property Rights (TRIPs) Agreement; (ii) Under the Transparency Clause, China is called upon to make available to WTO members, upon request, all laws and regulations and other measures relating to trade in goods and services, TRIPs or control of foreign exchange before these measures are enforced; (iii) China will publish, on a regular basis, official journals describing all laws, regulations and measures affecting trade in goods and services, and products under import and export licensing.

Institutional: (i) Under the *Transitional Product–specific Safeguard Mechanism* a provision is made for a WTO member to introduce safeguards against massive imports of Chinese goods which might cause market disruption. Market disruption is defined whenever 'imports of an article, like or directly competitive with an article produced by the domestic industry are increasing rapidly, either absolutely or relatively so as to be a significant cause of material injury or threat of material injury to the domestic industry'; (ii) Under the *Transitional Review Mechanism* WTO and its subsidiary bodies have been given a mandate to review, within one year after accession, China's implementation of the WTO Agreement and the related provisions of the Protocol; (iii) *Equal or Non-discriminatory Treatment* of national and foreign enterprises and individuals is required in respect of procurement of goods and services for production, prices and availability of goods and services by national and sub-national authorities, and the distribution of import and export licences and quotas.

Under the WTO Agreement China has made far-reaching commitments, many of them unprecedented and others far more stringent than those made by other developing countries. To some extent this may have been due to China's being a transitional economy, still not regarded as a fully-fledged market economy. Since the WTO aims at fostering freer trade, and is thus based on free market principles, China may have agreed to strict obligations in order to expedite its WTO membership; it may have feared that there may be higher costs of further delays in seeking to obtain additional concessions. Third, China's acceptance of such a heavy burden may simply be explained in terms of its confidence in its ability to accelerate the process of economic reforms which began decades ago.

China has agreed to open its domestic market further providing market access to most imported goods and services including large increases in import quotas of automobiles (see Chapter 5). It has also agreed to reduce tariff barriers on most important goods and has promised to abolish all quotas by 2005–2006. It has opened its hitherto closed domestic market in such services as telecommunications, banking, insurance, securities and professional services (see Chapter 6). It has agreed to abide by the rules and regulations of such other international agreements as GATS, TRIPs and TRIMs. China has granted trading rights to a large number of domestic and foreign companies as noted in the previous section. It has agreed to adjust and expand the list of enterprises under the designated trading system annually during the three-year transition period.[3] China is committed to abolishing import and export volumes as eligibility criteria for obtaining trading rights, and to reduce minimum capitalization requirements (applying only to wholly Chinese-owned enterprises) from RMB 5 million in the first year to RMB 3 million in the second year and RMB 1 million in the third year of the transition period (WTO, 2001a). As regards foreign enterprises, in the first year full trading rights to joint ventures with minority share of FDI will be granted, and in the two subsequent years, to joint ventures in which FDI has a majority share. At the end of the three-year transition, China will grant all enterprises, including private proprietorships, full trading rights to import and export all goods except those subject to state trading.

China has agreed to simplify the criteria and procedures for quota allocations. All requests will be approved if the relevant quota quantity exceeds total requests for allocations. In other cases, the criteria for allocations will include performance of applicants during the three years prior to accession. In cases where the average imports during this period amounted to less than 75 per cent of the quota allocation, the following criteria will be taken into account:

- Production or processing capacity in the case of intermediate products and raw materials.
- Experience and ability in producing, importing, marketing and servicing in global markets in the case of finished goods for wholesale and retail distribution.

In cases where average imports during the three years prior to accession exceed 75 per cent of the relevant quota, applicants will be allocated 10 per cent of the quota in the first year and the majority of any quota growth in the subsequent year (WTO, 2001a).

These above commitments and obligations on the part of China are quite far-reaching, which leads many observers to doubt China's willingness or ability to honour them. There are others who feel that the negative impact of these obligations on the Chinese economy and society might turn out to be unbearable and may thus reinforce tendencies towards non-compliance. We discuss in Chapter 8 the arguments for and against China's compliance of the WTO Agreement and argue that a scenario of non-compliance is unwarranted.

Under the terms of the TRIMs Agreement China will have to abolish local-content requirements that call upon foreign firms to use a certain minimum proportion of their inputs from local suppliers. It will also have to relax foreign exchange requirements under which these firms are required to export a certain proportion of their output to pay for imports. For example, in the case of automobiles China grants preferential import tariff rates to enterprises, which have high local-content (localization) rates (WTO, 2001b) (see Chapter 5). Local-content requirements have also been imposed by other developing countries. The local sourcing of inputs was 33 per cent in the Republic of Korea and 27 per cent in Taiwan (China) (Spinanger, 1984).

Abolition of local-content requirements may raise economic efficiency by reducing market distortions. But these measures, as we show in Chapters 3 and 5, can have adverse employment effects, at least in the short run. Backward linkages of foreign investments through local sourcing of inputs, for example, generate considerable *indirect* employment and lead to skill acquisition, technology improvements and improved managerial know-how. For instance, it has been shown that the Mexican *maquiadoras* (export processing and assembly activities), which use very few local inputs from Mexico, could significantly increase indirect employment if the use of local inputs were to be increased. The job multiplier estimate for domestic services and inputs is one indirect job for every four direct workers in the interior of Mexico and one for every five for border cities (see Fuentes *et al.*, 1993). It is estimated that for the Philippines, Thailand and ASEAN as a whole one or two jobs are generated indirectly (through backward linkages) for each job directly created by affiliates of transnational companies (UNCTAD, 1994: 195). Thus a possible trade-off between efficiency and employment needs to be recognized. Any growth in employment due to improved resource reallocation will occur only after a time lag.

The overall implications of China's acceptance of TRIMs, and investment liberalization after WTO membership are likely to be positive in terms of FDI inflows, output and employment growth. We discuss in Chapter 3 the positive impact of increased FDI inflows on employment in the wake of the WTO Agreement. However, one should bear in mind that these effects may not be realized immediately. OECD (2002: 354) estimates that FDI inflows will increase rather modestly reaching $45 billion during the first two years after accession. Subsequently they will grow more rapidly, reaching $100 billion by 2010. Furthermore, as we noted above, there is an uneven spread of FDI between the coastal regions and the hinterland. The eastern region, which is already more developed, is likely to benefit even more from WTO membership by receiving a disproportionately larger share of increased FDI inflows. Opening up of the service industries to FDI will also encourage the establishment of foreign firms in the coastal areas where infrastructure is better developed. It is not clear whether the government's preferential policies in favour of the western region will be successful in narrowing the FDI gap between the east and the rest of the economy. In Chapter 7, we discuss the possibility of a 'flying-geese' model at work within China whereby FDI and production activities could gradually shift towards the lower-cost hinterland as production costs rise in the coastal areas. The success of such an operation may depend considerably on the effectiveness of government policies. In fact, it is reported that the government has already closed down many loss-making textile firms in the coastal areas and subsequently re-established them in the non-coastal areas (see Chapter 7).

China has made many WTO commitments which are unique to it. For example, it is the only developing country which has allowed WTO members to continue to apply a safeguard mechanism against excessive textile imports from China until 2008. The WTO Agreement also allows WTO members to treat China as a non-market economy in cases of anti-dumping for fifteen years after accession. This means that they can determine dumping margins on the basis of third-party prices instead of Chinese prices. So far, after the European Union, China has faced the largest number of anti-dumping cases against it.[4] In July 2001, the representative of China at the WTO Working Party on China's accession expressed concern that certain WTO members 'imposed anti-dumping duties on Chinese companies without identifying or publishing the criteria used, without giving Chinese companies sufficient opportunity to present evidence and defend their interests in a fair manner, and without explaining the rationale underlying their determinations, including with respect to the method of price comparison' (WTO, 2001a).

The above actions are based on the treatment of China as a non-market economy and are clearly not in conformity with the non-discrimination principles of the WTO. This discrimination against transition economies is defended on the grounds that their exports are distorted by price controls and subsidies and do not reflect the true cost of production, an assertion which may not always be true (Yang, 2000). The bulk of commodity prices in China are now market determined.[5] Anti-dumping measures allowed under WTO rules, many of which may not be economically sound, will clearly limit China's market access opportunities, particularly in industrialized countries. This is likely to have potential adverse employment effects.

It seems rather odd that China accepted a discriminatory safeguard provision despite having complained about discrimination. China's motivation to do so remains unclear. Did China make this concession in exchange for some benefits such as the continuation of infant industry protection and balance of payments safeguards? (Yang, 1999).

In the past, China has suffered from import quotas imposed by industrialized countries on its exports, especially textiles and clothing. In principle, under the WTO Agreement China will benefit from an eventual abolition of these trade barriers. But quotas will be lifted only gradually, by 2005. Furthermore, as noted above, anti-dumping and safeguard clauses by industrialized countries will remain in force for several years. As we discuss in Chapter 5, at least in the case of textiles and clothing, restrictive trade arrangements may not offer any significant expansion for China's exports and employment immediately after China's entry into the WTO. Those who are optimistic about an expansion of these exports assume, rather unrealistically, that the abolition of Multi-Fibre Arrangement (MFA) will have immediate favourable effects on China's exports. Lardy (2002: 82) rightly notes that 'under the terms of the transitional product–specific safeguard clause in China's Protocol of Accession to the World Trade Organization, it will be fairly easy for the United States and other countries to impose restrictions on goods imported from China'.[6] This is because serious injury to the domestic industry is to be proved under the regular WTO Safeguard Mechanism whereas a simpler standard of market disruption is required under the transitional product–specific safeguards. The product–specific safeguard to which China has agreed will be in force for twelve years after accession whereas the textile restrictions are valid for only eight years. China's textile exports could also be restricted under the product–specific safeguard mechanism.

Many simulation studies (for a review see Gilbert and Wahl, 2002; OECD, 2002) have estimated the impact of trade liberalization on the Chinese economy in anticipation of the WTO Agreement based on an assumption of reduction of tariffs and non-tariff barriers. Most of these studies estimate a substantial negative impact. However, as we shall show in this book, most of these forecasts are exaggerated. If the first six months after accession in December 2001 are any guide, China's domestic market has not been flooded with imported goods even though China has been reducing tariffs and NTBs in preparation for accession. The total imports of foodgrains in the first half of 2002 increased by only 4.4 per cent. Imports of soybeans declined by 45 per cent during the same period. As we shall discuss in Chapter 4, many studies forecast a decline in agricultural prices in the wake of an increase in cheaper imports. But the price of rice actually went up in 2002. Furthermore, imports of wine and beer went down despite tariff reductions and quota elimination. The tariff on beer imports was reduced from 3.5 yuan per litre to 3 yuan per litre and some of the wine import licences were abolished. Shenzhen Customs statistics show that beer imports were reduced by 35 per cent in the first few months of 2002. The reason for this decline is that domestic beer production increased. In 1998, there were 95 joint ventures in beer production accounting for nearly 33 per cent of total beer production in China (*Shenzhen Business News*, 31 August 2002). Many observers expected that China's trade balance would be biased in favour of imports subsequent to China's accession. However, in reality, according to the Customs' statistics China's trade surplus in the first six months of 2002 rose by \$13.41 billion (*Bulletin of the Ministry of Foreign Trade and Economic Cooperation*).

Increased imports into the Chinese market and more fierce competition in both domestic and global markets are usually presented as the main explanation for a possible growth of unemployment in the wake of accession. We discuss this subject in Chapter 2 before examining the likely overall employment impact.

2 Trade liberalization, competition and employment

The standard trade theory traces favourable effects of trade liberalization on employment through (a) a shift in comparative advantage towards labour-intensive exports, and (b) a narrowing of the gaps between wages of unskilled and skilled labour. However, greater specialization need not necessarily induce an increase in global demand for labour-intensive goods to enable an increase in employment. The standard trade theory is based on such unrealistic assumptions as full employment, unified labour market and equal access to technology which do not apply to such developing economies as China charaterized by surplus labour and dualistic labour markets.

An early study linking trade and employment (Lydall, 1975) analyzed and estimated effects of trade through labour requirements per unit of value-added which vary across industries and countries (see Chapters 3 and 5 for estimates on China) and through multiplier effects defined as 'effects on employment in a developing country of an expansion of its internal demand just sufficient to induce an increase in its imports equal to the foreign exchange earned from its original exports...' (Lydall, 1975: 13).[1]

Two major factors are mentioned in the literature to explain changes in employment in developed and developing countries: trade competition and technological change. A few years ago Wood (1994) explained the decline in manufacturing employment in the North by increasing exports of labour-intensive manufactures from the South. He assumed that de-industrialization in such countries as the US resulted from a loss of industrial competitiveness in the global economy. However, Krugman and Lawrence (1994) argued that international trade was not the main cause of shrinking manufacturing employment and the declining real wages of less skilled workers in the US. Instead, de-industrialization was considered to be due more to such *domestic* factors as a shift in spending from manufacturing to services and to automation or labour-displacing technological change. Will a similar phenomenon occur in China after the WTO accession? In other words, will exports raise employment, or will increasing import competition and lack of competitiveness of Chinese SOEs reduce employment, particularly in the manufacturing sector? There is no simple answer to this question since not all SOEs are uncompetitive. Contraction of manufacturing employment will take place with or without accession due partly to technological unemployment and demand conditions. However, it is most unlikely that a substantial shift of spending away from manufacturing will occur in China in the foreseeable future.

One of the major difficulties in estimating the employment and output effects of China's WTO accession is that several other factors are at work at the same time. Even without accession, China has been undergoing structural transformation of agriculture and industry (see Chapters 4 and 5), for example, of SOEs, which leads to (and has already resulted in) labour redundancy. Separation of the employment and output effects from non-WTO induced factors is one of the most intractable problems. As we shall discuss in Chapters 4 and 5, most estimates of these short- and medium-term effects are exaggerated because they do not take into account structural adjustment that has been taking place for several years in preparation for WTO entry.

An assessment of the overall impact of international trade on the size of the manufacturing sector can be measured by the manufacturing trade balance (i.e. the difference between the amount of manufactured exports and imports. In the case of China, the manufacturing trade balance has been growing since the mid-1990s, with exports exceeding imports (see Table 2.1).

The impact of industrial competitiveness on China's trade after accession needs to be examined in the light of recent trends in the growth of trade by different types of industrial enterprises. These trends are analyzed below separately for domestic enterprises (state and non-state), SOEs and foreign-funded enterprises (FFEs). Figure 2.1 illustrates the relative importance of FFEs in China's rapid trade expansion. Table 2.1 shows that trade growth of FFEs was much more rapid than that of domestic enterprises during the 1980s and 1990s till 1997 when trade growth rates became quite similar for both. Several factors explain the more rapid trade growth of FFEs. First, FFEs started from a very low base. Second, government policy required FFEs to export a substantial proportion of their production. They had to balance their foreign exchange requirements which induced export expansion. Third, FFEs generally have better marketing channels and sales networks, which make it easier for them to export more.

The growth of import of FFEs was generally much higher until 1996, presumably to ensure better-quality inputs (particularly machinery) which might not have been locally available (see Table 2.2). Greater global competition after accession will require substantial increases in labour productivity through technological modernization, which may further increase FFEs' requirements for imports. This situation will be reinforced by the abolition after the WTO entry of local-content requirements that hitherto applied to joint ventures and foreign firms (see Chapters 1 and 5).

Domestic and foreign competition

Both domestic and foreign competition are relevant to the discussion on the employment impact of WTO accession. Porter (1990) discusses several factors which determine the existence and intensity of industrial competition such as the

Table 2.1 China's trade in manufactured goods (1991–99) (billion dollars)

	Total			Chemicals and related products			Goods classified chiefly by material			Machinery and transport equipment			Miscellaneous and other goods		
	Exports	Imports	Balance	Exports	Imports	Balance	Exports	Imports	Balance	Exports	Imports	Balance	Exports	Imports	Balance
1991	55.7	52.96	2.74	3.82	9.28	-5.46	14.46	10.5	3.96	7.15	19.6	-12.45	30.28	13.58	16.7
1992	67.94	67.33	0.61	4.35	11.16	-6.81	16.14	19.27	-3.13	13.22	31.31	-18.09	34.23	55.59	-21.36
1993	75.08	89.75	-14.67	4.62	9.7	-5.08	16.4	28.53	-12.13	15.28	45.02	-29.74	38.78	6.5	32.28
1994	101.3	99.13	2.17	6.24	12.13	-5.89	23.22	28.08	-4.86	21.9	51.47	-29.57	49.94	7.44	42.5
1995	127.3	107.67	19.63	9.09	17.3	-8.21	32.24	28.77	3.47	31.41	52.64	-21.23	54.55	8.95	45.6
1996	129.12	113.39	15.73	8.88	18.11	-9.23	28.5	31.39	-2.89	35.31	54.76	-19.45	56.44	9.13	47.31
1997	158.84	113.75	45.09	10.23	19.3	-9.07	34.43	32.22	2.21	43.71	52.77	-9.06	70.47	9.46	61.01
1998	163.1	117.29	45.81	10.32	20.16	-9.84	32.39	31.08	1.31	50.2	56.85	-6.65	70.2	9.21	60.99
1999	174.99	138.85	36.14	10.37	24.03	-13.66	33.26	34.32	-1.06	58.84	69.45	-10.61	72.52	11.05	61.47

Source: *China Foreign Economic Statistical Yearbook, 1996, 2000* (original in Chinese).

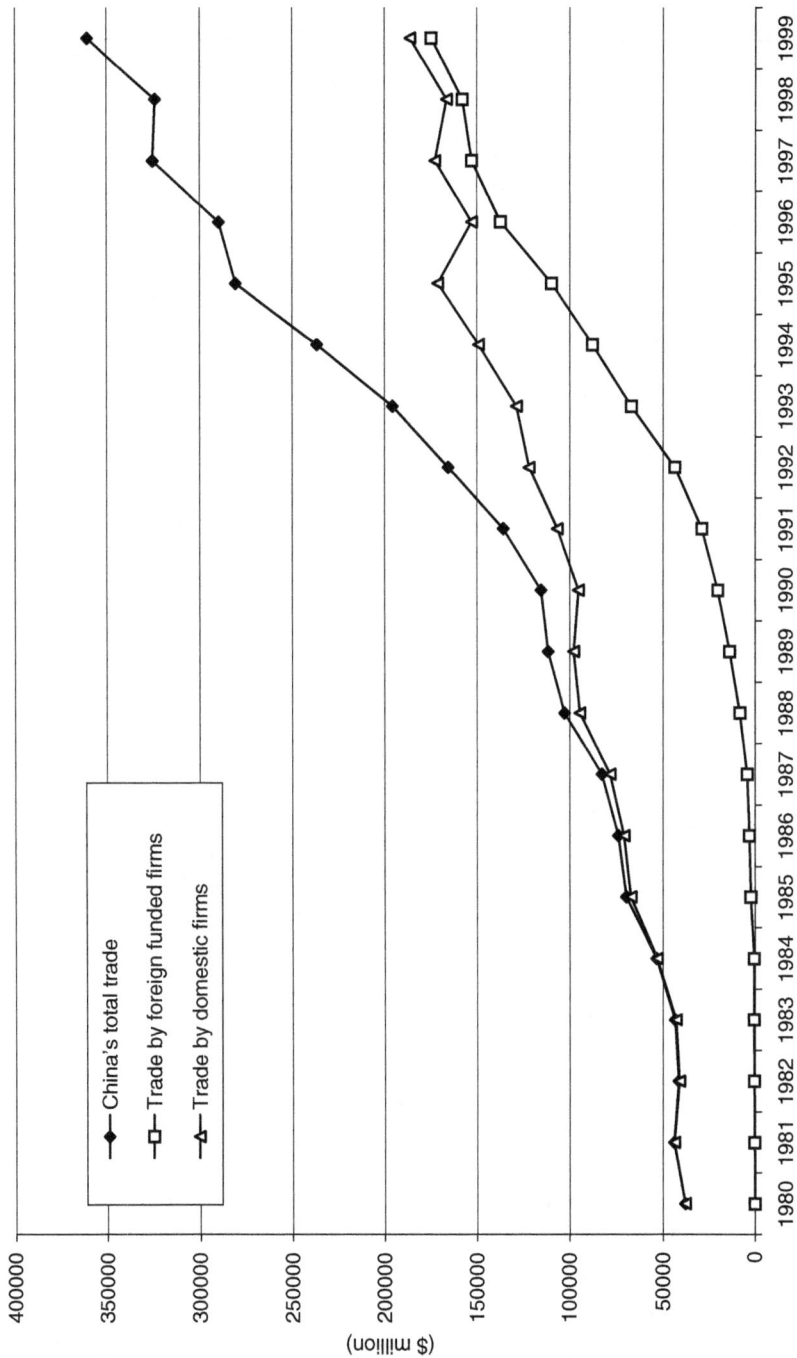

Figure 2.1 China's foreign trade by foreign and domestic firms (1980–99)

Source: *China Foreign Economic Statistical Yearbook 1996; 2000.*

Table 2.2 Trade, export and import growth rates of domestic and foreign-funded firms (1981–99)

	Trade growth rate			Export growth rate			Import growth rate		
	Total	Foreign firms	Domestic firms	Total	Foreign firms	Domestic firms	Total	Foreign firms	Domestic firms
1981	15.44	232.56	15.20	21.47	292.60	21.34	9.99	222.20	9.62
1982	−5.50	130.07	−5.94	1.41	63.43	1.32	−12.40	149.32	−13.22
1983	4.83	87.84	4.17	−0.40	524.85	−1.65	10.89	4.19	10.98
1984	22.76	−24.27	23.44	17.59	−79.13	19.05	28.14	38.61	28.00
1985	29.97	404.49	26.67	4.63	330.37	3.77	54.14	417.05	48.78
1986	6.11	27.57	5.35	13.13	96.17	12.22	1.56	17.74	0.73
1987	11.92	43.76	10.56	27.47	107.56	25.94	0.70	28.47	−0.97
1988	24.37	89.45	20.77	20.49	103.33	17.87	27.91	84.06	23.54
1989	8.65	67.12	3.58	10.56	100.01	5.69	7.00	53.06	1.66
1990	3.37	46.76	−2.71	18.18	59.04	13.96	−9.79	39.91	−18.47
1991	17.49	43.91	11.91	15.70	54.18	10.16	19.57	37.38	14.23
1992	22.05	51.02	14.18	18.23	44.07	13.03	26.34	55.98	15.65
1993	18.23	53.38	5.60	8.01	45.41	−1.60	29.00	58.64	14.58
1994	20.91	30.68	15.82	31.91	37.55	29.76	11.21	26.54	0.88
1995	18.70	25.30	14.81	22.95	35.04	18.09	14.25	18.91	10.31
1996	3.21	24.85	−10.68	1.53	31.21	−12.13	5.11	20.12	−8.55
1997	12.17	11.31	12.94	21.01	21.78	20.49	2.55	2.80	2.25
1998	−0.37	3.31	−3.63	0.50	8.09	−4.77	−1.50	−1.29	1.74
1999	11.32	10.67	11.94	6.11	9.47	3.46	18.15	11.95	25.65

Source: *China Foreign Economic Statistical Yearbook*, 1996, 2000 (original in Chinese).

Note: The domestic–foreign dichotomy is not so clear-cut in China since the FFEs also include equity joint ventures with Chinese enterprises besides wholly foreign-owned enterprises. Thus the above table includes the domestic enterprise element in foreign-funded enterprises.

threat of new entrants and of substitute products and services, the bargaining power of suppliers and buyers (consumers), and rivalry among existing competitors. A firm's industrial structure influences each of the above factors which in turn affect its cost, price and investment. Chinese firms that are already facing domestic competition are likely to be better prepared for import competition. They may also be in a better position to capture a share of the export market when the domestic market is saturated. In fact large excess capacity in Chinese industry will put pressure on domestic prices and the need to export.

Domestic competition

Domestic competition in China has grown thanks partly to a policy of decentralization which induced local governments to compete with one another in profit-making activities. (However, in the early stages many local governments tried to set up trade barriers against potential competitors.)[2] As we discussed in Chapter 1, under the WTO Agreement China's domestic market has been opened up to foreign goods and services, and foreign enterprises and joint ventures enjoy greater access to this market. The consequent increase in competition may lead to an erosion of market shares of inefficient domestic enterprises thereby resulting in loss of employment. Foreign firms will be able to capture a growing share of the domestic market through product differentiation and technology improvements. This is indicated by the fact that in 1998 investment in technology improvement by foreign firms was on average four times higher than that by domestic firms including SOEs.

The market structure of Chinese industry is characterized by different degrees of protection and competition. Industry ownership, technology level, entry barriers and the likely economic and social effects of accession, are illustrated in Table 2.3.

Table 2.3 Matrix of the impact of WTO accession on China's industry and economy

Market structure	Ownership structure	Entry barriers (import tariffs, NTBs)	Government subsidy	Status and impact of accession
Globally integrated/ competitive: competition in both global and domestic markets (e.g. shipbuilding, textiles, clothing, electronics)	State-owned, collective, town and village enterprises, joint ventures, or private	Low or zero	Zero	(a) *Economic* higher efficiency better market access (b) *Social* increase in employment through export expansion.
Segmented/ protected: segmentation of domestic and export as the former is protected (e.g. machinery and chemicals, and automobiles)	State-owned, collective, TVEs, joint ventures or private	Medium or high	Low or medium	(a) *Economic* improved efficiency better market access (b) *Social* loss of employment in inefficient enterprises; increase in employment in efficient ones.
Insulated: only competition in domestic market, closed to foreign entry (e.g. telecommunications)	State-owned	High	Medium or high	(a) *Economic* scope for raising efficiency better market access (b) *Social* loss of employment due to import competition; increase in employment through better market access.

While such industries as electronics and shipbuilding are competitive, and thus globally integrated, others, like petrochemicals and automobiles, are heavily protected. Generally, light consumer goods industries (e.g. bicycles, textiles and household appliances) are more open to competition than heavy industries (Liu and Woo, 2001).

Market shares and profits become more sensitive to production costs as the product market becomes more competitive. In order to maintain market shares, managers need incentives to work harder. In the absence of direct monitoring (which is difficult) privatization helps motivate managers. Using China's industrial census data for 1993 to 1995 for 2,000 counties and 4,000 firms, Shaomin Li *et al.* (2000) show that cross-regional competition is one of the major factors in the transition from public to private ownership. They note that SOEs in the north-eastern and north-western regions of China are less privatized since there are few private enterprises in the neighbourhood to offer competition. The coastal economies are more privatized than those of the hinterland since lower transport costs facilitate cross-regional competition.

Domestic competition among enterprises takes place in several forms, e.g. among SOEs, between SOEs and collective enterprises and private enterprises, and among private enterprises. A priori, competition may be more intense among enterprises under private ownership and less so among large firms under state ownership. On the basis of a World Bank/CASS/RCRE/SCRES 1990 Enterprise Survey Sample, Liu and Garino (2001) have tabulated Chinese industries by market characteristics (including state ownership) and show that most industries face competition although its degree varies according to the type of ownership and nature of industry. Sample enterprises were asked if they faced competition in sales and, if so, whether it was high or low. In Table 2.4 we rank industries in the descending order of the state's share and compare it with enterprise responses. A number of features of the table are worth noting. First, sample firms reported a high degree of competition in all industries except power supply and water supply in which the state's share is extremely high. Second, the intensity of competition is extremely high in the furniture industry in which the state's share is very low. Third, state ownership does not seem to correspond with low degree of competition; whereas some industries with a high state share face a high degree of competition (e.g. metal processing, machine building, food and chemicals), others such as coal mining do not indicate very severe competition. This suggests that economic reforms (e.g. encouragement of new entrants like joint ventures between domestic and foreign firms and a policy of improving SOE efficiency through competition from collectives and non-state enterprises) have had an effect. A few studies (Liu, 1996; 1998) argue that SOEs took account of competition in the 1980s in setting prices for their products.

Nowadays China is a mixed economy in which both government and market play a role in allocating resources whether a firm is subject to planning or purely market forces depending on the sector in which it operates. Competition has become more intense in recent years especially in consumer goods markets since

Table 2.4 State ownership and the degree of competition in Chinese industry

Industries ranked in descending order of state ownership	State share (%)	Degree of competition of sample firms (%)				Number of sample firms
		High	Moderate	Low	None	
Tobacco	97	81.8	9.1	0.0	0.0	11
Petroleum processing	97	22.2	66.7	0.0	11.1	9
Power supply	96	0.0	22.2	0.0	77.8	9
Water supply	92	0.0	18.2	0.0	81.8	11
Metal processing	84	62.1	36.8	0.0	1.1	87
Food	81	62.2	29.7	2.7	0.0	37
Chemicals	79	67.1	29.0	0.0	2.6	76
Coal mining and dressing	79	25.6	53.8	2.6	17.9	39
Beverages	72	89.7	6.9	0.0	3.4	29
Machine building	69	69.6	27.5	0.0	2.9	69
Electronic goods	68	75.8	12.1	3.0	9.1	33
Rubber goods	68	86.2	13.8	0.0	0.0	29
Textiles	57	54.5	39.4	3.0	3.0	66
Electric goods	51	81.6	10.2	0.0	8.2	49
Building materials	47	49.3	40.6	4.3	4.3	69
Timber processing	47	40.0	60.0	0.0	0.0	10
Plastic goods	24	57.7	34.6	0.0	7.7	26
Furniture	13	100.0	0.0	0.0	0.0	3

Source: Liu and Garino (2001).

shortages have disappeared in the wake of rapid growth. Competition has often led to a decline in prices, leading to a benefit for consumers.

Generally, domestic competition has had two main effects. First is the lower profitability of firms; over time both SOEs and non-state enterprises have suffered a decline in profitability. On the basis of firm-level World Bank data, Jefferson *et al.* (1994) show that profit rates have been declining in SOEs, urban collectives and TVEs, but export-oriented enterprises have been more profitable than non-exporting enterprises. However, competition is only one of the factors explaining low profitability noted by several authors (e.g. Fan *et al.*, 1998; McMillan and Naughton, 1993). They argue that economic reforms relaxed entry barriers and enabled non-state enterprises to compete with SOEs in given product markets. But while this argument may be valid, what explains the decline in profitability of TVEs and private enterprises? Firms can overcome this decline by raising productivity, which may call for the development of new products, research and development and cost-cutting investments (Hay *et al.*, 1994). The problem is that in many consumer goods sectors production capacity is well in excess of market demand. Therefore, firms in these sectors are forced to reduce price in order to induce consumers to buy. As a result profits are squeezed and adequate resources are not available for R&D and product innovations. The second effect of domestic competition is that many firms are turning their attention to international markets for raising their exports. Accession will induce these domestic firms to expand exports and foreign firms to develop China as a global manufacturing base.

Import competition and export competitiveness

The opening up of China's market to foreign (imported) goods will provide direct and indirect competition. Imported goods and services are in direct competition with Chinese ones, which may drive out inefficient activities and lead to a loss of output and employment. Indirectly, competition may grow in economic activities such as tradeables and financial and transport services. Greater foreign competition has an indirect effect of putting pressure on structural adjustment and the reallocation of economic activities from less efficient to more efficient ones. In the long run this can lead to higher growth and positive output and employment effects through a more optimal resource allocation.

Foreign competition, by lowering the price of Chinese exports relative to that of other countries and raising the price of imports could lead to a reduction in real earnings because China would have to sell its goods more cheaply but pay more for its imports. Developing countries as a whole suffered from such a decline in the terms of trade during the period 1980–95; so did such newly industrializing Asian countries as the Republic of Korea, Singapore and Thailand (see Yang and Vincs, 2000). China's terms of trade in manufacturing also declined during the 1993–2000 period, with the exception of 1994 and 1997 when they rose slightly (see Zheng and Zhao, 2002). In 1994 China significantly reformed its foreign exchange policy, which led to a depreciation of the yuan and an increase in China's export competitiveness (see Chapters 1 and 7). A slight increase in its terms of trade in 1997 is linked to the Asian financial crisis which led to a decline in import prices relative to export prices. During other years, China's terms of trade with both developed and developing countries declined. Zheng and Zhao (2002) group manufacturers into four categories: (a) labour-/resource intensive; (b) low-tech; (c) medium-tech; and (d) high-tech, and show that China's terms of trade declined for all these categories, with major declines occurring in the last two.

Export competitiveness

Different methods of assessing export competitiveness have been used in the literature. These include:

1   *A comparison of domestic and international costs and prices.* Generally, a static approach is adopted to compare costs of domestic producers against those of international producers. This method is not helpful when factor and product markets are characterized by different levels and degrees of

competition. Cost is only one among many factors that determine the competitiveness of an industry. As Liu and Woo (2001) note, firm costs are difficult to determine since information is private and confidential. Some firms may use this information for effective bargaining with government to introduce more favourable industrial measures. Furthermore, costs and prices do not indicate equilibrium or optimal conditions when the price structure is distorted, as is the case in China and many other developing countries.

2   *Changes in market shares.* As an indicator of competitiveness, market share though common, suffers from several limitations. Product differentiation and growth of niche markets can vitiate the measurement of market shares (Liu and Woo, 2001). Furthermore, causation may run both ways: competitiveness may be the cause of higher market shares as well as the result. For China this indicator is not very appropriate owing to its dualistic production and trade structures. High tariff barriers have created segmented domestic and export markets. Of course, this segmentation will gradually disappear in the post-accession period, but at present and in the foreseeable future competitiveness in the domestic market may not necessarily ensure similar competitiveness in export markets.

Liu and Woo (2001) and others have used the market share indicator to measure the competitiveness of Chinese industry after accession. They argue that industries that are already globally competitive are unlikely to be adversely affected by increased competition. Even SOEs, which are subject to different degrees of protection and some FDI restrictions, may survive increased import competition by entering into joint ventures with technologically advanced foreign firms. Import competition in the currently protected domestic market may have an adverse effect only in the short run; in the medium term it will be neutralized by alliances. However, it is uncertain whether a simple change in the ownership structure of industry will ensure beneficial employment effects. Privatization, takeovers, and mergers and acquisitions (M&As) may simply lead to rationalization rather than expansion, thus leaving unchanged the level of employment or reducing it. Competition is double-edged: while it will raise the efficiency of already competitive industries, it will lower the competitiveness of inefficient hitherto protected industries, especially SOEs involving adverse employment effects.

During the reform period, China first opened up its light consumer goods sector to competition. Although it maintained relatively higher import duties on these goods, entry barriers in light industry were low for both domestic and foreign enterprises. The ownership structure in light industry has become much more diversified due to the restructuring of SOEs and the establishment of new private domestic and foreign-funded enterprises. Many joint ventures have been established between domestic enterprises of different ownership types as well as between domestic and foreign enterprises. As a result, the market shares of SOEs and collectives have declined whereas those of foreign-funded enterprises (including those owned by overseas Chinese) and domestic private enterprises have increased (see Table 2.5). Apart from the policies of reform and opening up, product differentiation and technology upgrading also played an important part in diversifying the ownership structure of light industry. It is estimated that in 1998 investment in technology improvement by foreign firms was, on average, four times higher than that by domestic firms including SOEs. China attracts foreign companies for two main reasons: its huge market potential and cheap labour. It is increasingly becoming a manufacturing base of the world thanks to these factors, combined with the availability of modern technologies and low-cost transportation. This trend will accelerate after WTO accession.

3   *Productivity differences.* Export competitiveness reflected in export shares has been attributed to productivity differences across countries which in turn are affected by the level of R&D and the sophistication of the technology used. Long before competitiveness indices were developed (see below), several authors (e.g. Balassa, 1963; MacDougall, 1951) underlined the importance of cross-country productivity differences in explaining differences in export shares. MacDougall compared differences in relative productivity and relative export volumes between the US and the UK; they concluded that in twenty out of twenty-five industries covered the American output per worker was more than double that of the UK and accounted for the bulk of the export market. Balassa showed that productivity differences explained 64 per cent of the variance in export shares.

Table 2.5 Changes in market shares in Chinese light industry by enterprise ownership (%)

Industry/ownership	1990	1992	1994	1996	1998
Light Industry					
Domestic enterprises	97	95	87	82	77
of which: SOEs	52	49	39	36	28
Foreign-funded	3	5	6	10	13
Overseas Chinese	–	–	7	8	9
1. *Bicycles* (top 10 firms)					
SOEs	–	40	43	43	23
Overseas Chinese	0	0	4	8	26
2. *Household Appliances*					
Domestic	–	–	–	52	58
of which: SOEs	–	–	–	38	40
Foreign-funded	–	–	–	31	20
Overseas Chinese	–	–	–	17	22

Source: *China Light Industry Yearbook* (in Chinese).

Note: Markets share estimates are based on total sales.

Comparative advantage vs competitiveness

Comparative (cost) advantage

The standard trade theory (Heckscher-Ohlin-Samuelson-Stolper model) stipulates that countries specialize in those traded goods in which they enjoy natural comparative advantage. Thus, in general, developing countries with abundant labour will specialize in labour-intensive exports whereas developed countries with labour shortages but relative abundance of capital (both physical and human) will concentrate on the export of capital-intensive and skill-intensive goods.

The above standard trade theory is based on several well-known but unrealistic assumptions, namely, uniform technology, undifferentiated products, factor price equalization and absence of economies of scale. These assumptions may render the theory less useful for analyzing actual trade patterns of countries.

Does the traditional theory apply to Chinese exports? Are they based on the principle of natural comparative advantage? These are some of the questions discussed below. In agriculture, crop-specific shifts in trading suggest a movement towards comparative cost advantage. For example, exports of such land-intensive commodities as foodgrains and oilseeds have declined whereas those of more labour-intensive commodities such as fruits and vegetables and animal products have risen (Huang and Rozelle, 2002). By the end of the 1990s, these latter exports accounted for about 80 per cent of agricultural exports (Huang and Chen, 1999). This situation was the direct result of trade liberalization.

For manufacturing, comparing Guangdong and Shanghai, Lardy (1992) notes that the former's product mix was initially weighted in favour of light industrial goods in which China had a comparative advantage during the 1980s. Also Panagariya (1993: 60–61) argues that the share of Chinese exports of light industrial goods expanded rapidly. He concludes that 'to the extent that light industry is labour intensive relative to heavy industry, this situation was consistent with China's comparative advantage'. On the other hand, Lo and Chan (1996) argue that growth of China's exports, particularly the recent expansion of exports of machinery and electronic goods – the non-labour intensive exports although some may be labour-intensive – is not based on the comparative-cost principle, but, instead, on the competitiveness of its industries. The share of machinery and transport equipment in total exports increased from 6 per cent in 1987 to 25 per cent in 1995, while exports of computers and other electronic goods have also expanded significantly in recent years. Non-traditional, medium- and high-tech products largely accounted for the significant increase in China's exports during the 1990s. Compared to 1990 the shares of medium and high-tech products in China's total exports in 2000 were 10.6 and 9.9 times respectively, whereas those of labour-intensive and low-tech products were only 4.6 times and 5.1 times respectively (Zheng and Zhao, 2002).

The Lo-Chan argument that the rapid expansion of China's non-traditional exports is inconsistent with its comparative advantage is misleading and may simply be due to a misinterpretation of the concept. It is not the *static* notion of the concept but its *dynamic* element that is relevant to the discussion. In the process of economic development and structural change, a developing economy is constantly moving up the technological ladder (through learning-by-doing, accumulation of capital and skills, and better management); this shifts its comparative advantage gradually from labour-intensive to technology-intensive goods. In Chapter 5, we show that China's revealed comparative advantage (RCA) (see p. 31) in textiles and clothing, a labour-intensive industry, has been declining during the 1990s. As we show in the following section, what Lo and Chan call 'competitive advantage' may simply be another name for 'dynamic comparative advantage'.

Lo and Chan (1996: 7) note that 'the Chinese economy is heading towards a pattern of intra-industry instead of inter-industry international specialization', which is again not consistent with the theory of comparative advantage. In principle, one can argue that China will specialize in labour-intensive operations even if the industry is capital- and technology–intensive. Although data limitations do not permit a detailed analysis of intra-industry trade, data on capital-labour ratios and average labour productivity suggest that such industries as electronics are actually capital-intensive. In a rapidly growing economy like the Chinese, its capital stock may be growing faster (albeit from a low base) than that of its trading partners, particularly developing countries. As a result, the overall capital intensity of its exports will tend to grow.

China's access to foreign markets will depend, *inter alia*, on the *price* and *quality* competitiveness of its exports. These are essential ingredients for productivity growth. The fact that China's exports of clothing, toys, footwear and electrical machinery continued to grow in the wake of the Asian financial crisis suggests the competitiveness of these products despite the depreciation and realignment of other Asian currencies (see Bhalla, 2001). Porter (1990) argues that it is difficult to achieve both price and quality competitiveness simultaneously since raising product quality and differentiation are costly. The historical experiences of such countries as Japan and the Republic of Korea show that the manufacturing industry first exploits a cost-based advantage before using its market position to exploit other advantages based on product quality.

China's recent experience in exports of manufactures is similar to that of Japan and the Republic of Korea in the sense that emphasis was initially placed on labour-intensive exports in which China enjoyed a cost advantage. Zheng and Zhao (2002: 30) note that 'emphasis has long been on quantity rather than quality – on the extension of export volume rather than the enhancement of product quality'. Quality improvements have been slow due to lack of innovations. However, WTO membership and greater competition in both domestic and foreign markets in the future will certainly put pressures on Chinese and foreign enterprises (based in China) to raise productivity and product quality.

Revealed comparative advantage

The most frequently used concept of comparative advantage in the economic literature is that of 'revealed comparative advantage' (RCA) of countries in individual commodities and manufactured goods (Balassa, 1965). An estimation of direct and indirect labour and capital coefficients does not provide an appropriate measure of comparative advantage when inter-country differences exist in productivity and efficiency. Therefore, relative export shares may be a better measure for revealing the comparative advantage of a country in a particular good or industry. Cost considerations are necessary but not sufficient. Such non-price factors as quality, repair and maintenance facilities, and the size of an economy are equally important in determining a country's *dynamic* comparative advantage.

The RCA is estimated on the basis of a comparison of a country's relative shares in world exports of individual commodities and changes of these shares over time. The RCA index is measured as:

$$RCA = (X_{ij}/X_{wj})/X_i/X_w, \tag{1}$$

where X_{ij} is exports of country i of commodity j; $X_{wj\ i}$ is total world exports of commodity j; $X_{i,}$ total exports of country i, and X_w, total world exports. The above formula is based on the market share principle since (X_{ij}/X_{wj}) represents the market share of country i in commodity j, and (X_i/X_w) represents a country's export market share in total world exports.

Changes in China's RCA indices for primary products and manufactured goods are shown in Table 2.6. The table shows that China's initial comparative advantage in resource-intensive products in the 1980s has given way to comparative advantage in labour-intensive manufactured goods in the 1990s. We have not reported yearly estimates of RCA indices which show that in 1992 to 1994 only processed foods had an RCA index greater than unity. The RCA index for labour-intensive manufactured materials and finished manufactures (SITC 68) increased significantly, reaching a peak at 2.07 in 1997 (Yue and Hua, 2002).

Competitive advantage

Some authors (notably Porter, 1990) argue that a distinction needs to be made between comparative cost advantage, which refers only to the advantage due to cost differences, and competitive advantage, which captures many additional factors (e.g. technology, better macroeconomic and microeconomic policies, superior management and market information, economies of scale, and country size). They argue that while comparative advantage may be necessary, it is not sufficient to explain trade patterns. For example, the historical experiences of such countries as Japan and the Republic of Korea show that countries with few natural resource endowments can capture export markets in capital-intensive goods. This has also been the recent experience of China, which has succeeded

Table 2.6 Changes in RCA indices for China's primary products and manufactures (1980–2000)

Product item	1980	1985	1990	1995	2000
I. Resource-intensive products					
Primary processed goods					
Processed foods (SITC 0)	1.72	1.94	1.46	0.94	0.76
Beverages and tobacco (SITC 1)	0.49	0.46	0.48	0.83	0.28
Crude materials (SITC 2)	1.41	2.00	1.23	0.72	0.51
Refined fuels (SITC 3)	0.89	1.79	0.83	0.54	0.46
Animal and vegetable oils (SITC 4)	0.52	0.79	0.64	0.60	0.09
II. Labour-intensive products					
Secondary goods					
Materials and finished manufactures (SITC 68)	1.48	1.34	1.69	2.00	1.78
III. Technology-intensive goods					
Chemicals (SITC 5)	0.82	0.69	0.70	0.64	0.51
IV. Capital-intensive products					
Machinery and equipment (SITC 7)	0.11	0.10	0.49	0.53	0.81

Source: Yue and Hua (2002). Estimates are based on data from *Statistics Canada, China Customs Statistics* (1998–2000), and UNCTAD *International Trade Statistics Yearbook* (1998).

Note: The categories 'resource-intensive', 'labour-intensive', 'capital-intensive' and 'technology-intensive' are not watertight. They may overlap. For example, although machinery and equipment is generally capital-intensive, it may also include some labour-intensive items.

in exporting capital-intensive products (see above). While factor costs may be important for labour-intensive and resource-based industries, they are less so for skill- and technology-intensive industries whose existence is a precondition for productivity growth. Porter (1990) argues that it is not natural factor endowments but man-made efforts by a firm to improve efficiency, develop new products (or introduce product differentiation) and make innovations which can occur regardless of factor intensity. An economy's productivity and competitiveness depend on that of its firms and their subsidiaries.

A firm must have a business strategy which Porter likens to the shape of a 'diamond' with four distinct elements: (a) *the quality of factor inputs* (e.g. skilled and unskilled labour, infrastructure, physical capital endowment); (b) *demand conditions* at home and abroad, determined by the level of sophistication of consumers and how demanding they are in terms of quality and variety of the products and services; (c) *related and supporting industries* (e.g. availability and quality of local suppliers, and the state of development of industrial clusters); and (d) *the context for firm strategy and rivalry* (e.g. corporate investment strategy, business environment, macroeconomic policies). Scholars who favour a selected number of national champions would argue that domestic competition and rivalry might be wasteful. Porter, however, believes that these champions are generally not globally competitive, and that rivalry facilitates competitiveness by creating pressures to innovate and raise standards of product quality. The above four elements need to be combined with a firm's corporate strategy to exploit potential competitive advantage. Porter notes that government and non-governmental organizations (e.g. universities, trade associations, and the private sector) are important agents for improving the business environment. Furthermore, differences in economic structures, social values, culture and institutions of a given society can also explain growth in productivity and competitive advantage.

Porter's concept of competitive advantage is thus rooted in an analysis of corporate strategy rather than in economic analysis (see Lall, 2001b). It bears striking similarities to the concept of *dynamic* comparative advantage which envisages improvements in innovation and infrastructure to increase competitiveness. Warr (1994) notes that Porter's criticism of the comparative advantage concept rests partly on a misunderstanding of the concept and partly on a confusion between the economic success of a firm and of a nation. Like comparative advantage, competitive advantage is also dynamic and keeps evolving over time, depending on learning-by-doing and changes in innovations, products and processes. Indeed, the traditional concept of comparative advantage has been modified to take account of these factors (see Caves *et al.*, 1993; Deardorff, 1984; Krueger, 1984).

With increasing globalization of competition a number of countries, including China, have considered advantages of locating industries in other countries (offshore) through transnational corporations (TNCs) and their subsidiaries. Chinese TNCs have been increasing their presence in other Asian countries, Western Europe and the US in search of resources, better market access and modern technology (see Zhan, 1995; and Chapter 7). In some industries, proximity to buyers may be more important for acquiring access to local skills and for developing relationships with key customers. Proximity may also be essential for marketing and the provision of such services as banking and insurance.

Competitiveness indices

International competitiveness is difficult to measure both analytically and empirically. Apart from questions about the meaningfulness of *national* competitiveness (Krugman, 1994), problems of appropriate data and estimations are also formidable. Notwithstanding these problems, a number of measures of a firm's (and a country's) competitiveness have been used in the literature. These are briefly reviewed below.

The World Economic Forum (WEF) index

The competitiveness index developed by the WEF is one of the most frequently quoted indices of global competitiveness.[3] Based on Porter's concept of competitive advantage discussed above, it emphasizes technological dynamism as one of the important determinants of competitiveness. It is concerned mainly with microeconomic factors although good macroeconomic management is noted as a facilitating factor. As Lall (2001b:1506) notes, the WEF index leans heavily towards free trade and free markets and 'a competitive setting with full exposure to international markets is the primary requirement of success'. This is not surprising considering that WEF is mainly a business forum even though the index was derived mainly by professional economists.

WEF ranks countries based on two quantitative indices of national competitiveness: the Current Competitiveness Index (CCI), and the Growth Competitiveness Index (GCI). In the words of WEF (2000), the CCI 'aims to identify factors that underpin high current productivity and hence current economic performance measured by the level of GDP per person, whereas the GCI aims to measure the factors that contribute to the future growth of an economy measured by the rate of change of GDP per person. . .'. Thus the notion of competitiveness is equated with that of productivity.

Although the CCI and GCI are meant to measure national competitiveness, microeconomic variables are used for determining productivity and micro-economic performance of firms. The microeconomic performance is determined by the 'quality of the microeconomic business environment' and 'the sophistication with which companies or subsidiaries based in a country compete' (Porter, 2000).[4] The GCI is based on three indices: (i) the economic creativity index (which includes current technological efforts in the form of R&D, and technology imports); (ii) the finance index (financial accessibility, interests rates and the current state of the capital market); and (iii) the international index (measuring import barriers and capital account liberalization). Both indices are based on questionnaire surveys and business perceptions – a qualitative and subjective indicator – rather than on hard data that are often available (e.g. on R&D).

The WEF index suffers from several analytical and measurement problems. There seems to be a confusion between the macroeconomic and microeconomic underpinnings of the analysis. The transformation and aggregation of micro results into a national index for ranking of countries is confused (for a detailed critical assessment of the WEF index, see Lall, 2001b).

The rankings of competitiveness on the basis of the CCI for 1998 to 2000 are shown in Table 2.7. China's ranking is compared with that of other selected developing and developed countries. Several odd features of these rankings are worth noting. First, there are wide fluctuations in rankings from one country to another during a short three-year period. This suggests that the index and rankings are subjective and arbitrary. For example, China's ranking goes down from 42 in 1998 to 49 in 1999 and then improves again to 44 in 2000. It is difficult to find any reasonable explanation for this see-saw movement. Second, the Indian ranking is higher than the Chinese for 1999 and 2000, which is implausible. China's export performance is much better than that of India, which demonstrates its greater competitiveness in global markets. Perhaps the authors

Table 2.7 Global competitiveness ranking of China and other selected countries

	GCI	CCI			Company operations ranking			Ranking by quality of business environment		
	2000	2000	1999	1998	2000	1999	1998	2000	1999	1998
Asia										
China	41	44	49	42	38	31	35	45	50	44
Hong Kong (China)	8	16	21	12	23	24	17	14	18	11
Singapore	2	9	12	10	15	14	12	5	12	6
Taiwan	11	21	19	20	18	17	16	21	22	21
Malaysia	25	30	27	27	30	25	34	30	31	26
Philippines	37	46	44	45	43	34	41	46	46	45
Thailand	31	40	39	37	47	43	37	40	39	36
Indonesia	44	47	53	51	51	47	52	47	52	51
Vietnam	53	53	50	43	50	41	36	52	49	43
India	49	37	42	44	40	48	50	37	43	42
Korea, Rep. of	29	27	28	28	25	27	24	28	30	28
Japan	21	14	14	18	4	4	7	19	19	19
Other countries										
Argentina	45	45	40	34	45	39	30	44	40	34
Mexico	43	42	34	39	42	30	29	43	35	41
Brazil	46	31	35	35	29	32	27	32	37	39
South Africa	33	25	26	25	26	28	33	25	25	25
Israel	19	18	20	21	13	18	21	20	20	20
UK	9	8	10	5	11	13	9	9	8	5
Canada	7	11	8	6	16	12	15	8	4	3
USA	1	2	1	1	2	1	2	2	1	1

Sources: WEF (2000); Porter (2000).

of the CCI believe that China is less globally integrated than India because of the language barrier and poorer technology licensing and marketing. A comparison of balance sheets for the two countries in the WEF Report shows that in technology licensing India ranks 1 whereas China ranks 50. Third, China's ranking for 2000 is close to that of Argentina and Mexico, both of which have an inferior economic record in terms of growth and export performance. In fact, Porter (2000: 49) notes that 'the performance of India and Brazil may be pulled down by their political complexity and the existence of large populations outside the mainstream economy'. There is no mention of China in this context although China also has a very large population, and its greater political stability should qualify it for a higher ranking.

The innovation index

The US Council on Competitiveness developed this index to measure the innovative capacity of seventeen OECD countries, including the US. It uses patents held by a country internationally as an index of innovative capacity. Panel data for each year between 1973 and 1996 were used to measure the innovation index to reflect the global competitiveness of a country (see Porter and Stern, 1999: 25). Porter and Stern note that 'while competitiveness in the short term can be improved by cost cutting and deficit reduction, national innovative capacity is a lynchpin of national industrial competitiveness in the long run'. The index is estimated on the basis of economic, technological and skill variables, e.g. R&D expenditure and personnel, per capita income, expenditure on secondary and tertiary education as a proportion of GDP, and industrial patents.

In the final stages of estimating the index, eight emerging economies have also been included: China, India, Ireland, Israel, Malaysia, Singapore, the Republic of Korea and Taiwan (China). Little discussion is provided on the results for these economies other than a graph which shows that (a) Singapore will be ahead of all other emerging economies in 2005, followed by Taiwan (China) and the Republic of Korea, and (b) China, India and Malaysia are technologically stagnant. The authors note that these countries 'have registered virtually no international patenting through the mid- to late 1990s, in sharp contrast to countries such as Taiwan or Israel' (p. 37). Their conclusions are based on a highly limited assumption, that innovative capacity is measured only by patents. Generally, in developing countries non-patented innovations on the shop floor are more important than the patented ones. Minor incremental technology improvements and learning-by-doing sometimes explain significant productivity increases. The results would be substantially different if these incremental innovations were included. The use of patents biases the results in favour of developed countries. Patents are only a partial measure of domestic innovation since they ignore the use of imported technology and innovations (see Lall, 2001b). Second, the use of per capita GDP as a determinant of innovation seems rather peculiar. Third, quantitative estimates of the index are vitiated by the fact that the economic, technological and skill variables used in the multiple regressions can be multi-collinear.

The unit labour cost index

While the above two indices are rooted in business studies and strategies, the unit labour cost index is mainly used by economists to determine competitive advantage. Several relative cost measures are in use, but the most common among them is the relative unit cost of labour in the manufacturing sector (see Boltho, 1996). Mazumdar (1993) uses the unit cost of labour in dollars as an indicator of interactions between labour market functioning and macroeconomic policies and international competitiveness. The unit cost of labour is decomposed into the three following components which are crucial for determining export competitiveness of tradeable goods and services:

- wage–productivity ratio;
- ratio of domestic to foreign prices; and
- the rate of foreign exchange.

The unit cost of labour is defined in dollars (U_c) in terms of its three components as follows:

$$U_c = \frac{W}{V} \cdot \frac{1}{e} \tag{2}$$

Where, W – is wages per worker, V – value-added per worker, e – the exchange rate.

Equation (2) can also be expressed as:

$$
\begin{aligned}
\dot{U}_c &= \dot{W} - \dot{V} - \dot{e} \\
&= (\dot{w} + \dot{P}_c) - (\dot{v} + \dot{P}_p) - \dot{e} \\
&= (\dot{w} - \dot{v}) + (\dot{P}_c - \dot{P}_p) - \dot{e}
\end{aligned} \tag{3}
$$

where w is the real wage (in terms of consumer goods), v – an index of physical productivity of labour, $\dot{P}_c$, an index of the cost of living, and $\dot{P}_p$, an index of prices of manufactured goods. The dot above the letters in equation (3) represents proportionate rate of change.

Equation (3) captures changes in the three elements of the unit cost of labour index mentioned above: $(\dot{w} - \dot{v})$ indicates the wage–productivity gap; $(\dot{P}_c - \dot{P}_p)$, shift in the ratio of domestic to foreign prices, and $\dot{e}$, the change in the nominal exchange rate.

Assuming that $\dot{P}_c$ is the price of non-traded goods and $\dot{P}_p$ the price of traded goods, the second element (i.e. ratio of domestic to foreign prices) is equivalent to the domestic real exchange rate (DRER). This is particularly true for the open economies of China and Southeast Asia.

The third element is the change in the exchange rate which is crucial in determining export competitiveness. In principle, an overvalued exchange rate will discourage exports by making them more expensive relative to imports, whereas a more realistic exchange rate will make exports more competitive (see below).

Unit cost of labour in China

For our purposes in this book, the macroeconomic or national competitiveness indices are less meaningful than the microeconomic ones. After all, in the post-WTO period the relevant issue is the competitiveness of Chinese enterprises with foreign enterprises.

Wage–productivity ratio

China's industry will be competitive in the export market if productivity (real value-added per worker) grows faster than the real wage per worker. Table 2.8 shows industrial wage–productivity ratios using real wages (deflated by consumer price index) and product wages (deflated by product–specific price deflator). Between 1980 and 1995, the real wage–productivity ratio declined after rising; so did the product wage–productivity ratio. Both real and product wages rose much more rapidly than labour productivity which would militate against competitiveness. Figure 2.2 compares wage–productivity ratios for traditionally export-oriented industries (e.g. food products, textiles and garments and footwear) and traditionally import-competing industries (e.g. iron and steel, industrial chemicals and transport equipment) from 1984 to 1995. As import-competing industries tend to be more capital-intensive, wages and labour productivity in these industries were consistently higher than in export-oriented industries throughout this period. However, the gap in wage–productivity ratios between the export-oriented and import-competing industries was much wider during 1987–93 than during 1984–86 and 1993–95 (see Fig. 2.2). The curves for the two industries show that the wage increase surpassed productivity increase; the gap between the curves represents the relative growth of the two factors (wages and labour productivity) in the two sectors. The gap indicates that the wage has been growing faster in export-oriented industries than in import-competing industries in which SOEs dominate. An interesting point to note is that the gap also reflects that export-oriented industries (which are generally non-state) could afford the increase in wages whereas SOEs in import-competing industries were restricted to do so by government control and their own financial limitations. However, in the early 1990s and after, the latter were able to catch up with the former by entering export market, laying off workers and by introducing further reforms and restructuring. This may partly explain the convergence in the wage–productivity ratios in the two sectors in the early 1990s.

Table 2.8 Industrial wage–productivity ratios in China (1980–95)

Year	Wage (1,000 yuan per person at 1980 prices)		Labour productivity (1,000 yuan per person at 1980 prices) (3)	Wage–productivity ratio	
	Deflated by consumer price index (1)	Deflated by product–specific price deflator (2)		Real wage– productivity (3)/(1)	Product wage– productivity (3)/(2)
1980	747	747	3.18	0.40	0.40
1985	875	941	4.24	0.48	0.45
1990	988	1,110	4.73	0.48	0.43
1995	1,406	1,948	5.55	0.39	0.28

Source: Based on data in Woo and Ren (2002).

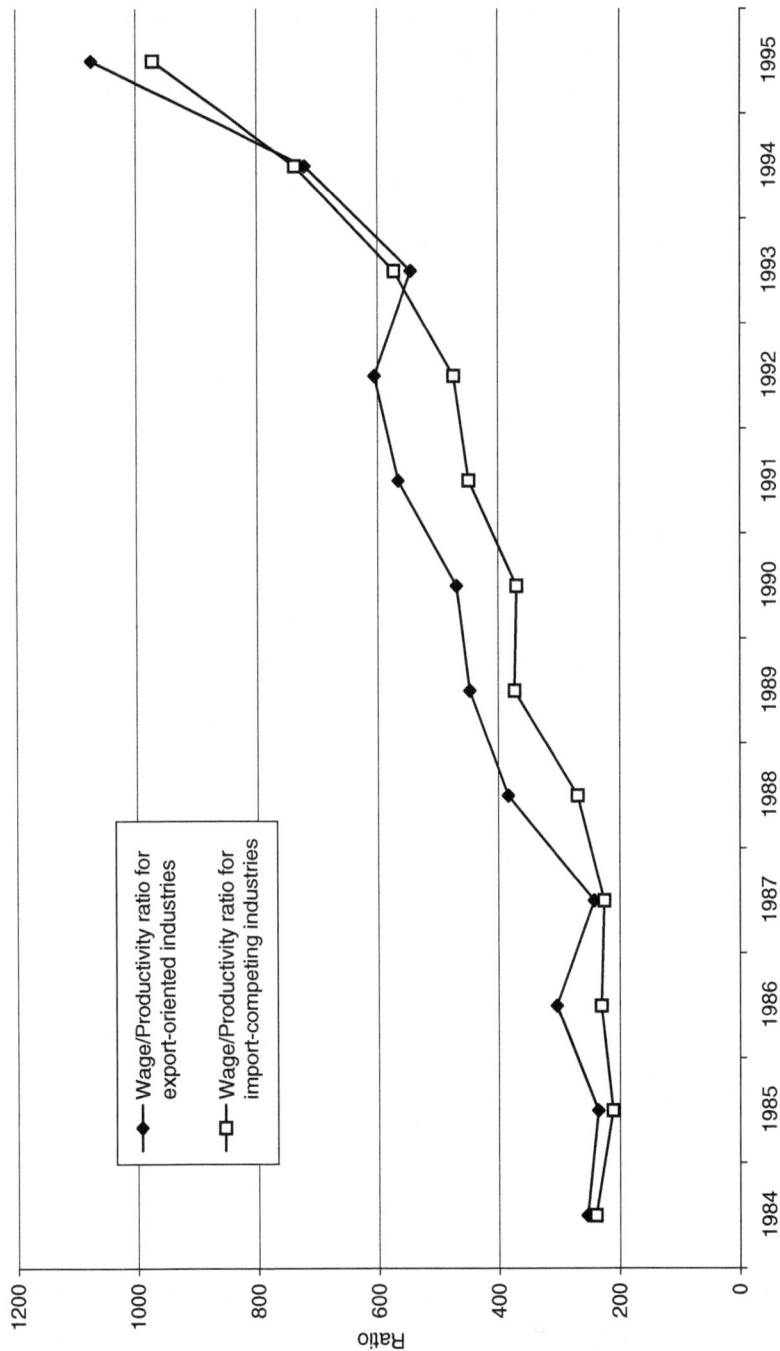

Figure 2.2 Wage–productivity ratios for China's export-oriented and import-competing industries (1984–95)

Sources: Based on industrial census data, annual industrial survey data and interpolations to obtain annual estimates. See Woo and Ren (2002).

In Table 2.9 we compare China's wages per worker, value-added per worker and the unit labour costs in manufacturing with other Asian countries for the periods 1980–84 and 1995–99. The table shows that China continues to enjoy a labour-cost advantage over many Asian countries, which are its competitors in several products in third markets. In China, the labour cost per worker in 1980–84 was the second lowest after Sri Lanka, whereas in 1995–99 it was the fourth lowest after Sri Lanka, Bangladesh and Vietnam. In terms of labour cost per unit of value-added, China ranked the lowest in 1980–84, whereas in 1995–99 it ranked fifth lowest after Thailand, Sri Lanka, Indonesia and the Philippines.

UNCTAD (2002) compares wages and unit labour costs in manufacturing between China and a selected number of developing and industrial countries. It shows that although wages in such countries as Chile, Mexico, the Republic of Korea and Turkey are much higher than those in China, unit labour costs (average wages divided by manufacturing value-added) are lower because their industrial productivity is much higher than it is in China. As we noted above, such inter-country comparisons may not be very reliable since market situations vary across countries. In China, the price structure is known to be more distorted than in many other countries, which can influence the results. Further limitations of cross-country comparisons of unit labour costs arise because of differences in the output and skill composition of manufacturing and in the coverage of labour costs. Notwithstanding the above limitations, unit labour costs and market access are important factors in determining a country's global competitiveness in particular industries. These factors are discussed in detail in Chapter 5 which provides case studies of Chinese textiles and clothing, automotive industry and household appliances.

Ratio of domestic to foreign prices

As a large proportion of manufactured goods from China is now exported, we can assume that the index of manufactured goods prices is equivalent to the index of traded goods. The consumer budget consists of many non-traded services such as transport and housing. In the case of China, rice is a major item of consumption which is also traded. But China has so far maintained price controls on rice for social considerations. The objective is to administer the rice price in such a way that the farmer (producer) gets a reasonably high price whereas the consumer buys it at a relatively lower price which might still be higher than the world price.

The rate of foreign exchange

The exchange rate policy can determine export competitiveness and the extent and composition of imports and exports. The nominal exchange rate (NER) is the official rate of exchange of a country's local currency which may imply its over- or under-valuation relative to foreign currencies. For example, an overvalued

Table 2.9 Wages, labour costs and productivity in manufacturing in China and other Asian countries ($ per year)

Country	Agricultural wage (1)		Labour cost per worker in manufacturing (2)		Value-added per worker in manufacturing (3)		Labour cost per unit of value-added in manufacturing 4 = 2 divided by 3	
	1980–84	1995–99	1980–84	1995–99	1980–84	1995–99	1980–84	1995–99
China	349	325	472	729	3,061	2,885	0.15	0.25
Bangladesh	192	360	556	671	1,820	1,711	0.30	0.39
India	205	245	1,035	1,192	2,108	3,118	0.49	0.38
Indonesia	–	–	898	1,008	3,807	5,139	0.23	0.20
Japan	–	–	12,306	31,687	34,456	92,582	0.36	0.34
Korea, Rep. of	–	–	3,153	10,743	11,617	40,916	0.27	0.26
Malaysia	–	–	2,519	3,429	8,454	12,661	0.30	0.27
Philippines	382	–	1,240	2,450	5,266	10,781	0.23	0.23
Singapore	–	4,856	5,576	21,317	16,442	40,674	0.34	0.52
Sri Lanka	198	264	447	604	2,057	3,405	0.22	0.18
Thailand	–	–	2,305	2,705	11,072	19,946	0.21	0.13
Vietnam	–	442	–	711	–	–	–	–

Source: World Bank, *World Development Indicators*, 2001.

exchange rate would discourage exports by making the price of exports relatively higher than that of imports. As we noted above, prior to reforms China kept the exchange rate overvalued to facilitate the import of cheap capital goods and intermediate products from abroad, a policy which may have encouraged capital intensity in production well above the level dictated by factor endowments.

Depreciation of the exchange rate over time is favourable to export expansion, which is supported by the Chinese experience following economic reforms. The Chinese yuan was initially overvalued, but it has been gradually depreciating (see Fig. 2.3). The real exchange rate in the 1990s was less than half of what it was in the early and mid-1980s. Figure 2.4 shows that China's NER and REER diverged significantly till the early 1990s when they started converging. Over the past decade China has devalued the yuan so that its official rate of exchange reflects closely its real market value. The convergence of the NER and REER suggests that the Chinese foreign exchange market (which was quite distorted in the 1980s) has become much less distorted with greater price liberalization and lower implicit taxation or subsidies.

Figure 2.4 compares China's REER with that of Japan, Malaysia, the Philippines and Singapore (changes in the NER are not reported as they are very close to the REER). It shows that the Chinese REER in 1985 was well above that of these other Asian economies. However, REERs started converging after 1994. The Chinese REER continues to be closely aligned to that of the neighbouring economies, which suggests that: (a) domestic prices in China are converging with those of its trading partners, and (b) that China's nominal rate of protection is declining.

As we noted in Chapter 1, in 1994 China introduced a unitary exchange rate which was allowed to fluctuate within limits. The official rate of exchange against the US dollar changed from 5.8 yuan to 8.7 yuan, representing a nominal devaluation of the yuan by 33 per cent. This depreciation of the currency had a positive stimulating effect on China's exports, which in 1994 and 1995 rose by an annual rate of nearly 32 per cent and 23 per cent respectively (Zheng and Zhao, 2002).

However, contrary to what one would expect, the export prices of China's manufactured goods did not decline in the wake of the nominal devaluation of the yuan in 1994. The price index of China's manufactured exports in 1994 was actually 4.7 per cent higher than that for 1993. With the exception of low-tech export products, whose price index fell by 3.4 per cent, all other categories of manufactured exports showed a price increase, thanks to the strength of global market demand. Another reason for the failure of China's export prices to drop is that the *real* devaluation of the yuan was only about 10 per cent as against the *nominal* decline of 33 per cent. This is so because even before 1994, the higher exchange rate of 8.7 yuan to the dollar was used for over 80 per cent of the country's export transactions. Finally, the effect of depreciation of the yuan on China's exports of processed goods was limited (Zheng and Zhao, 2002).

The exchange rate has been fairly stable since 1994. It remained stable even during the 1997 Asian financial crisis when most currencies of the Southeast

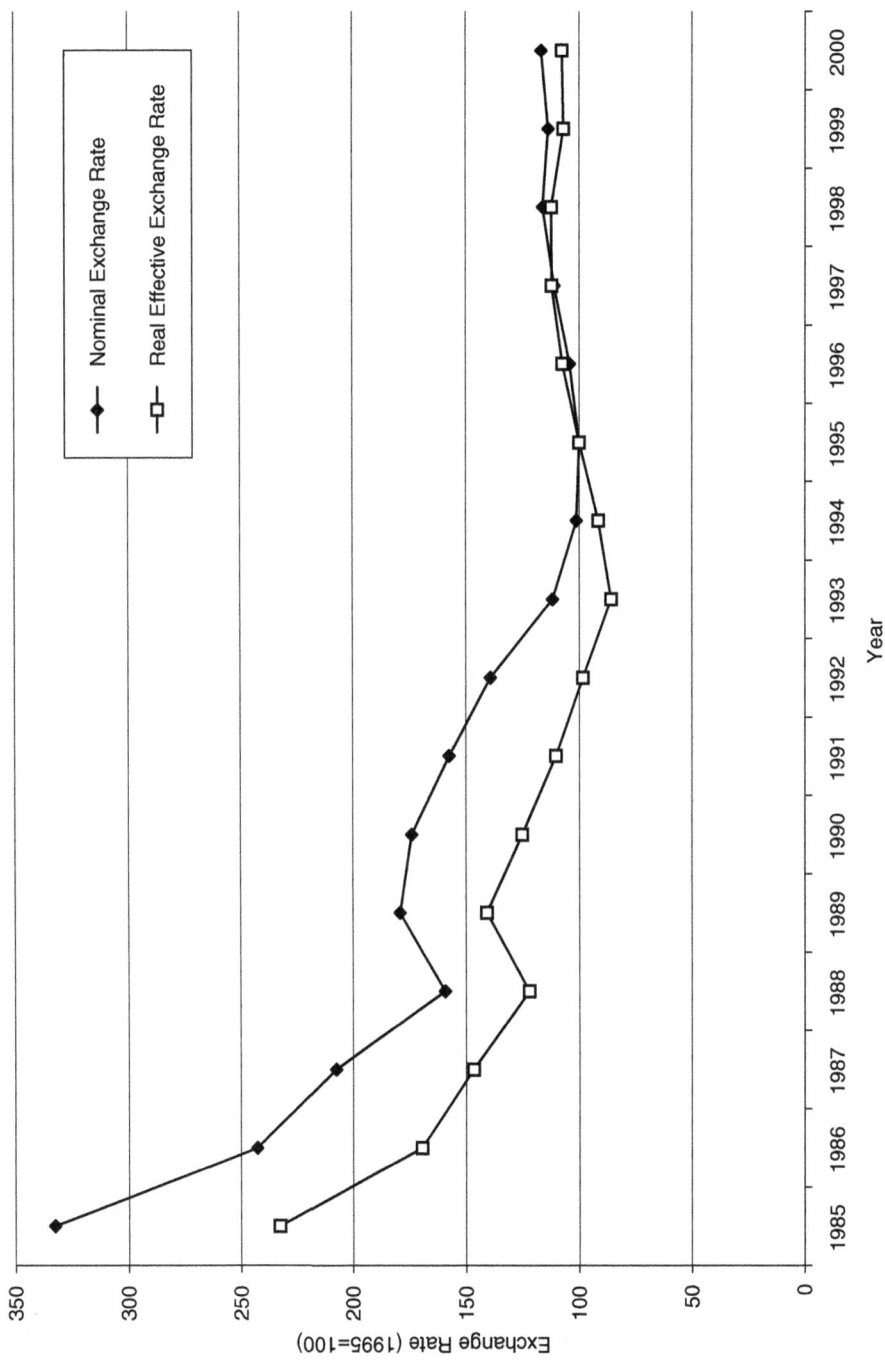

Figure 2.3 China's nominal and real effective exchange rates (1985–2000)

Source: Based on *IMF: International Financial Statistics Yearbook.*

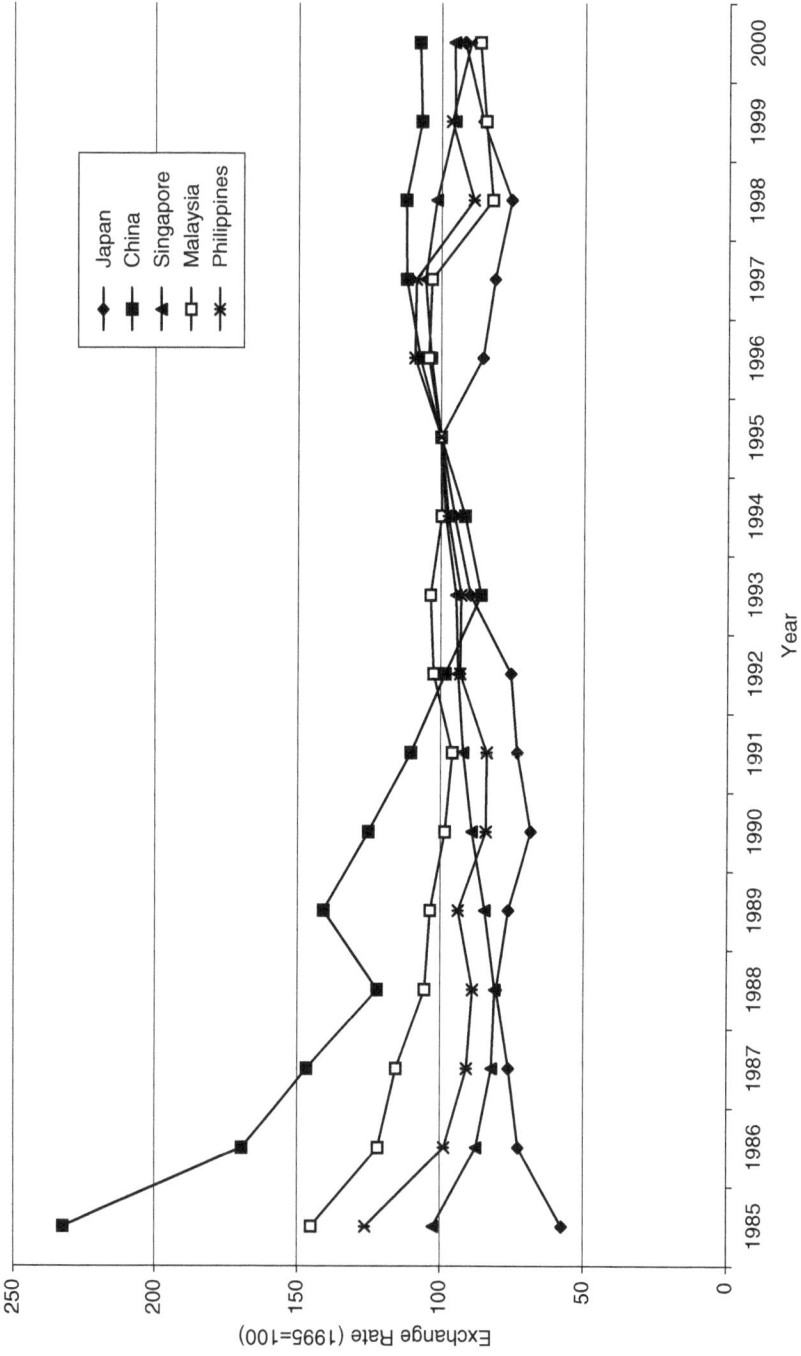

Figure 2.4 Changes in real effective exchange rates: China and selected Asian countries (1985–2000)

Source: Based on *IMF: International Financial Statistics Yearbook.*

Asian economies were realigned. The stable exchange rate, combined with low inflation since the early 1990s, has provided macroeconomic stability which is essential for investor confidence in the Chinese economy.[5] Macroeconomic stability has enabled China to benefit by expanding exports and attracting foreign direct investment. Low inflation reduces firms' costs and breeds investor confidence. If macroeconomic stability can be sustained in the post-accession period, China will be successful not only in expanding exports and attracting more FDI, but also in generating/maintaining growth and employment in its domestic as well as export sectors.

Having provided some historical and analytical background in this and the previous chapter, we turn in Chapters 3 to 6 to the possible employment impact of China's WTO accession.

3 The impact of accession on employment

Chapters 1 and 2 discussed the main features of China's accession to the WTO and the implications of further trade liberalization on competition and employment. In this chapter we discuss the likely overall employment impact of accession on China. Chapters 4 to 6 examine the sectoral employment implications in agriculture, industry and services respectively.

To understand the employment impact of accession, we first examine the current unemployment situation and its causes, and inter-sectoral employment trends over time. In the light of this information we make an assessment of the implications of accession on employment or unemployment in China.

The current unemployment situation in China

Generally speaking, the total labour force in a country is composed of the employed and unemployed population. However, official unemployment statistics vary across different economies and countries due to different definitions and concepts. This is particularly true when we consider unemployment in China. First, the official unemployment statistics refer only to the urban areas including towns, but excluding vast rural areas where there are currently about 130 million redundant workers. Second, the unemployment figures take into account only those who have registered. They exclude those who are still on the payroll but are not actually working (e.g. *xiagang*), whether they are paid or not, or paid fully or partially. Third, unemployment registration includes only people in the age range of 16–50 for males and 16–45 for females, and those who have the ability to work and who want to work, while the official retirement age is 60 years for men and 55 years for women. Therefore, the registered unemployment age is 10 years shorter than the official working age, which understates the true level of unemployment.

China has been experiencing rapid growth in unemployment since the economic reforms started in 1978. Official estimates indicate that during the Tenth Five-Year Plan (2001–2005), the registered unemployment rate will reach 3.5 per cent. Half the provinces will be able to reabsorb only about 50 per cent of the laid-off workers. Rural redundant labour will continue to increase. Urban unemployment in China has also become more serious. The hidden unemployment or excess workers (*fuyu renyuan*), who are redundant in urban and rural areas, are estimated to be of the order of about 30 million, or nearly one-third of SOE workers (Solinger, 2001). Hu (2001) estimates that the unemployment rate for 2000 is 8.3 per cent (see Table 3.1). Hu's unofficial estimates of urban unemployment are based on the assumption that 60 per cent of laid-off workers find new employment so that 40 per cent remain unemployed. Another unofficial estimate of urban unemployment by Gu (1999) is even higher: rising from 4.4 per cent in 1993 to 9.4 per cent in 1997.[1]

Variations in unofficial unemployment estimates is a symptom of the difficulties with recent data on unemployment. Data inadequacies and inconsistencies do exist and need to be borne in mind in interpreting the above results. For example, in the case of official statistics on laid-off workers, there is confusion between annual lay-offs and cumulative figures. Difficulties also arise due to adjustments by the National Bureau of Statistics (NBS) of the total urban unemployment figure on the basis of data obtained from the sample surveys on population changes. Rawski (2002: 2) notes that 'it illustrates the wide range of uncertainty surrounding basic information underpinning any analysis of recent trends in China's economy'.

Employment characteristics

Since economic reforms, employment in China has been characterized by the following features: first, reduction in employment in the state sector has, to a very large extent, been matched by an increase in employment in the non-state sector, especially the private sector, which has been growing at an annual rate of more than 20 per cent with net job creation of about 6 million (see *People's*

Table 3.1 Official and unofficial rates of urban unemployment in China

Year	No. of registered unemployed (million)	Official unemployment rate (% of registered urban population	Unofficial unemployment rate (% of registered urban population
1985	2.4	1.8	n.a.
1990	3.8	2.5	n.a.
1993	4.2	2.3	3.3–3.7
1994	4.8	2.6	3.6–4.1
1995	5.2	2.9	4.0–4.7
1996	5.5	3.0	4.9–5.9
1997	5.7	3.1	5.6–6.9
1998	5.9	3.1	7–8
1999	6.2	3.1	8–9
2000		3.1	8.3

Sources: *Labour Statistical Yearbook* for data on registered unemployed; *China Statistical Yearbook* for official rates; Hu (1998, 2001 cited in Rawski, 2002) for unofficial rates.
n.a. = not available.

Daily, 5 July 2001). Second, employment has been shifting from the primary and secondary sectors to the tertiary sector. Many rural people have migrated to urban areas to work in such activities as domestic help, cleaning, maintenance and repair, building and construction, restaurants and so on. Although there are no reliable estimates of rural-to-urban migration (and estimates vary), it is generally agreed that the number of rural migrants to urban areas has increased during the 1990s. Goodkind and West (2001) quote a figure of 100 million of the so-called floating population (*liudong renkou*) (these are seasonal migrants and residents in new urban areas whose permanent household registration remains unchanged) in 1997 as an estimate of the Chinese Ministry of Public Security.[2] Hua (2000, cited in Goodkind and West) forecasts an increase in the floating population to 160 million by 2010. Although some of these migrants are seasonal workers, many stay permanently in the urban areas. Third, a large proportion of laid-off workers becomes permanently unemployed. In many cases the number of migrant workers exceeds that of laid-off workers. Migrant workers are more successful than laid-off workers in obtaining jobs, presumably because employers do not have to pay them social benefits. Gu (1999) notes that many enterprises employ temporary migrant workers while at the same time abolishing many formal jobs.[3] This suggests that the Chinese labour market may be gradually becoming flexible as a result of such official measures as greater autonomy to firms to recruit and lay off workers and to use contract labour (Bodmer, 2002). Rawski (2002) alludes to this phenomenon of 'possible large-scale substitution of informal for formal workers' as one of the reasons for the slow growth of labour demand in the formal sector after 1995.

It is increasingly difficult for laid-off workers to be re-employed in conditions of labour oversupply. According to an official statistical bulletin, in the first half of 2001, of the 7.69 million laid-off workers, 0.79 million succeeded in obtaining other jobs; the re-employment rate was only 11 per cent.[4] A survey of labour demand and supply in 59 large and medium cities estimated that there was only 0.65 job for every job seeker (*People's Daily*, 30 July 2001).

Some studies suggest that economic growth in China will involve a shift in production towards capital- and technology-intensive goods, which will require fewer workers. The employment elasticity of output in China is estimated at only 0.1 or less, which means that for every 1 per cent GDP growth rate, demand for additional employment will be very limited. Although the Chinese economy maintains a 7–8 per cent growth rate, employment elasticity has been declining. In 1980, a 1 per cent GDP growth rate led to an increase in employment by 0.33 per cent; in 1999 the figure dropped to 0.05 per cent (*People's Daily*, 30 July 2001; Wang, 2000). It will be difficult to increase employment simply by promoting economic growth if current trends continue. Although employment elasticity of output and of exports can improve as a result of policy changes and an increase in global demand for labour-intensive goods, it is unlikely that it will rise significantly considering that capital-intensity of manufacturing is also rising. Woo and Ren (2002) note that only four out of ten industries considered had a positive employment elasticity of export.

A decline in real wage may also raise employment in future through greater demand for labour in domestic and export industries. However, as we noted in Chapter 2, wages have been rising faster than productivity so far. Thus if present trends continue, employment expansion would be adversely affected.

The regional dimension

The extent and seriousness of unemployment and lay-offs vary a great deal across regions and provinces. Furthermore, there are considerable variations by types of ownership of enterprises (see Table 3.2). In the coastal areas, employment generation is highly concentrated in a few provinces. For example, in 1999 five provinces – Guangdong, Hebei, Jiangsu, Liaoning and Shandong – provided 29.5 per cent of total employment in the country, and 62.6 per cent of total coastal employment. These five provinces provided the most significant SOE employment in 1999, accounting for nearly 64 per cent of total coastal SOE employment and nearly 28 per cent of total SOE employment in China. They accounted for 68 per cent of coastal employment in urban collectives, and 33 per cent of total Chinese employment in urban collectives. These provinces accounted for 54 per cent of employment in coastal non-state enterprises (including private enterprises), or 34 per cent of employment in all non-state enterprises. In the non-coastal areas, six provinces, namely Anhui, Heilongjiang Henan, Hubei, Hunan, and Sichuan, accounted for 28 per cent of total employment and 53 per cent of total non-coastal employment in 1999.

These provinces accounted for 50 per cent of total non-coastal SOE employment and 28.6 per cent of total SOE employment in China. They accounted for 31 per cent of China's urban collective employment and 60 per cent of such employment in non-coastal areas. The non- coastal areas accounted for 21 per cent of China's total non-state employment and 77 per cent of the non-coastal total (see Table 3.2).

Lay-offs are a phenomenon of Chinese SOEs and urban collectives. Joint ventures and private enterprises do not over-hire. Lay-offs by SOEs in the non-coastal provinces (e.g. Heilongjiang, Hubei, Hunan and Jilin) are generally higher than those in the coastal provinces, although there are such exceptions as Liaoning and Tianjin, which together accounted for 12.6 per cent of total lay-offs in China, and 44.5 per cent of SOE lay-offs in the coastal areas. The above four non-coastal provinces alone accounted for 31 per cent of total SOE lay-offs in China and nearly 46 per cent of SOE lay-offs in the non-coastal areas/provinces (Table 3.2).

Historically, heavy machine-building and other industries such as textiles, armaments and chemical engineering were located in the hinterland for military and security reasons. (The problem was particularly acute in such north-eastern provinces as Heilongjiang, Jilin and Liaoning.) These industries use old technologies and production facilities which are being modernized; large-scale lay-offs is a natural consequence. This process of technological modernization will become much more rapid following accession. China will

Table 3.2 Employment and worker lay-offs in coastal and non-coastal areas by ownership categories (1999) (1000)

	SOEs			Urban collectives			Other enterprises			Total		
	Employ-ment	Laid-off workers	(%)	Employ-ment	Laid-off workers	(%)	Employ-ment	Laid-off workers	(%)	Total employ-ment	Total laid-off workers	(%)
National total	85,721	6,525	7.61	17,118	2,589	15.12	18,463	257.4	1.39	121,302	9,371.5	7.72
I. Coastal Areas												
Tianjin	1,185	144.8	12.2	305	52.0	17.05	627	1.2	0.19	2,117	198.0	9.35
Beijing	2,876	29.0	1.01	497	2.8	0.56	950			4,323	31.8	0.73
Hebei	4,474	196.8	4.4	686	55.5	8.09	592	2.6	0.44	5,752	254.9	4.43
Liaoning	4,472	678.0	15.2	1,141	452.5	39.66	852	29.0	3.40	6,465	1,159.5	17.93
Shanghai	2,197	98.5	4.48	394	36.0	9.14	1,081			3,672		
Jiangsu	4,555	170.5	3.74	1,427	100.3	7.03	1,379	11.3	0.82	7,361	282.1	3.83
Zhejiang	2,242	56.3	2.51	731	46.0	6.29	1,111	2.5	0.22	4,084	104.8	2.57
Shandong	5,799	143.1	2.47	1,207	82.7	6.85	1,249	3.2	0.26	8,255	229.0	2.77
Fujian	1,795	29.3	1.63	371			1,122			3,288		
Hainan	688	38.9	5.65	46	4.4	9.56	82	0.2	0.24	816	43.5	5.33
Guangdong	4,499	135.1	3.00	1,227	123.6	10.10	2,210	7.2	0.32	7,936	265.9	3.35
Guangxi	2,442	127.6	5.23	311	5.2	1.67	313	1.8	0.57	3,066	134.6	4.39
Total for coastal areas	37,224	1,847.9	4.96	8,343	961.0	11.52	11,568	59.0	0.51	57,135	2,867.9	5.02
II. Non-coastal areas												
Guizhou	1,628	109.6	6.73	217	19.7	9.08	201	0.8	0.398	2,046	130.1	6.36
Sichuan	4,052	296.3	7.31	824	103.9	12.61	732	29.9	4.08	5,608	430.1	7.67
Chongqing	1,612	135.1	8.38	361	57.8	16.01	289			2,262	192.9	8.53

Table 3.2 Employment and worker lay-offs in coastal and non-coastal areas by ownership categories (1999) (1000) (Continued)

	SOEs			Urban collectives			Other enterprises			Total employ-ment	Total laid-off workers	(%)
	Employ-ment	Laid-off workers	(%)	Employ-ment	Laid-off workers	(%)	Employ-ment	Laid-off workers	(%)			
Yunnan	2,366	58.8	2.48	288	5.5	1.91	268			2,922		
Hunan	3,864	524.5	13.57	623	226.8	36.40	270	7.0	2.59	4,757	758.3	15.94
Hubei	4,449	414.5	9.32	767	205.5	26.79	606	39.4	6.50	5,822	659.4	11.33
Henan	4,753	262.6	5.52	1,458	121.9	8.36	1,207	12.7	1.05	7,418	397.2	5.35
Anhui	2,866	287.6	10.03	741	136.4	18.41	589	4.6	0.78	4,196	428.6	10.21
Jiangxi	2,498	261.9	10.48	371	59.6	16.06	272	4.7	1.73	3,141	326.2	10.38
Heilongjiang	4,552	740.5	16.27	891	394.2	44.24	526	83.0	15.78	5,969	1,217.7	20.40
Jilin	2,696	339.7	12.60	494	117.1	23.70	389	5.3	1.36	3,579	462.1	12.91
Inner Mongolia	2,133	129.2	6.06	304			393			2,830	129.2	4.56
Shanxi	2,945	200.5	6.81	523	49.0	9.37	453	1.9	0.42	3,921	251.4	6.41
Shaanxi	2,802	325.0	11.60	332	102.9	30.99	328	8.2	2.50	3,462	436.1	12.59
Gansu	1,704	156.9	9.21	269	17.0	6.32	134	0.04	0.03	2,107	173.94	8.25
Qinghai	468	61.1	13.05	55	0.9	1.64	13			536	62.0	11.57
Ningxia	523	39.5	7.55	54	3.7	6.85	78	0.3	0.38	655	6.6	1.01
Xinjiang	2,426	87.5	3.61	190	6.1	3.21	140	0.5	0.36	2,756	94.1	3.41
Tibet	159			11			5			175		
Total for non-coastal areas	48,496	4,430.8	9.14	8,773	1,628	18.56	6,893	198.34	2.88	64,162	6,257.14	9.75

Source: Data supplied by the Ministry of Labour.

Note: The laid-off workers are the total figure at year-end, which is the previous year-end total plus new lay-offs minus those who were re-employed during the year.

be unable to sustain or regain its export market shares without increasing efficiency.

Unemployment rates are generally lower in the coastal provinces (with greater economic activity and higher growth rates) than in the non-coastal provinces. Hu's (1999) comparison of official and actual unemployment rates by provinces shows that the latter are much higher. For example, the actual rates estimated by Hu for Hebei, Jilin, Jiangsu, Jiangxi, Henan and Hunan are more than double the official rates of unemployment (see Fig. 3.1).

Some fear that import competition after China's accession will exacerbate the problem of regional differences in employment, unemployment and real incomes. The agricultural sector (see Chapter 4) and SOEs are viewed by many observers to be particularly vulnerable. Wang (1999) argues that inland provinces suffer most from global competition because their economies (unlike those of the coastal provinces) are undiversified and depend on a limited number of key crops. Their limited financial resources and poor natural endowments will prevent them from restructuring agriculture and industry. However, this argument implicitly assumes that cooperation between the coastal and non-coastal provinces (to be strengthened further under the Western Development Strategy) will not work. As we argue in Chapter 7, the flying-geese model of trade and development is likely to operate within China. Given proper incentives and policies, this should lead to a narrowing of regional differences. We further argue that China can maintain its global competitiveness in such labour-intensive exports as textiles and clothing by relocating production to non-coastal areas (see Chapter 5).

Employment and labour surplus in SOEs

One of the major reasons for the pessimistic forecasts of the employment impact of accession is the low competitiveness of China's SOEs which were hitherto protected but are now exposed to global competition. It is therefore useful to examine the recent employment situation in China's SOEs prior to WTO entry. However, a look at the employment situation over time in SOEs in isolation is not helpful. We need to compare the declining employment in SOEs with the increase in employment in the private sector and other ownership types (e.g. joint ventures, cooperatives and limited liability corporations) (see Fig. 3.2). While employment in SOEs has been consistently declining since 1995 and in urban collectives since 1993 even without the accession, that in TVEs, private sector and other ownership categories has been rising. This trend (also noted in the automotive industry in Chapter 5) is likely to continue after China joins the WTO. However, it is unclear whether TVE employment will grow siginificantly. China's 1995 Industrial Census revealed that employment statistics in TVEs compiled by the Ministry of Agriculture were highly exaggerated. Actual TVE employment does not appear to have grown since 1996–97. Rawski (2002) argues that TVE employment in 2000 was about 90 million, much lower than the official figure of 127 million for 1999.

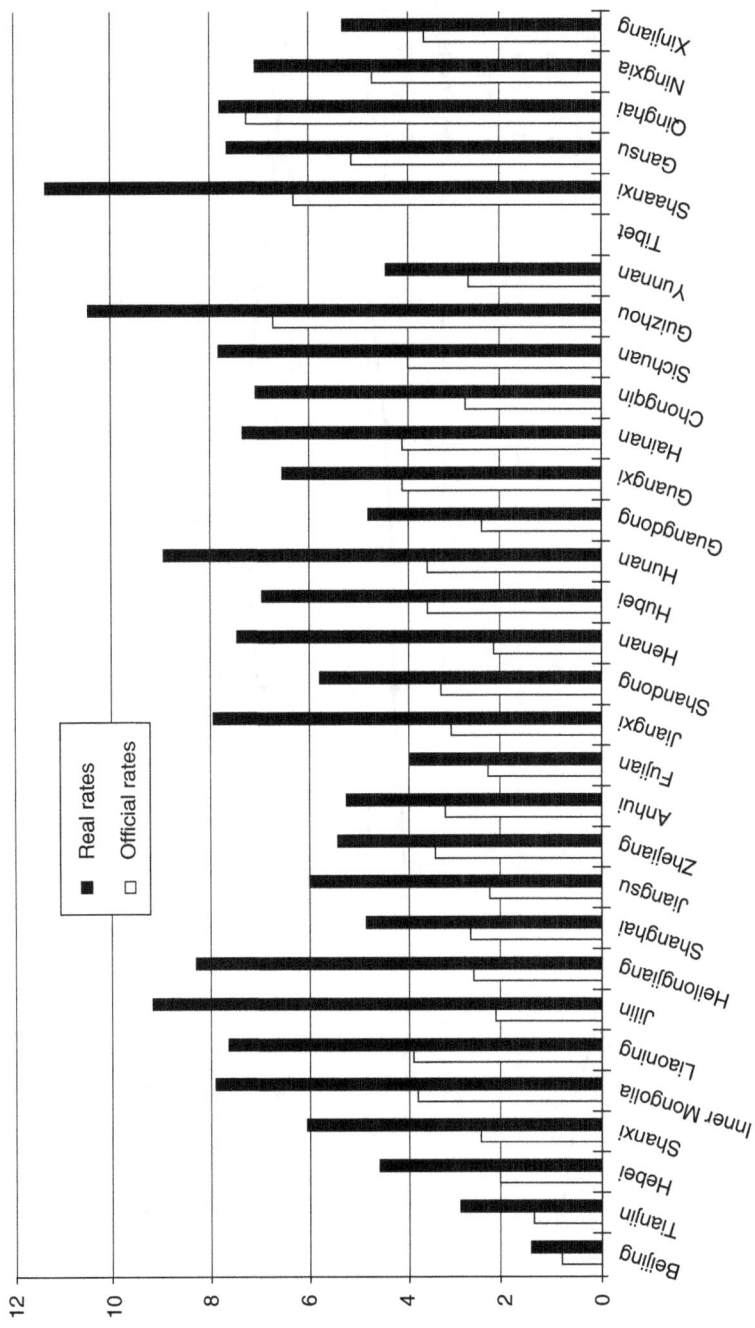

Figure 3.1 China's provincial unemployment rates (%)

Source: Hu (2000), cited in Wang (2000).

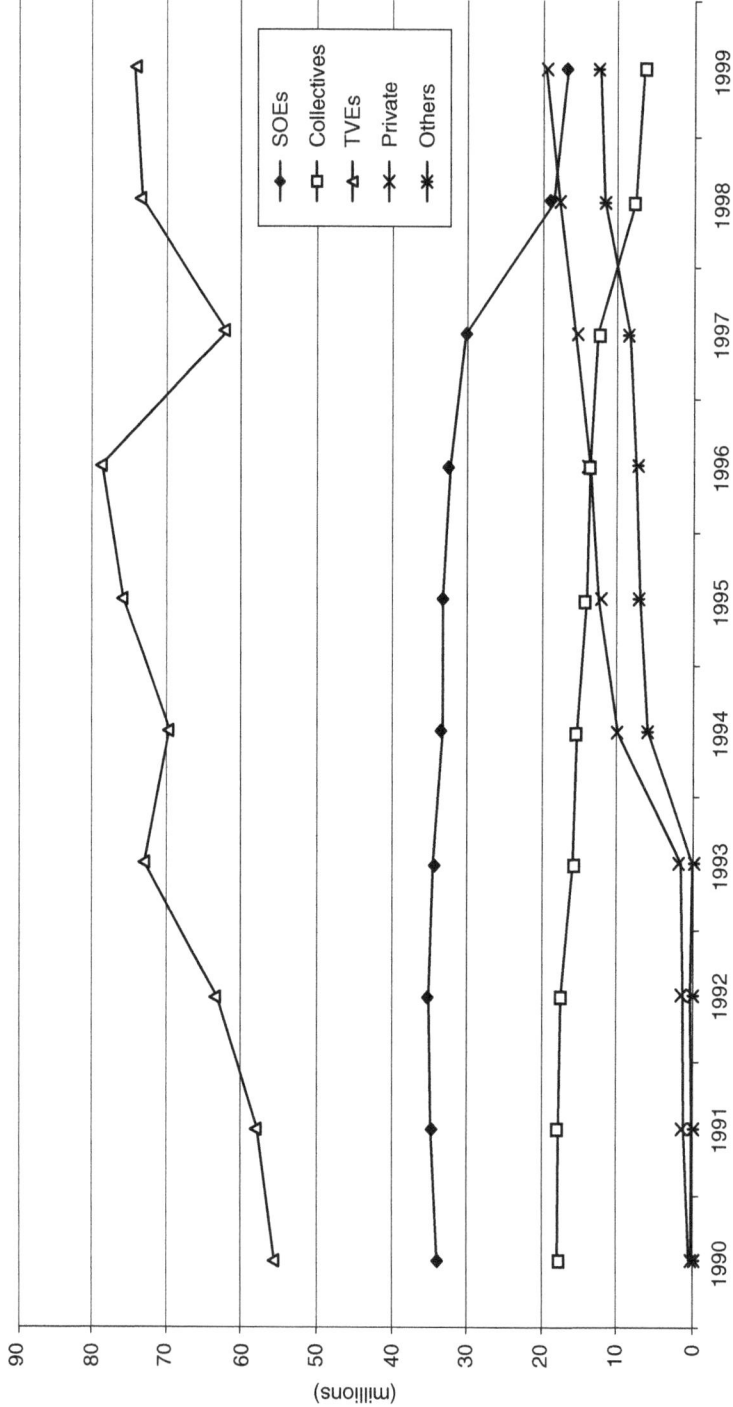

Figure 3.2 Employment in Chinese SOEs and other ownership types (1990–99)

Source: Based on *China Labour Statistical Yearbook*, various issues.

The diversity of ownership in China's manufacturing sector, noted above, is the direct result of a gradual marketization of the economy since 1980, which reformers believed would facilitate domestic competition. Indeed, initially China did not privatize; rather it encouraged the growth of TVEs to provide competition to SOEs (see Bhalla, 2001). However, since 1995 small and medium SOEs have been privatized, whereas large SOEs remain state-owned. The latter benefit from subsidies, either directly by the government or indirectly by commercial banks owned by the state.

There are two distinguishing features of SOEs compared to collectives and non-state enterprises. First, many of the SOEs (about one-third of the total) are making losses and thus are less competitive. Empirical estimates show that their total factor productivity has been rising, although not as fast as that of collective enterprises and TVEs.[5] Second, most large SOEs are concentrated in capital-intensive sectors, whereas the non-state sector is engaged in all kinds of activities, especially labour-intensive ones in which China has a comparative advantage. Town and village enterprises (TVEs) and joint ventures account for a substantial value and volume of China's exports, whereas SOEs are less important exporters. Thus China's trade sector is quite dualistic.

Employment data in manufacturing SOEs by type of industry are hard to find. Therefore, it is not possible to determine any time trend. However, we have some data for 1998 to 2000, which show the importance of such industries as machinery manufacturing, textiles, petroleum processing and non-metal mineral products (Table 3.3).

Various official and unofficial estimates of labour surplus in Chinese SOEs are now available. Two notable features of these estimates are: (a) their wide range and (b) their partial and micro nature. Estimates vary, depending on the assumptions and perceptions of enterprise managers, since most of the estimates are based on interview surveys. Lim *et al.* (1996: 31) estimate labour surplus in Chinese industrial SOEs and other forms of ownership on the basis of an ILO field survey undertaken in February–March 1995. 'In job' labour surplus was estimated by asking enterprise managers whether the same level of output could be achieved with fewer workers, and if so, by what percentage. The responding enterprises noted that labour could be cut by 17 per cent of their current total workforce. Among all the ownership categories, the highest level of labour surplus was reported in joint stock companies (18.9 per cent) followed by labour service enterprises (16.4 per cent) and state-owned enterprises (15.6 per cent).

The above data based on managers' responses needs to be interpreted with care. Of course, there is no doubt that most SOEs are overstaffed. We do not question the existence of surplus labour, but the feasibility of removing it, at least in the short run, would pose serious problems in a labour surplus economy, particularly since WTO accession will exacerbate the unemployment situation noted earlier.

The official estimates of excess labour in different types of enterprises are presented in Table 3.4. In addition to the 'in job' labour surplus, a phenomenon peculiar to China is that of 'on leave' surplus labour (*xiagang* or lay-offs), which

Table 3.3 SOE employment in Chinese manufacturing sectors (1998–2000)

Sector	1998 (000)	% of total manufacturing employment	1999 (000)	% of total manufacturing employment	2000 (000)	% of total manufacturing employment
National total	19,007	100	16,652	100	14,321	100
Food processing	974	5.1	836	5.0	677	4.7
Textiles	2,119	11.1	1,769	10.6	1,504	10.5
Garments and other fibre products	167	0.9	154	0.9	136	0.9
Leather and related products	86	0.4	74	0.4	64	0.4
Timber processing (bamboo, cane)	133	0.7	109	0.6	96	0.7
Furniture making	35	0.2	26	0.2	21	0.1
Papermaking and paper products	390	2.0	308	1.8	245	1.7
Printing	345	1.8	312	1.9	278	1.9
Stationery, educational and sports goods	41	0.2	31	0.2	25	0.2
Petroleum processing	508	2.7	486	2.9	429	2.9
Chemicals and chemical fibres	1,979	10.4	1,721	10.3	1,455	10.1
Medical and pharmaceutical products	440	2.3	408	2.4	364	2.5
Rubber products	172	0.9	152	0.9	133	0.9
Plastic products	146	0.8	119	0.7	94	0.6
Non-metal mineral products	1,493	7.8	1,305	7.8	1,132	7.9
Smelting/processing of metals	2,259	11.9	2,045	12.3	1,811	12.6
Metal products	314	1.6	270	1.6	196	1.4
Machinery manufacturing	2,554	13.4	2,188	13.2	1,832	12.8
Transport equipment	1,774	9.3	1,664	10.0	1,459	10.2
Electric equipment and machinery	643	3.4	557	3.3	469	3.3
Electronics and telecommunications	462	2.4	378	2.3	336	2.3
Instruments, meters	258	1.3	217	1.3	179	1.2
Other manufacturing	132	0.7	126	0.7	148	1.0

Source: *China Labour Statistical Yearbook* (original in Chinese).

Note: Percentages may not add up to 100 due to rounding.

Table 3.4 Estimates of surplus labour in Chinese SOEs and other enterprises (000)

	1993	1994	1995	1996
All SOEs	544	1,202	6,570	6,593
Manufacturing SOEs	308	677	4,314	3,233
Urban collectives	–	314	2,101	2,845
Other enterprises	–	61	155	212

Source: Data supplied by the Ministry of Labour. – = not available.

Note: Surplus labour includes lay-offs. Data on surplus labour are not available since 1996. It may be because such data are replaced by those on lay-offs and unemployment.

represents a phased labour redundancy in SOEs. The policy of *xiagang*, an important element of Chinese urban reforms, was launched in 1997 although some experiments were carried out as early as 1994. The policy was designed to resolve SOE problems of overstaffing and economic inefficiency by laying off redundant workers.[6] Although these workers vacate their posts, they continue to be paid a partial salary or allowances for a specified period during which they are encouraged to look for alternative jobs. In contrast, fully redundant workers do not benefit from such assistance, although they may receive some unemployment benefits from the local labour bureaux.

There was a dramatic increase in 'on leave' workers which may be explained by an increase in the number of SOE bankruptcies (see Yang and Tam, 1999). From 1998 to the first half of 2002, 17 million workers were laid off (*Xinhua News*, 11 November 2002). Initially, *xiagang* applied to bankruptcies and closures only, but its coverage gradually widened to include the following: (i) those with reduced salary; (ii) those who retired or left on prolonged leave; and (iii) those awaiting reassignment within the enterprise (Lee, 2000). *Xiagang* is a case of slow retrenchment no doubt, which softens the blow of social hardship, but it continues to remain a financial burden on SOEs. The total cost to SOEs of paying surplus workers is estimated to be 96 billion yuan, which was twice the total profits of SOEs in 1997 (Lee, 2000).

Redundant labour is concentrated mainly in SOEs and urban collectives. This is not surprising considering that in the pre-reform period, the Chinese government used SOEs as an employment-generating mechanism to ensure full employment. It expected enterprises to employ not only workers who were not necessary for production, but also to provide jobs to their children. Government subsidies to SOEs continue to finance the wages of such workers.

Females accounted for a substantial proportion of lay-offs in SOEs urban collectives and other enterprises. Older workers (35–46 years) predominate among those laid off and a substantial proportion have low educational qualifications (see Table 3.5). Both these factors – older age and low education – renders their retraining and re-employment difficult. There is evidence that, faced with the problem of massive lay-offs and resulting social instability, the Chinese Government has often discouraged SOEs from shedding surplus labour.

Table 3.5 Characteristics of laid-off workers by ownership categories in 1998 (000)

	SOEs	(%)	Urban collectives	(%)	Other firms	(%)
Lay-offs at the end of 1997	6,918		2,665		301	
Additional lay-offs during 1998	5,622		1,570		197	
Reduction of lay-offs during 1998	6,592		1,721		261	
Of which: re-employed during 1998	6,099	100.00	1,518	100.00	222	100.00
SOEs	1,663	27.27	148	9.75	21	9.46
Non state-owned firms	1,687	27.66	552	36.36	62	27.93
Private self-employed	2,581	42.32	781	51.45	135	60.81
Total laid-off workers at the end of 1998	5,948	100	2,514	100	307	100
Of which: female workers	2,684	45.12	1,132	45.03	110	35.83
Of which: 35 years and below	2,106	35.41	708	28.16	103	33.55
35–46 years	2,473	41.58	1,129	44.91	117	38.11
Above 46 years	1,368	23.00	677	26.93	87	28.34
Of which: Middle school and below	3,301	55.50	1,537	61.14	163	53.09
Secondary school	2,211	37.17	822	32.70	119	38.76
College and other high education	436	7.33	156	6.21	25	8.14

Source: Data supplied by the Ministry of Labour.

Although in theory the Chinese government now allows SOEs to lay off workers, in practice labour market flexibility (hiring and firing) is not common due, in part, to the failure or lack of a comprehensive social security system and limited resources for social welfare at the level of local governments. Labour mobility is restricted by the fact that, once they leave SOEs, workers forgo social welfare benefits of housing, education and health services (and even pensions). These benefits are not available to workers under other forms of ownership (e.g. joint ventures, and collective and private enterprises). Nevertheless, SOEs competing in the export market are increasingly permitted to hire and fire workers (see Box 3.1 describing a visit to an SOE factory in Guizhou province where employment is not guaranteed). After China's accession restructuring of the labour market and a shift from guaranteed permanent employment to more flexible contract employment is bound to become a common practice, especially as a means of reducing production costs.

The official figures of *xiagang* given in Table 3.5 may be underestimated. Solinger (2001: 676) notes that 'officially counted *xiagang* staff and workers relate only to those that the government knows about and so amount to just a portion of this group, excluding what are probably millions of other individuals who have lost their jobs since the late 1980s'. In fact, there are incentives to both understate and overstate *xiagang* workers and their re-employment. First, the central government may have a tendency to underestimate *xiagang* in order to show that the unemployment situation in urban areas is better than it actually is. On the other hand, at the local level there may be an opposite tendency, to exaggerate the figures in order to obtain greater subsidies for the needy. The Chinese government has also launched a nationwide re-employment programme besides subsidizing enterprises which employ laid-off workers (Gu, 1999). Second, local governments may have an incentive to overstate numbers trained and re-employed in order to attract investment and training funds from the central government.

There are many institutional constraints to re-employment of laid-off workers. First, the laid-off workers have a tendency to seek state jobs in order to avail of security and welfare benefits. However, the number of jobs in the state sector have been shrinking rapidly. Besides this demand factor (the availability of jobs), the supply side of the problem also, that is, changing of the incentive structure facing laid-off workers seeking re-employment, is equally important. Gu (1999) notes that the *daiwei* (worker units) system of welfare socialism is still in place, which discourages job seekers from seeking private-sector employment. Removal of institutional barriers to mobility between the state and non-state labour markets is therefore essential.

Worker lay-offs are only one element in employment reduction. Other elements include early retirements, normal retirements, natural attrition, and unemployment due to technological, structural and cyclical phenomena.[7] But the *xiagang* (or furlough) policy of lay-offs was preceded by policies of labour redeployment not involving lay-offs: transferring redundant workers to such subsidiary enterprises as hotels and restaurants, and 'labour service companies' (Rawski, 1999). We mentioned earlier that more and more SOE workers have

Box 3.1 **Visit to a state-owned enterprise in Guizhou Province (Southwest China)**

On 9 April 2001, the authors visited Zhenning Hongbeiye Limited, a subsidiary of Guizhou Redstar Development Corporation. It was set up in October 1995 by its parent company, Qingdao Redstar Chemical Industry Group, a large state-owned company producing non-organic salt products. In 1994, since market conditions for the chemical industry were not favourable, the parent company decided to transfer some production to locations close to natural resources and raw materials: Zhenning Bouyi and Miao Autonomous County that have abundant heavy crystal stone, limestone, coal resources and power supply. A nationally-designated poor county, it is a partner-county of Qiaodao in a scheme under which the cities in the eastern areas assist the western region in alleviating poverty.

Zhenning Hongbeiye company produces carbon-acid barium and carbon-acid strontium, the products with wide industrial applications, especially for making TV or computer glass screens. Majority of its products are exported to American, European and other international markets. They are of a high quality and globally competitive. Many international suppliers have stopped production to buy products from this factory.

The factory is run quite differently from its parent company. The majority of its workers are hired locally. There are about 800 workers on the site we visited. They are employed on a contract basis and do not enjoy guaranteed employment for life as was the case formerly. For new workers, a probationary period of three months has been introduced. No worker can be transferred to a contract position unless he or she fulfils the minimum performance requirements. Every year a comprehensive assessment of workers' performance is undertaken and 5 per cent of the top performers are awarded extra bonus. The bottom 5 per cent are placed on a three-month probation. A worker must leave the factory at the end of the probationary period if he/she cannot find an alternative job within it. The wage structure consists of a basic wage plus a bonus: about one-third consists of the basic wage and two-thirds is performance-related payment. Unlike many other SOEs, this factory had no obligation to provide such social services as health and education for its workers.

The workforce is mainly recruited from among former retired soldiers, school-leavers and farmers. Extensive training is given to new workers.

The initial production capacity of 45,000 tons annually was raised to 80,000 tons in 1998, and at present, it is 120,000 tons.

lost their jobs as a result of restructuring, sale of enterprises or bankruptcies. Almost half of the laid-off or unemployed workers simply cannot find new jobs, and many prefer to take early retirement or seek state-sector employment (dubbed as an 'aristocratic' mentality of laid-off workers).[8] Even when some get re-employed, they find jobs mostly in the non-state or private sector. Thus the state sector in industry will be much smaller after accession in respect of both output and employment. Additional jobs will be created mainly in the private sector. It is estimated that during 1995–97, China's domestic private enterprises created more jobs than those in state, collective and town and village enterprises. The contribution of the private sector to employment in the 1990s is known to have been underestimated, as some private enterprises are reluctant to register for fear of being taxed, and others are disguised as rural or urban collectives (Zhu, 1998). Private and individual enterprises play a very important role in providing job opportunities to laid-off workers. From 1990 to 2001, 30 million new jobs were created in the private sector, accounting for 40 per cent of the total number of new jobs created during this period (*Xinhua News*, 11 November, 2002).

Loss-making SOEs in China are known to have raised wages and disbursed bonuses.[9] This is evidenced by the relatively constant share of the wage bill of industrial SOEs between 1981 and 1995, despite falling employment and profitability (Perkins, 1999). Between 1985 and 1996, the average real wage of SOE workers increased by 50 per cent, which was double that of workers in collective enterprises (Huang *et al.*, 1999). Under the Chinese enterprise reforms, bonuses (not exceeding 25 per cent of the basic wage bill) were allowed in order to induce greater labour productivity. There are indications that wage bonuses and allowances paid by many SOEs to compensate for increases in cost of living were well in excess of this ceiling, even when these enterprises made losses. Under increased global competition after accession, China will not be able to afford massive wage increases which are inimical to improving its industrial competitiveness.

The employment impact of accession

Many quantitative forecasts exist of the implications of China's WTO entry on output, exports and imports. Gilbert and Wahl (2000a) reviewed thirty such studies most of which are based on computable general equilibrium (CGE) models using the Global Trade Analysis Project (GTAP) data base. None of those studies reviewed estimate the overall employment impact of accession. The main reason why CGE models do not indicate an impact on the overall level of employment is the overwhelming dominance of the neoclassical assumptions, especially with regard to China, which is still a transition economy with imperfect factor and product mobility. UNCTAD (2002) notes that CGE models make an implicit assumption that labour moves rapidly in response to new incentive structures. Furthermore the models are of a comparative static nature with no explicit time dimension. However, since it is generally assumed that wages will adjust to clear the labour market, the CGE models implicitly take a long-term view.[10] Second, as most studies make neoclassical assumptions of full employment and wage flexibility, unemployment is regarded as a temporary phenomenon. There is only one study by Xu and Chang (2000), which is explicitly concerned with the impact of *unilateral* tariff reductions of 25 or 50 per cent, not of *multilateral* tariff reductions associated with accession, on structural employment in China.

Xu and Chang argue that the estimates of the potential structural unemployment effect of China's trade liberalization (which some believe is as much as 20 million jobs) is highly exaggerated. Their estimates suggest that a 50 per cent across-the-board tariff cut would lead to a temporary loss of 4 million jobs.[11] If tariff cuts are introduced only in one particular sector, for example, heavy industry, a 50 per cent tariff cut would lead to a decline of employment by 0.6 million workers (see Table 3.6). While the Xu-Chang estimates are more conservative than others (e.g. Zhang *et al.*, 1998), who also examine the impact of unilateral tariff reduction and estimate 11 million job losses, there is no certainty that their estimates are more reliable. Furthermore, another limitation of the Xu-Chang estimates is that they are based on the old 1992 Social Accounting Matrix (SAM) for China, which does not reflect the recent situation. Whether the employment impact of unilateral tariff reductions is low or high depends very much on the assumptions one makes. This *unilateral* action by China implies that its trading partners may not take similar action, in which case China's exports to these partners would suffer thus causing adverse employment. Its imports might increase substantially, leading to adverse terms of trade. However, multilateral tariff reductions under the WTO Agreement are different in the sense that China's trading partners, especially major ones like the US and the EU, also have accepted some reciprocal obligations to open up their markets to China's exports. Thus, in principle China should be able to expand its employment in the tradeable sectors more under *multilateral* than under *unilateral* tariff reductions.

Invariably forecasts of unilateral or multilateral tariff reductions are simulations based on (often arbitrary) assumptions, since facts about China's accession became known only at the end of 2001. It is not our intention to add to

Table 3.6 Employment effects of unilateral tariff reductions by China

Nature of tariff cuts	*Employment effects of: (million workers)*	
	25 per cent tariff cut	*50 per cent tariff cut*
Across-the-board tariff cuts	−2.0	−4.1
Tariff cuts only in manufacturing	−0.2	−0.4
Tariff cuts only in heavy industry	−0.3	−0.6
Tariff cuts only in light industry	−1.2	−2.3

Source: Xu and Chang (2000).

this large body of quantification and forecasting. We believe that CGE model forecasting of such a complex exercise as implications of the WTO entry with no clear counterfactual may not be useful particularly since the forecasts do not take account of the substantial trade, investment and foreign exchange liberalization which has already taken place (see Chapter 1). The various estimates are based on such unrealistic assumptions as the existence of equilibrium conditions in factor and product markets, and generally perfect labour mobility. While it is true that some of the models (e.g. Gilbert and Wahl, 2002b; Yang and Huang, 1997; Zhai and Li, 2000) have attempted to relax these assumptions by introducing imperfect labour mobility, they are generally subject to other stringent assumptions as well. Furthermore, many of these forecasts are based on high tariff rates which prevailed in the mid-1990s, but which China has unilaterally and significantly reduced since then.[12] Forecasts based on such assumptions are bound to overstate the impact of WTO membership, as we shall show in subsequent chapters. Gilbert and Wahl (2002a: 720) conclude: 'given the inherent uncertainty over specification, parameters and data, we should guard against interpreting CGE results too literally'.

The issue of the employment impact of China's accession is concerned with identifying which tradeable and non-tradeable sectors will absorb the unemployed after China's entry to the WTO. To answer this question we need to examine current trends in inter-sectoral employment and shifts between the primary, secondary and tertiary sectors. Figure 3.3, which plots the evolution of employment shares of these sectors between 1952 and 1998, shows that throughout this period, the primary sector remained the major absorber of labour, followed by the secondary sector until 1994 when its share was overtaken by the tertiary sector. There has been a sharp decline in employment growth in manufacturing despite FDI inflows into this sector (Rawski, 2002). It is widely believed that the following traditional labour-intensive export sectors will benefit within five years after accession: textiles and clothing, food processing, construction and service sectors.[13]

The trend towards greater employment in the tertiary sector (both numbers of workers and share of total employment) is likely to continue and become more significant in the post-accession period. This is particularly so since agriculture already absorbs a very large proportion of workers. Under the WTO Agreement (see Chapter 1), barriers that restrict entry into many service industries (especially, telecommunications and financial services) will be removed. These barriers were introduced mainly to protect the pricing power and profits of SOEs. Their relaxation after accession is likely to expand employment in such services as telecommunications by increasing competition, reducing prices and increasing volume (see Chapter 6).

Ianchovichina *et al.* (2000) compare changes in China's output and employment in selected industries, with and without accession for the period 1995–2005 (see Table 3.7). They show that a positive gain in employment of unskilled workers will occur in the following industries: foodgrains, meat and livestock and dairy products, clothing and electronics. On the other hand,

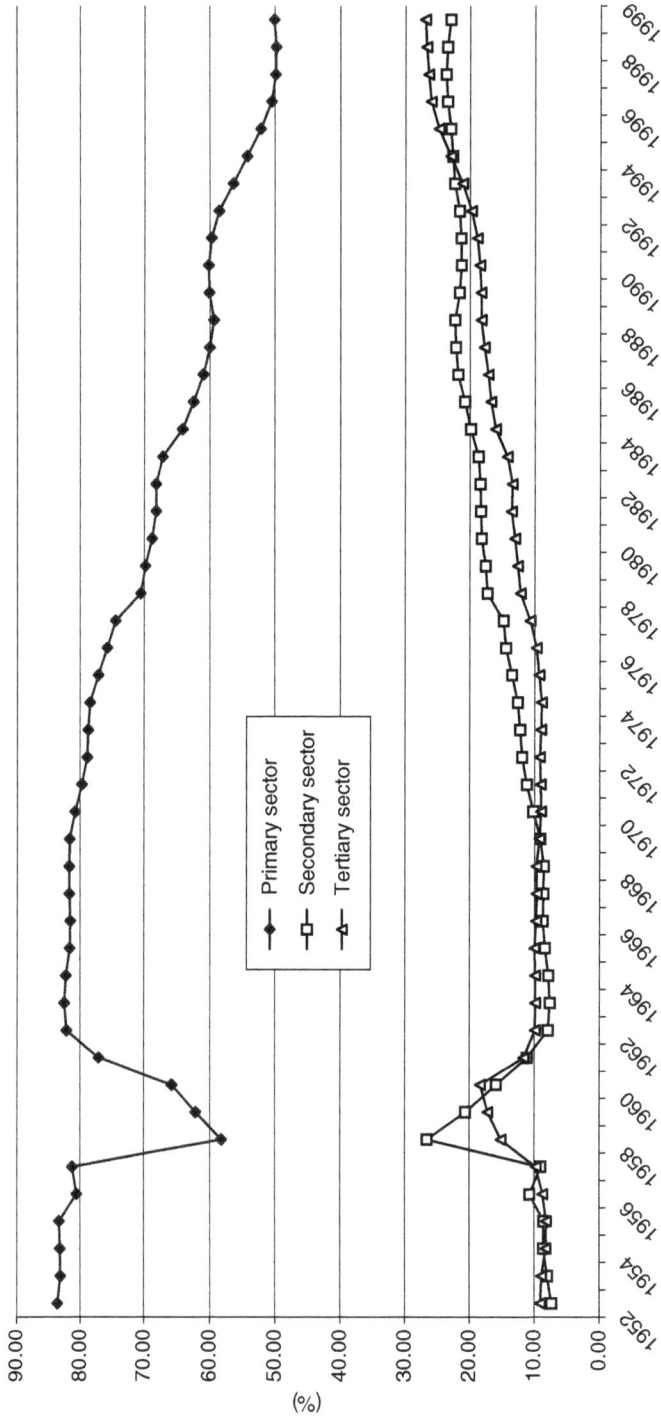

Figure 3.3 Sectoral employment shares in China (1952–99)

Source: *China Statistical Yearbook*, various issues.

Table 3.7 Output and employment changes in selected Chinese industries/sectors (percentage change between 1995 and 2005)

	Output		*Employment of skilled labour*		*Employment of unskilled labour*	
	Without accession	*With accession*	*Without accession*	*With accession*	*Without accession*	*With accession*
Foodgrains	46.3	44.5	30.1	28.5	19.4	17.9
Feedgrains	28.9	26.9	14.4	12.6	7.2	5.5
Oilseeds	32.4	32.3	17.7	17.7	10.3	10.2
Meat and livestock	75.0	81.3	63.0	69.8	41.5	47.3
Dairy	74.9	84.4	60.6	70.5	35.0	43.2
Other agriculture	53.2	50.0	37.2	34.3	28.6	25.8
Other food	50.5	51.8	−11.0	−10.7	−34.5	−34.3
Beverages/tobacco	80.7	13.8	2.2	−36.1	−24.8	−53.0
Extractive industries	61.9	60.2	63.7	60.8	54.9	52.2
Textiles	71.6	88.0	6.2	15.5	−24.8	−18.3
Clothing	57.0	263.5	2.4	134.4	−27.5	65.9
Wood and paper	103.6	93.9	27.8	20.9	−9.5	−14.5
Petrochemicals	105.8	98.6	14.8	10.0	−18.7	−22.2
Metals	135.7	126.2	30.5	24.3	−7.6	−12.0
Automobiles	189.6	−3.8	53.1	−51.2	8.4	−65.5
Electronics	142.5	169.1	38.2	52.1	−2.2	7.6
Other manufactures	131.7	125.5	45.0	40.1	2.7	−0.8
Utilities	103.2	101.2	0.4	−1.5	−28.9	−30.3
Trade/transport	110.9	114.4	0.8	1.3	−36.4	−36.1
Construction	147.9	149.0	119.7	119.9	49.7	49.7
Business/finance	104.6	105.1	26.4	25.9	−10.5	−10.9
Government services	85.0	85.9	56.3	56.6	10.7	10.8

Source: Ianchovichina *et al.* (2000).

Notes: The above simulations are based on a new version of the Global Trade Analysis Project (GTAP) model. Projections for population and unskilled labour were made by summing up the average growth rates between 1995 and the projected 2005 data. The skilled labour projections were based on forecasts of growth in the stock of tertiary educated labour.

employment will decline in beverages and tobacco, textiles, wood and paper, petrochemicals, automobiles, trade/transport and utilities. We find the estimates of substantial increases in agricultural output and employment implausible considering that foodgrains, feedgrains and oilseeds are land-intensive crops in which China has no comparative advantage. Estimates by Zhai and Li (2000) of a decline in output and employment in such agricultural commodities as rice, wheat and cotton is a more likely scenario. These sectors are protected by heavy import quota restrictions, which will have to be gradually lifted under the WTO

Agreement. However, as we show in Chapter 4, the concept of employment is much less clear-cut in agriculture than in manufacturing. Therefore, the more relevant issue is not so much employment or unemployment as agricultural and rural incomes. Of course, employment is more easily defined in the rural non-farm sector than in agriculture.

According to the principle of dynamic comparative advantage discussed in Chapter 2, after China's accession production should shift away from wheat towards such labour-intensive crops as fruit, flowers and vegetables generating substantial incremental employment. Domestic prices for these commodities are much higher than world prices. For example, the domestic price for rice is higher than the world price by 40 per cent, wheat by 10 per cent, maize by 60 per cent, soyabean by 40 per cent, and oil by 30 per cent. However, in other primary export products including meat, fishery products, vegetables, fruits, tobacco leaves, China will still maintain a comparative advantage as these products do not need much land and they can utilize redundant labour, and workers who are idle during low seasons. In these products, China is more competitive in the international markets: the price of meat is 57 per cent lower than the world price, beef 84 per cent lower, lamb 54 per cent lower, apples 41 per cent lower and oranges 47 per cent lower (Yu and Yu, 2001).

There is consensus that China's accession to the WTO will make a positive contribution to GDP growth. However, opinions differ as to the precise magnitude of increase in the growth rate: an optimistic estimate is 3 per cent of GDP growth, whereas the more conservative estimate is 0.5 per cent (see Yu *et al.*, 2000; *Life Times*, 27 December 1999).

Estimates of the employment impact vary widely, from 12 million jobs added to millions of jobs lost. Zhang *et al.* (1998) note that the short-term costs to China of trade liberalization (as we noted above, they study the impact of *unilateral* tariff reductions instead of *multilateral* actions through the WTO accession) will be substantial 'both in terms of the loss of domestic output (a drop of about $40 billion, or 32 per cent of pre-liberalization output in the protected sectors) and lost jobs (about 11.2 million workers in the protected sectors). Salomon Smith Barney, the investment bank, estimates that within five years after WTO entry China will have 40 million people unemployed: 5–10 million rural workers, 10 million laid-off SOE workers, and 20 million non-SOE workers (*Far Eastern Economic Review*, 5 October 2000). These forecasts need to be viewed against the official benchmark for end 2001 of the total registered urban unemployed of nearly 7 million, not including 5.15 million workers laid off by SOEs.[14]

The employment impact will vary depending on the assumptions made about the employment elasticity of output, the extent to which imported goods will replace domestic goods, and the magnitude of bankruptcies of inefficient state and non-state firms. Estimates of employment elasticity by sector and time periods show that it has declined in the primary and secondary sectors (see Table 3.8). On the basis of the average elasticity for 1995–99 and the employment figure for 1999, we estimate that for 1 per cent of GDP growth, jobs

Table 3.8 Sectoral employment elasticities of output in China (1955–99)

Period	Primary	Secondary	Tertiary
1955–59	−9.64	0.57	1.83
1960–64	2.70	−0.15	0.99
1965–69	1.10	0.12	2.32
1970–74	0.50	1.35	0.39
1975–79	−0.05	−0.19	3.98
1980–84	−0.09	0.89	0.70
1985–89	0.52	0.29	0.43
1990–94	0.22	1.00	2.00
1995–99	−0.07	0.09	0.51

Source: Estimated on the basis of GDP and employment data from the *China Statistical Yearbook* and the *China Labour Statistical Yearbook*.

Note: Elasticity in each period is an average of annual figures.

in the primary sector will be reduced by 250,000 and those in the secondary and tertiary sectors will increase by 150,000 and 970,000 respectively. But this static analysis may overstate the increase in unemployment in the primary sector, since for every 1 per cent GDP growth rate, this sector's contribution will be smaller than 1 per cent under current and future economic conditions. Employment reduction in the primary sector may simply nullify an employment increase in the secondary sector so that the net increase for every per cent GDP growth would be just under one million. This estimate is more or less consistent with the data for job creation since 1993, which was about 7 million a year (Niu, 1999).

We are aware that estimates of employment elasticities of output reported by different authors are different due to the different period coverage and whether they are annual estimates or averages of three or five years. The fluctuations in estimates reflect the nature of China's transitional economy. We notice that up to 1995, the elasticity for the secondary sector is reasonably high but it declined afterwards. We believe this is due partly to the preparations for WTO accession and partly to deepening of SOE reforms. Both the government and people had expected China to enter WTO earlier, which put pressure on enterprises to become more efficient in order to survive. As a result more workers were laid off to raise efficiency, which led to a decline in employment elasticity. However, this decline may be stopped in future through trade liberalization following accession. Greater specialization in labour-intensive exports can lead to an increase in employment elasticity for the manufacturing sector (Ghose, 2000). We believe that the elasticity may not increase dramatically but it will recover to its previous acceptable level with an increase in such exports. We expect that employment elasticity for the tertiary sector will also increase. Thus as a whole the employment prospects may improve gradually.

Obviously the impact of accession will not be evenly spread across sectors and industries. Most observers believe that the potential for employment growth is minimal in such sectors as agriculture, automobiles and machinery and instruments. According to a recent report, during seven years following accession, employment will decline by 9.66 million in the agricultural sector (or 3.6 per cent of the total), 4.98 million in automobiles (or 14.5 per cent of the current employed workforce), and 5.82 million in machinery and instruments (or 2.5 per cent of current employment) (*Beijing Evening News*, 18 November 1999).

China's integration into the global economy will deepen after accession. Changes in global demand for Chinese exports during the current world economic slowdown could adversely affect economic activities in China. However, there are factors which could offset the negative impact of the slowdown. First, since China is a large economy, its size will enable it to weather external shocks better. Second, the Chinese economic cycle is not synchronized with the world economy; China has been growing rapidly in the past even when other countries have been growing slowly. Third, the predominance of cheap labour-intensive goods in its export structure may enable China to increase its exports, since consumers in advanced countries may become more price conscious when their incomes and jobs are under threat. A good example is the successful expansion of Chinese exports to Japan when the Japanese economy was slowing down; China's trade with Japan has soared especially since 1993. In 2000, the total trade volume between the two countries reached $87.5 billion, of which China exported $50 billion to Japan. Thirty per cent of China's exports consisted of textiles and clothing, 26 per cent, mechanical products, and 11 per cent, food and vegetables. Due to China's cheap labour, low-cost production and a potentially very big market, many Japanese companies (e.g. Toshiba TV and washing machines) have shifted some or all of their production to China (see Chapter 5).

Generally speaking, the impact of accession on employment in China was already being felt long before China formally became a member of WTO, since the entry negotiations dragged on for several years. Thus the Chinese people became aware of the challenges that membership would entail and industries had time to adjust and reorganize. But the industrial sector has not kept pace with the required adjustment. It is not the government's intention to maintain the state sector's dominant position in terms of output and employment. With or without accession, economic reform and structural change will, no doubt, have profound consequences for Chinese industry, society and its people.

According to official estimates, during the Tenth Five-Year Plan period (2001–2005) 8 million new entrants will be added to the job market each year in the urban areas in addition to a total of 10 million workers laid-off from SOEs. Therefore, the total labour supply in the urban areas is estimated at about 50 million during this period. Apart from urban labour supply, there are 40 million rural surplus workers wishing to transfer out of agriculture (*People's Daily*, 26 March 2001). Lower GDP growth and more capital- and technology-intensive development will reduce the demand for labour. The government expects that registered unemployment will increase from 3.3 per cent to 5 per cent during

2001–2005. Second, accession will encourage more foreign direct investment into China as a result of which more jobs will be created. China has increasingly become the world's manufacturing base due to its abundant and cheap labour supply. Multinational companies have relocated many of their product lines from developed countries to China. So far foreign investments have concentrated mainly on industry and property development. In 1999, investment in these sectors accounted for 84 per cent of the total (see Yu and Yu, 2001). It is expected that such activities as retailing, distribution, and tourism will create more employment opportunities when entry restrictions are relaxed on sectors in which foreign companies are permitted to invest. Third, China's services sector will expand to provide services related to different stages of exports. As more foreign companies set up businesses in China, they will require various services from accountants, lawyers, engineering and other consultants and supporting staff.

The negative employment impact of accession will be felt through import competition and the closure of inefficient domestic firms, especially SOEs, after the withdrawal of subsidies. However, there are no estimates concerning the likely number of firm closures. In the post-accession period, China will import those products which are more expensive to produce within the country (e.g. feedgrain and oilseeds), or those of superior quality or which use advanced technology not available in China. Of course, it cannot be ruled out that individual firms could go bust due to poor management or bad investment. More and more quality goods are now assembled and processed in China and domestic firms, joint ventures or relocated foreign firms gradually switch to the manufacture of technologically advanced products.

Impact on wage and income inequalities

In China wide wages and income disparities exist between the urban and rural areas, between different regions and between SOEs and other types of ownership. Trends in money and real urban wages show that all categories (namely, SOEs, TVEs and other forms of ownership) other than collectives witnessed a widening gap. Contrary to what one would expect in conditions of lay-offs and rising urban unemployment, real wages actually rose in the second half of the 1990s (Rawski, 2002).

There were wide and growing regional income inequalities even before accession (see Wang and Hu, 1999), partly due to the differences in unemployment rates discussed above. The generally higher unemployment rates in the non-coastal areas are reflected in the lower wages in these areas compared to those in coastal areas. In addition, regional income inequalities have widened since the early 1990s. Wang (2000) identifies two phases of China's economic reforms in this context. In the first phase (1978–93), all social groups benefited from reforms, although some benefited more than others. In the second phase (1994 onwards), worsening unemployment and income inequalities made some social groups absolutely worse off. The losers were mainly farmers and workers engaged in SOEs. However, these two phases are not all that distinct considering that in 1988 (the first phase) more than one-third of urban households were reported to have suffered a fall in their real incomes, which led to social unrest and riots in 1989.

A third phase of regional wage and income disparities envisaged to coincide with WTO accession in 2001, is likely to accentuate the disparities experienced during the second phase. Increasing imports from abroad will put downward pressure on wages in general and on unskilled wages in particular. While more rapidly growing coastal provinces will be able to weather the external shocks, the inland provinces are likely to suffer greater incomes and employment losses especially in provinces with a heavy concentration of inefficient SOEs. Several studies (e.g. IMF, 2000; Zhai and Li, 2000; Yang and Huang, 1997) have predicted a rise in rural–urban income disparities subsequent to China's accession.

Unskilled wages are estimated to grow twice as fast as wages of skilled workers between 1995 and 2005 (see Ianchovichina *et al.*, 2000). This is partly because China's unskilled labour during this period will grow by 12 per cent compared to 43 per cent growth for skilled labour (see Ahuja and Filmer, 1995). It is not clear whether WTO accession will have a particularly strong upward effect on the wages of unskilled and skilled workers. Simulations by Ianchovichina *et al.* do not show significant wage differences with or without accession during 1995–2005. For example, wages of unskilled labour are expected to increase by 83 per cent without accession, and by 87 per cent with accession during this period. It is not certain that an increase in wages will have an equalizing effect. As we discuss in Chapter 4, tariff reduction on agricultural commodities after accession will lead to an increase in cheap agricultural imports with which Chinese small farmers will be unable to compete. According to a 'conservative' estimate by the US Department of Agriculture, China will import annually an additional $1.6 billion worth of US grains, cotton, oilseeds and related products by 2005 (cited in Wang, 2000). Wheat, corn, cotton and oil have historically been the main staple crops in the interior provinces. A decline in agricultural prices, though beneficial for consumers in general, will hurt small producers. The result will be a decline in farm incomes in the predominantly agricultural provinces of the hinterland. Zhai and Li (2000) conclude that rural household welfare will decline and urban welfare will increase (see Chapter 4).[15]

4 Agriculture

China's large population size and a significant proportion of its people living in rural areas suggests that WTO accession will have significant implications for its agricultural sector and the rural population. The Chinese agriculture is generally considered to be very vulnerable to tariff reductions resulting from trade liberalization under the terms of accession. The former Chinese Premier Zhu Rongji openly expressed his concern about the negative impact of accession on China's agriculture and rural incomes. Reduction of tariff and non-tariff barriers will raise import competition for Chinese agriculture resulting in lower prices which will depress farmers' incomes. In this chapter we discuss China's commitments in terms of agricultural trade, the short and long-term effects of tariff reductions on resource allocation, and rural incomes. We argue that the agricultural impact of accession is better understood in terms of the effects on rural incomes than on rural unemployment. The latter is a more ambiguous concept in the case of agriculture than the concept of the working poor.

Although China has made commitments to rely more on market forces in agriculture, at present prices remain controlled and a substantial amount of agricultural production is still subject to government procurement. China's agriculture is oriented mainly towards domestic consumption and its agricultural exports are limited to small quantities of traditional food products. Imports of food are allowed mainly to overcome shortfalls in foodgrains production in order to ensure food security for China's population. As Miner (1998: 211) notes, 'China is a minor player (in world agricultural trade) apart from wheat where on average it accounts for about 10 to 12 per cent of total imports'. WTO accession, which is in direct conflict with China's current policy of food security and self-sufficiency, may force China to import cheaper foodgrains and other food products in the interests of a more efficient allocation of resources.

China's commitments under the Agreement

Before joining the WTO, China took various measures to control imports of agricultural products such as quotas, export and import licences and other import restrictions. At the same time, only designated state trading companies were allowed to conduct imports and exports of agricultural products. The mainstream trade measures remained intact although China allowed more agricultural imports. China's agricultural exports increased by more than two-fold while imports of agricultural products increased by only 84 per cent. Thus China enjoyed agricultural trade surplus from 1980 to 1994.

Chinese agriculture is subject to state trading in foodgrains. Private companies are not permitted to import or export foodgrains, vegetables oils or cotton. Government controls output, marketing, domestic prices, and the distribution of foodgrains through import quotas or licences issued through the Ministry of Foreign Trade and Economic Cooperation (MOFTEC).

Under the WTO Agreement the above controls are to be gradually phased out and trade in agriculture is to be liberalized. On 15 November 1999 China and the United States signed a bilateral agreement under which China made many concessions including market access to American agricultural products. Under this bilateral agreement, by January 2004, tariffs on agricultural products will decline sharply, from an average level of 31 per cent to about 14 per cent. (Under the WTO Agreement, overall average tariffs on agricultural products will be reduced from 22 per cent to 17.5 per cent.) Selected tariff cuts by agricultural commodity under the US–China agreement are shown in Table 4.1.

China will set up new tariff-rate quotas (TRQs) replacing the current import control and licensing system. Under the system, there is a cap of total amount of imports for which lower tariff (10 per cent) is applied and any amount above the quotas will be levied a higher duty. A specific proportion of TRQs will be reserved for non-state trading companies. This provision is intended to ensure that the Chinese government does not manipulate imports through state-trading corporations. Foreign companies will be allowed to apply for and obtain import licences to directly import agricultural commodities into China. Before China's accession, the ability of foreign companies to trade commodities under state control was strictly limited because the right to engage in trade was restricted to

Table 4.1 Selected tariff cuts on Chinese agricultural commodities (%)

Item	Base tariffs	Tariffs in 2004
Beef	45	12
Pork	20	12
Poultry	20	10
Citrus	40	12
Grapes	40	13
Apples	30	10
Almonds	30	10
Wine	65	20
Cheese	50	12
Ice cream	45	19

Source: US–China Bilateral Agreement.

a small number of state-owned trading companies. China promised to administer TRQs on the basis of economic rather than political criteria to ensure a transparent and consistent system for allocating TRQ shares and to ensure that quota-holders are not impeded in utilizing their quotas. TRQs will be redistributed to other end users who may be interested in importing in the event of their non-utilization. TRQs will be shared between the state and private trading companies. If a TRQ share reserved for a state trader is not contracted for by October of any given year, it will be reallocated to non-state traders.

State trading will still be maintained for certain sensitive commodities including wheat, corn, rice, cotton and soybean oil. Trading rights for these products will be phased out gradually. State trading and monopoly of the government procurement agencies will be gradually phased out. The state agencies will compete with private companies, both domestic and foreign, in the procurement of foodgrains directly from the farmers, for example.

China has agreed to abolish all export subsidies on agricultural products. This commitment is particularly likely to hurt China's potential exports of corn, rice, and cotton, which in the past have displaced US products in third-country markets.

After tough negotiations with its trade partners China agreed to cap its future spending on farm subsidies at 8.5 per cent of the value of domestic farm production, the level between 10 per cent allowed by developing countries and 5 per cent applicable in developed countries. The cap will give China room to provide greater assistance to farmers since China's agricultural subsidy is currently only about 2 per cent.

Chinese agriculture will be vulnerable due to a greater risk of external shocks and uncertainty about ensuring regular food supplies to feed China's population. Since the Revolution China has adopted the policy of food self-sufficiency. Considerations of food security are so paramount that China planned to import no more than 5 per cent of its food requirements from abroad. China feared that food could be used as a weapon against it in conditions of political tensions with big powers like the US (Fewsmith, 2001b).

Following accession agricultural trade liberalization will encourage China to import large quantities of food in the wake of declining food production at home and continuing high food demand. Indeed, cheaper, better-quality and higher gluten-content foodgrains (e.g. wheat) are likely to flood the Chinese domestic market. Wen (1999) estimates that wheat imports from the US alone could amount to 9.3 million tons followed by corn, 7.2 million tons, and rice, 5.3 million tons. Several other economic implications of accession will include changes in the commodity terms of trade, convergence of domestic and world prices of foodgrains, and increase in food imports especially of processed foods for urban consumers.

Rural labour supply

We noted in Chapter 3 that China suffered from large rural labour surpluses. Labour intensity of Chinese agriculture is one of the highest among the major grain-producing countries in the world. For example, it is 50 times higher than the world average and 100 times higher than that in Australia and Canada (ILO, 1998; World Bank, 1997). Agricultural labour productivity remains extremely low due to limited arable land per capita (see below), large rural population and the low level of technology.

According to official estimates, in 1999 there were 469 million rural workers of whom 367 million (or 78.4 per cent) were engaged in agricultural activities. The share of non-farm workers was 16.2 million (or 3.5 per cent). There are wide inter-provincial variations in the magnitude and shares of farm and non-farm rural labour force (Table 4.2).

Wang (2000) estimates that rural labour force increased from 347 million in 1980 to 519 million in 2000, figures which are higher than the official estimates shown in Table 4.2. These differences are due to differences in the data sources, namely, census data and agricultural statistics. While the former includes all persons working for more than ten days during a year, the latter includes only persons who work more than two months a year (Cai *et al.*, 2002: 49).

In future, the rate of growth of rural labour force will be slower thanks to urbanization and one-child family planning policy.[1] Assuming that TVE employment growth and rural–urban migration will be slower than during the 1990s, Wang predicts the total rural labour force in 2010 to be of the order of 530 million. Agricultural labour force in the same year under two alternative assumptions will be 304 million and 274 million respectively (Table 4.3).

It will be difficult to absorb such massive agricultural labour force within the rural sector considering a deceleration of TVE employment growth from 12 per cent in the 1980s to only 3 per cent in the 1990s (Wang, 2002). It is unlikely that this growth rate will pick up in the near future as the problems of the TVE sector continue to grow.[2]

China's comparative advantage in agriculture

China is very short of arable land compared to many other developing countries such as India. Arable land per capita in China is much lower (Table 4.4). With the exception of Japan, China has the lowest figure among the selected countries. It is estimated that cropland is shrinking at a rate of 1 per cent per annum. Limited by natural resource endowment China is at a disadvantage compared with developed countries. Not only is arable land per capita in China very small, the climatic conditions are also worse. China's agricultural areas are seriously affected by droughts and floods due to the influence of monsoon climate. Overcoming droughts and floods requires construction of irrigation systems and dams which add to agricultural costs. In the US a farmer cultivates hundreds of hectares of land and in Europe, a smaller but substantial number of hectares, while a Chinese household possesses an average of only 0.4 hectares. In developed countries all farm products are for commercial sales while in China a major portion of agricultural produce is for farmers' own consumption.

Table 4.2 Rural labour force and its composition in China and its provinces (1978–99)

Year & region	Farming, forestry, animal husbandry and fishery (million)	(%)	Rural industry (million)	(%)	Rural building (million)	(%)	Rural transport and storage (million)	(%)	Rural retail, whole sale & catering (million)	(%)	Others non-agricultural activities (million)	(%)	Total (million)
1978	284.56												
1980	298.08												
1985	303.52	81.9	27.41	7.4	11.30	3.0	4.34	1.2	4.63	1.2	19.46	5.2	370.65
1987	308.70	79.2	32.97	8.5	14.31	3.7	5.63	1.4	6.07	1.6	22.33	5.7	390.00
1988	314.56	78.5	34.13	8.5	15.26	3.8	6.07	1.5	6.57	1.6	24.08	6.0	400.67
1989	324.41	79.2	32.56	8.0	15.02	3.7	6.14	1.5	6.52	1.6	24.74	6.0	409.39
1990	333.36	79.4	32.29	7.7	15.23	3.6	6.35	1.5	6.93	1.7	25.93	6.2	420.10
1991	341.86	79.3	32.68	7.6	15.34	3.6	6.55	1.5	7.23	1.7	27.27	6.3	430.93
1992	340.37	77.7	34.68	7.9	16.59	3.8	7.06	1.6	8.14	1.9	31.18	7.1	438.02
1993	332.58	75.1	36.59	8.3	18.87	4.3	8.00	1.8	9.49	2.1	37.03	8.4	442.56
1994	326.90	73.2	38.50	8.6	20.57	4.6	9.08	2.0	10.84	2.4	40.65	9.1	446.54
1995	323.35	71.8	39.71	8.8	22.04	4.9	9.83	2.2	11.70	2.6	43.80	9.7	450.42
1996	322.60	71.2	40.19	8.9	23.04	5.1	10.28	2.3	12.62	2.8	44.16	9.8	452.88
1997	324.35	70.6	40.31	8.8	23.73	5.2	10.58	2.3	13.82	3.0	46.84	10.2	459.62
1998	326.26	70.3	39.29	8.5	24.54	5.3	10.88	2.3	14.62	3.1	48.74	10.5	464.32
1999	329.12	70.2	39.53	8.4	25.32	5.4	11.16	2.4	15.85	3.4	47.99	10.2	468.97
Beijing	0.71	43.0	0.35	21.1	0.13	7.7	0.12	7.2	0.10	6.2	0.24	14.8	1.65
Tianjin	0.82	48.1	0.44	26.0	0.11	6.6	0.10	6.1	0.11	6.3	0.12	7.0	1.69
Hebei	16.40	61.8	3.82	14.4	1.98	7.5	0.91	3.4	1.30	4.9	2.14	8.0	26.54
Shanxi	6.55	66.9	1.14	11.6	0.50	5.1	0.53	5.4	0.43	4.3	0.66	6.7	9.79
Inner Mongolia	5.26	84.6	0.16	2.6	0.19	3.1	0.10	1.7	0.13	2.1	0.36	5.8	6.21
Liaoning	6.43	68.5	0.77	8.2	0.51	5.5	0.36	3.8	0.47	5.0	0.85	9.0	9.39
Jilin	5.20	82.8	0.21	3.4	0.20	3.1	0.13	2.1	0.18	2.9	0.36	5.7	6.27
Heilongjiang	7.45	83.2	0.34	3.8	0.23	2.5	0.17	1.9	0.25	2.8	0.52	5.8	8.95

Table 4.2 Rural labour force and its composition in China and its provinces (1978–99) (*Continued*)

Year & region	Farming, forestry, animal husbandry and fishery (million)	(%)	Rural industry (million)	(%)	Rural building (million)	(%)	Rural transport and storage (million)	(%)	Rural retail, whole sale & catering (million)	(%)	Others non-agricultural activities (million)	(%)	Total (million)
Shanghai	0.90	35.1	1.11	42.9	0.11	4.3	0.06	2.1	0.11	4.3	0.29	11.2	2.58
Jiangsu	15.05	55.5	4.46	16.4	2.50	9.2	0.93	3.4	1.02	3.8	3.15	11.6	27.09
Zhejiang	10.74	51.4	4.46	21.3	1.05	5.0	0.66	3.2	1.20	5.7	2.80	13.4	20.90
Anhui	19.91	73.1	1.52	5.6	1.53	5.6	0.55	2.0	0.87	3.2	2.86	10.5	27.24
Fujian	7.80	64.2	1.31	10.8	0.76	6.2	0.36	2.9	0.54	4.5	1.37	11.3	12.14
Jiangxi	10.60	68.6	0.88	5.7	0.59	3.8	0.21	1.4	0.31	2.0	2.86	18.5	15.46
Shandong	24.74	68.4	3.43	9.5	2.86	7.9	1.10	3.1	1.46	4.0	2.60	7.2	36.20
Henan	32.99	76.5	3.10	7.2	2.41	5.6	0.92	2.1	1.42	3.3	2.27	5.3	43.11
Hubei	12.11	68.4	1.17	6.6	1.00	5.6	0.43	2.5	0.70	3.9	2.29	12.9	17.70
Hunan	20.74	73.8	1.81	6.4	1.17	4.2	0.47	1.7	0.77	2.7	3.13	11.1	28.10
Guangdong	15.31	57.5	3.82	14.4	1.89	7.1	0.72	2.7	1.13	4.2	3.77	14.2	26.65
Guangxi	16.03	77.1	0.61	2.9	0.79	3.8	0.32	1.5	0.47	2.3	2.58	12.4	20.80
Hainan	1.72	79.9	0.06	2.6	0.07	3.4	0.06	2.8	0.08	3.9	0.16	7.4	2.15
Chongqing	9.55	71.1	0.58	4.3	0.72	5.3	0.18	1.3	0.31	2.3	2.10	15.6	13.43
Sichuan	27.35	72.0	1.70	4.5	1.94	5.1	0.51	1.4	1.02	2.7	5.47	14.4	37.98
Guizhou	14.27	82.6	0.62	3.6	0.30	1.7	0.18	1.0	0.29	1.7	1.62	9.4	17.28
Yunnan	16.55	86.6	0.51	2.7	0.49	2.6	0.35	1.8	0.34	1.8	0.87	4.5	19.11
Xizang	0.92	90.9	0.01	1.3	0.02	1.5	0.02	1.7	0.01	1.4	0.03	3.1	1.01
Shaanxi	10.09	76.1	0.64	4.8	0.72	5.4	0.34	2.6	0.44	3.3	1.03	7.8	13.26
Gansu	6.90	75.0	0.30	3.3	0.40	4.4	0.19	2.0	0.19	2.1	1.22	13.2	9.19
Qinghai	1.44	83.1	0.06	3.5	0.04	2.6	0.05	2.6	0.04	2.1	0.11	6.1	1.73
Ningxia	1.53	79.6	0.07	3.5	0.09	4.7	0.07	3.7	0.06	3.2	0.10	5.3	1.92
Xinjiang	3.07	89.6	0.08	2.2	0.04	1.2	0.07	2.0	0.10	2.9	0.07	2.1	3.43

Source: Based on data from *China Statistical Yearbook 2000.*

Table 4.3 Rural labour, TVE employment and rural-urban migration in China (2000–2010) (million)

Year	Agricultural labour	Rural labour (statistics)	Rural labour (adjusted)	TVE employment	Rural-urban migration
1980	318	347	30	–	317
1990	473	473	93	14	366
2000	499	519	128	47	344
2010					
(assumption 1)	304	530	149	77	304
(assumption 2)	274	530	149	107	274

Source: Wang (2002).

Notes:
(1) Rural labour is adjusted according to the national census data.
(2) Number of rural-urban migration is estimated on the basis of MLSS (Ministry of Labour and Social Security) and National Bureau of Statistics (NBS) data for 1999.
(3) Agricultural labour is estimated by deducting TVE employment and rural-urban migration from rural labour.
(4) For the period 2001–10, the growth rates for rural labour and TVE employment are assumed to be respectively 0.2 per cent and 1.5 per cent.
(5) Rural-urban migration is assumed to be 3 million per year under assumption 1 and 6 million per year under assumption 2.

Table 4.4 Per capita arable land in China and other selected countries (sq. metres)

Country	Arable land per capita
China	1,033
India	1,644
Iran, Islamic Rep. of	2,560
Brazil	3,208
France	3,129
Japan	359
United States	6,457

Source: Crook (2001).

In April 2000, China accepted the first shipments of US pork and beef to start implementing the US deal. China's producers will be major losers because tariff cuts and freer imports will mean domestic grains like corn and soybeans must compete with higher-quality imports. Cheaper meat imports will threaten the domestic livestock industry. Based on the principle of international division of labour, a country will be influenced by its competitive advantages. This is also the case for China's agricultural sector. China's main comparative advantage lies in a large supply of cheap labour and labour-intensive activities. In agriculture, the natural resource conditions and technologies used by Chinese farmers suggest that in general China does not enjoy a comparative advantage in producing foodgrains, cotton, edible oil, and sugar, which are land intensive. However, within China there are variations across different regions. Because per capita arable land increases as one moves from the eastern region to middle China and western China these regions' relative advantage in producing land-intensive crops varies. Comparative advantage in labour-intensive crops moves in the opposite direction to that for land-intensive crops. The majority of existing agricultural workers will continue to be engaged in agriculture for some time to come because of the self-sufficient nature of agricultural activity, and the near zero opportunity cost of labour particularly during the slack seasons.

Due to the lack of cultivable land, productivity of major foodgrains is quite low and cheap foreign imports will drive many farmers out of production if China forgoes its right to protect domestic farmers. But from the viewpoint of international division of labour, China should encourage labour-intensive and high value-added products for export, such as fishery, vegetables, fruits, flowers and processed agricultural products. In exchange for these exports China should import land-intensive products such as foodgrains, oilseeds, cotton and tobacco leaves. This crop specialization, which will be reinforced following accession, has already been taking place for a number of years.

China will need to concentrate on high-quality wheat production in the Yellow River and Huaihai areas, sweet corn and soybean production in north-east China and eastern part of Inner Mongolia, cotton production in Xinjiang Autonomous Region, beef and lamb in central plains, and dairy products in North China, oranges, rape-seeds planting in the Yangtze River, apple cultivation in Shaanxi and Bohai Sea, aquatic products in coastal areas and along rivers and lakes. Thus in the long run China will need to focus on structural adjustment and optimization of its agricultural production.

Following WTO entry, agricultural inputs (e.g. fertilizers and pesticides) could become cheaper through increase in their imports into the Chinese domestic market. This should benefit the process of China's agricultural modernization. The cheapening of the imports of such agricultural inputs as pesticides, fertilizers and feedgrains should provide a fillip to the pig industry to meet the growing urban demand.

China enjoys a *dynamic* comparative advantage in the exports of animal husbandry products, fruits, vegetables, cut flowers and aquatic products. These are more labour-intensive goods whose domestic prices are 30–40 per cent lower than international prices. The lower prices of such land-intensive commodities as foodgrains in the past were due mainly to the government's procurement power (it bought foodgrains at prices even lower than production costs in order to maintain low consumer prices for urban residents). Since 1985 the reform of the foodgrain purchasing system has resulted in a gradual increase in prices of foodgrains and other agricultural products (see Chapter 3).

China can switch some of its production from foodgrains to other products in which it enjoys a comparative advantage. However, it will be difficult to realize possible gains in the short term because it takes time for the agricultural sector to adjust production to satisfy international market demand in terms of quality, sanitary and phyto-sanitary requirements.

Table 4.5 Exports of primary and manufactured goods ($ billion)

	Total export	Primary goods	% of total	Manufactured goods	% of total
1980	18.12	9.11	50	9.01	50
1999	194.93	19.94	10.2	174.99	89.8

Source: *China Statistical Yearbook* 2000.

Liberalization of trade in agriculture will lead to a shift from food crops to cash crops, which are more lucrative in the world market. This will involve changes in relative factor and product prices. A shift towards export crops and processed food products may lead to the degradation of such natural resources as forests. But there is no clear-cut evidence on this point.

Since China adopted the economic reforms and open-door policy, it has not only achieved rapid export growth, but also experienced dramatic shift of export structure from primary goods to manufactured goods. From 1980 to 1999, China's total exports increased by more than ten-fold to $194.93 billion from $18.12 billion. The share of primary goods exports dropped from 50 per cent to only 10.2 per cent, while the share of manufactured goods exports increased to 89.8 per cent (Table 4.5), roughly comparable to Japan, Germany and Israel. However, China's manufactured goods exports concentrate mainly on labour-intensive low value-added goods, accounting for 72.3 per cent of the total manufactured goods, while the export share of capital and technology-intensive goods is only 27.7 per cent of the total. The situation is the reverse in developed countries; the export of labour-intensive goods is normally below 30 per cent and that of capital and technology-intensive goods more than 70 per cent.

The impact of accession on rural incomes and employment

The impact of WTO accession on rural incomes and employment in China's agricultural sector and rural economy is quite different from its impact on other sectors. Chinese agriculture has some special characteristics, which are quite different from those in developed and other developing countries. First, in China the production unit, a household, is generally very small. Second, the agricultural seasons are limited mainly to spring and autumn with almost no work during the rest of the year due to the small size of land available per household. Third, as most farmers are self-employed (landless workers are almost non-existent) they do not get paid immediately after work effort but only when their crops are sold. Fourth, many rural household members find temporary jobs in urban areas to do construction and building work to support their families and purchase seeds and tools and other production inputs. Finally, only about 30 per cent of crops is sold with the bulk kept for self-consumption. Therefore, low prices of agricultural products will only affect farmers' incomes from the marketed part of their output. As a result, income from crops may decrease which may act as a disincentive to grow more crops. The grain prices are too low to cover production costs considering that incomes of rural households engaged in grain production have been stagnant during the 1990s. Nevertheless, a minimum of crops will have to be grown for farmers' own consumption.

One of the most profound impacts on China's agricultural sector may be its adverse effect on farmers' incomes due to lower international prices for agricultural products (see below). Following accession, the rate of growth of farmers' incomes is likely to slow down thus adversely affecting the whole economy. Uncertainty of supply from abroad could also have political implications and profound effects on world market of agricultural products. In 1995, China imported 20.8 million tons of foodgrains (which is about 4 per cent of China's total consumption in that year) at a price of $179 per ton. In 1996, the average price increased to $242 per ton, that is, up by 35 per cent in a single year. Any disruption in grain supply or sudden increase in prices could have a detrimental effect on rural incomes and the economy generally. Import of food instead of its domestic production will also involve loss of rural employment (see below).

Currently domestic prices of wheat and other agricultural prices are much higher than the world prices due to high demand, low land–labour ratio, and higher production costs. There will be a downward pressure on domestic price of foodgrains and other products with greater imports of grains from abroad. This may be a good thing for Chinese consumers who will pay lower prices (welfare effect). But producers (especially small farmers) will experience a decline in their incomes due to lower prices. The Chinese Academy of Social Sciences (CASS) estimates that Chinese farmers will suffer a loss of incomes of 5.5 billion yuan as a result of an increase of wheat imports into China from 2 million to 5 million tons (Yu *et al.*, 2000).

Jiang (2002) reports rather surprising results that the tariff cuts under the WTO accession will lead to larger increases of real incomes among rural households than among urban households. This is because rural output will increase while urban output will fall. Jiang argues that current tariff rates for grains within the tariff-rate quota (TRQ), that is 0 to 3 per cent, is consistent with WTO requirements, and tariff cuts may not, therefore, reduce domestic agricultural production. Second, of late domestic prices of rice and wheat have been much lower than the world c.i.f. prices. One needs to be careful in interpreting Jiang's simulation results, which are based on a general equilibrium model in which only the WTO tariffs are considered. Furthermore, the simulation results ignore the impact of capital flows.

Incomes of rural households can worsen if cheaper imports are allowed to compete with domestically produced crops. Cheap foreign imports following the implementation of the WTO Agreement will exert pressure on the already depressed agricultural prices. For example, during the Ninth Five-Year Plan period (1996–2000), wheat production cost rose by 22.6 per cent but its sale price went down by 36.4 per cent, even though the domestic price of wheat is still 200 yuan per metric ton ($24.18), which is higher than prevailing international price. The situation is similar for corn, the production cost of which increased by 19.2 per cent while the sale price dropped by 36.4 per cent.

A real dilemma faces China's policy-makers. The people most likely to be hard hit by WTO accession are those who are poverty stricken and live in the remote western areas in the hinterland. For the Chinese agriculture the WTO Agreement will lead to consequences that the Chinese leadership is trying to avoid, that is, making the poor even poorer. The Agreement is likely to help those who are already better off, namely, urban consumers and those living in the eastern part of China, probably at the expense of the poor in the central and western regions. These rural people had made sacrifices in the past: before 1949 when the People's Republic of China was founded, farmers from central and western China contributed their lives and food products to fight against the Japanese invaders. Throughout the whole period of building up of a socialist economy farmers were exploited by the deliberate government policy of higher prices for industrial products and low prices for food and foodgrains in order to finance industrialization. Once again the rural poor will have to make sacrifices: this time bearing the brunt of agricultural trade liberalization.

Rural employment

China will still reserve the right to protect its agricultural sector and rural incomes by tariff quotas to restrict the total imports of major agricultural products to 4–5 per cent of total demand. If China uses up all the import quotas, in theory, other things being equal, it could reduce demand for farm workers by the same percentage as it replaces the same proportion of domestic production. So it could reduce farming employment by up to 17.5 million (or 5 per cent of the total rural labour force engaged in farming). But the matter is not so simple. The impact of WTO accession on agricultural employment in China could be much less dramatic than the figure suggests. First, since it might not be possible to use up the total quotas, total imports could be much less than the allowed quota. Second, lower prices mean that Chinese farmers may need to sell more crops to obtain the same income, thereby raising output. As a result the demand for labour may be maintained. Third, even if farmers reduce production farming will not disappear unless better job opportunities are available. This is because a large proportion of farm produce is for own consumption – as noted above. Therefore, the total number of workers engaged in farming may not decrease in the same proportion as reduction in the demand for domestic agricultural products. What is certain is that reduction of tariffs and increase in the import of foodgrains from abroad will lead to a reduction in agricultural prices, and hence rural household incomes from farm activities.

Effects of the opening up of China's agricultural market on rural employment and incomes depends on the realization of the TRQs. Some observers estimate the effect in terms of the displacement of 3.5 million to 25.8 million rural workers (Ma and Lan, 2002). These estimates are based on different scenarios of

Table 4.6 Estimates of the impact of TRQs on rural incomes and employment in China

Different scenarios: TRQs realization	33.3%	66.7%	100%
Job reduction (million)	3.5	14.5	25.8
Job reduction as % of total rural workers	1.1	4.4	7.8
Total loss of income (billion yuan)	6.5	22.7	39.7
Income loss per person losing job (yuan)	1,538	1,569	1,835
Income loss per rural worker (yuan)	20	69	121

Source: Based on Ma and Lan (2002).

the realization of TRQs using data for 2000 on total rural net income and the number of people engaged in farming, and assuming that cultivated land per worker is 7 mu (0.47 hectares (Table 4.6).

According to the WTO commitments, China reduced import tariffs on agricultural products from 18.8 per cent to 15.8 per cent in 2002. Many observers had expected foreign agricultural products, especially foodgrains, and feedgrains flooding into China and hurting rural incomes and employment (*China Economic Times*, 21 March 2003). However, reality turned out to be quite different from the predictions. In 2002, China managed to increase manufacturing exports as well as expanded exports of agricultural products. It exported $13.5 billion worth of agricultural products, an increase of 13 per cent over the previous year. The import total was worth $10.2 billion, an increased of 2 per cent, raising the agricultural trade surplus to $3.3 billion.

In terms of import quotas, except for sugar, palm oil and wool, for which tariff rate quotas (TRQs) reached 70 per cent, only a small proportion of the quotas were filled for other commodities, for example, wheat 7.4 per cent, corn 0.2 per cent, rice 6 per cent and bean oil 34.6 per cent.

There are several reasons why China did so well in the first year of WTO accession. The first is that the world prices for wheat and corn rose by 25 and 30 per cent respectively due to a reduction in grains harvested in Australia and the United States. It is estimated that wheat output was reduced by 7 per cent in the US and 20 per cent in Australia. The second explanatory factor is the exchange rate. The Chinese currency is pegged to the US dollar, which depreciated against other major currencies by nearly 8 per cent. This helped to improve the terms of trade for Chinese agricultural products. Third, many predictions did not fully take into account the costs of transportation of goods to China. When these costs are added the differences between prices of imported commodities and those of local products are considerably reduced. This did not make imported goods particularly favourable compared to local goods. For instance, f.o.b. prices for corn were $94 per metric ton, which would rise to $146 once transportation costs are included. This figure is not very different from the domestic price of $150 (*China Economic Times*, 21 March 2003).[3]

The impact of accession on rural employment will vary across sectors and regions. Generally speaking, the regions producing land-intensive goods (e.g.

foodgrains) will be adversely affected. The surveys suggest that the shares of the labour force engaged in farming activities is different in different part of China. In 1998, it was 63.9 per cent in East China, 79.1 per cent in Central China and the highest at 81.62 per cent in West China. These figures reflect the natural resource endowments and economic activities across China. Thus, the latter two regions in the hinterland are likely to suffer greater rural unemployment than the eastern coastal region.

A number of authors have made forecasts of the output and employment impact of the accession in different agricultural commodities (Table 4.7). These estimates vary widely due to the different and often simplistic assumptions on which they are based. They do not consider transportation costs, which will add a substantial amount to the original cost of agricultural commodities. Furthermore, changes in prices over time are difficult to predict and can improve or worsen the terms of trade for China's agricultural sector. Finally, changes in the rate of foreign exchange are equally difficult to predict.

One thing is certain. The negative job implications of accession will not be as serious as many estimates have suggested. First, reduction in the demand for domestic agricultural goods does not imply that farmers producing these goods will become unemployed. For example, the land used for cultivating rapeseeds can be used to grow other crops which may fetch higher prices. So rural workers will still have work to do. Second, it may just mean the reduction of working days (underemployment) rather than total loss of employment. Third, as we mentioned above, the employment concept is less applicable to the agricultural sector in China where a large proportion of household members are self-employed and produce for own consumption regardless of the market demand situation. Therefore, the effect of accession on self-employed in the subsistence economy might be minimal. Land holdings are so small that farmers have little scope of improving their living standards appreciably even when price of marketed output rises significantly. The real solution to low rural incomes and poverty lies in the creation of job opportunities outside agriculture and a reduction in the total number of people relying on agricultural activities. While this process will occur with or without accession, the WTO entry will speed it up.

Concluding remarks

There is no doubt that in the long run the WTO Agreement can result in a win–win outcome for China and its trading partners. However, tariff reduction and agricultural trade liberalization is a two-edged sword and can hurt some while benefiting others. In terms of staple agricultural products such as wheat, corn, cotton and oilseeds, China has been able to and can continue to produce enough quantities of food for its own consumption. But it can maintain self-sufficiency only at a high production cost due to low labour productivity and lack of land resources. In China the unit of agricultural production is very small and the average size of arable land per capita very low. These diseconomies of scale lead to higher unit costs of labour and other inputs.

Table 4.7 Forecasts of agricultural output and employment in China

Commodity	Employment (million)	(%)	Output (billion yuan)	(%)
Zhai and Li (2000) (1995–2010)				
Rice	−2.5	−2.8	−4.6	−1.4
Wheat	−5.4	−14.2	−17.2	−9.0
Cotton	−5.0	−22.6	−11.7	−12.6
Other non-grain crops	1.5	1.9	11.3	1.8
Livestock	1.0	5.0	73.7	5.7
Forestry	0.05	1.4	1.3	1.1
Fishery	0.09	1.3	4.2	1.0
Wool	−0.1	−37.5	−3.0	−37.0
Wang (1999) (1995–2010) (% change)				
Rice		0.7		1.3
Wheat		−16.1		−15.7
Other grains		−9.2		−8.8
Non-grain crops		0.6		1.0
Livestock		2.5		3.2
Dairy and meat		0.5		1.7
Processed food		−0.4		1.0
Agriculture		−0.7		0.4
Forestry and fishery		0.7		0.9
Anderson et al. (2002) (2002–2007) (% change)				
Rice		−2.0		−2.1
Wheat		−2.0		−2.1
Oilseeds		−4.0		−7.8
Feedgrains		−3.0		−2.2
Vegetables & fruits		−4.0		−3.4
Livestock and meat		1.0		1.3
Forestry, fishing & mining		−1.0		−0.9
Dairy products		−2.0		−2.1
Beverages and Tobacco		−33.0		−33.1
UNCTAD (2002) (1997–2005) (% change)	Unskilled	Skilled		
Grains, vegetables, fruits	−7.7	−8.3		−4.8
Oilseeds	−60.6	−61.5		−53.5
Beverages & tobacco products	−35.3	−38.8		−38.7
Other crops	−12.1	−12.7		−8.8
Dairy products	−1.9	−4.7		−3.8

Sources: Anderson *et al.* (2002); Wang (1999); UNCTAD (2002); Zhai and Li (2000).

Notes: (1) Anderson *et al.* (2002) is a GTAP simulation model of the effects of trade reforms between 2002 and 2007. The 1997 data base is aggregated into 25 sectors and projected to 2001 and 2007 on the basis of World Bank projections. The study focuses on the additional commitments by China to be implemented between 2002 and 2007 (relative to the revised base case in which China's reforms only up to 2001 are considered. The initial base period case assumes: (a) China retains its protection policies as of 1995, (b) all other countries fully implement their Uruguay Round obligations before 2005, (c) Taiwan fulfils its commitments under the terms of its WTO accession. (2) Zhai and Li (2000) use a 41 sector 10 households (five rural and five urban) recursive dynamic model which incorporates China's two trade regimes, namely, ordinary trade and processing trade. They quantify the impact of the following four aspects of the accession: (a) tariff reductions in industrial sectors, (b) reduction of NTBs in industrial sectors, (c) agricultural trade liberalization, and (d) phasing out of MFA quota on textiles and clothing. Wang (1999) estimates are based on a GTAP model.

China's accession to the WTO has brought about both challenges and opportunities to the agricultural sector of the country. There is general agreement that China's agricultural sector must introduce structural adjustments and reforms with or without WTO accession. There is no hope for the Chinese rural population to prosper when so many people rely on so little resources for their livelihood. Accession will certainly encourage and speed up the transition process in agriculture. On the one hand, more opportunities are being offered to China to take advantage of the surplus and cheap labour by participating in the global economy. On the other hand, imports of cheap agricultural goods will make the transfer of labour from agricultural activities more urgent, especially from grain crop cultivation to other potentially higher income-earning crops and activities.

The transfer of resources from agricultural to non-agricultural activities has already been taking place, which has led to an increase in labour productivity. According to a report by Morgan Stanley's Asia Pacific department, the redistribution of rural labour to non-rural activities contributes about 1.2 percentage points in annual increase in labour productivity. China's agricultural sector will become more profitable as labour productivity continues to rise. Following accession the commercial potential of the agricultural sector is likely to grow in the future.[4]

It is clear that China cannot solve problems of poverty and low rural incomes as long as the rural population remains tied to land. The elasticity of demand for food is very low; as incomes rise people demand more high-quality and non-grain foodstuffs such as meats, vegetables, milk products and fruits. In the case of China, it can be predicted that the share of rice in consumption of grains will decline relative to that of wheat and coarse grains.

In the long run, the WTO Agreement will enable China to optimize rural resource allocation and speed up the process of transition to a modern industrial and service economy.[5] Implications for China's industrial and service sectors are discussed in Chapters 5 and 6.

5   Industry

We noted in Chapter 3 that employment growth in China's manufacturing sector has been slowing down for the past several years. A much smaller proportion of the Chinese labour force is employed in industry than in the primary or tertiary sectors.[1] Process of industrial rationalization and restructuring led to this situation long before China's entry into the WTO. The initial strategy of concentration on heavy industry (which is generally capital-intensive) during the pre-reform period may have also been responsible for low employment generation in the sector relative to its contribution to output. China's policy of setting up a few large 'national champions' (like the Korean *choebel*) to compete with global industrial giants after accession may have also contributed to the problem.

As we noted in Chapter 1, China has made major commitments under the WTO Agreement to offer market access to foreign firms in different economic sectors. Increased market access will, however, be more dramatic in agriculture and services sectors which were hitherto highly protected. The impact of accession may not be as serious in the industrial sector which has already been exposed to domestic and global competition (OECD, 2002). However, even in this sector the impact may be important in such protected industries as automobiles (see p.97). The nature and precise magnitude of the impact will depend on the competitiveness of these industries and the growth of domestic demand for their products. Many Chinese and Western observers are quite optimistic about the future of China's large industrial enterprises assuming that global competition in the wake of accession will lead to greater efficiency and competitiveness. There are others (e.g. Nolan, 2001b) who portray a bleak picture and argue that despite important progress over the last decade or so none of China's large industrial enterprises have become globally competitive.[2]

How will exports, output and employment of particular industries be affected by China's accession? The main purpose of this chapter is to answer this question. We discuss below cases of textiles and clothing, a global competitor, automobiles, a highly protected industry, and household appliances in which competition in the domestic market has led Chinese firms to take over market shares of foreign firms.

Textiles and clothing

China is one of the largest producers of textile products in the world, and the textile industry plays an important role in its economy. China's textile exports as a proportion of the world exports of textiles increased from 2.6 per cent in 1970 to 13.2 per cent in 1998 (see Table 5.1). This increase in exports was achieved in a very difficult international market environment. Developing-country exports faced quantitative restrictions by industrialized countries, which included global quotas, bilaterally negotiated quotas and unilateral quotas.[3] The textile sector remains China's biggest foreign exchange earner. The average annual trade surplus generated by textile exports during the period 1994–98 was more than $2.4 billion, higher than the surplus generated by any other sector. However, the industry shows a declining trend in terms of shares of output, employment and export (see Table 5.2 and Fig. 5.1). Since 1996 the ranking of industry dropped from 1 to 2 among the export sectors (surpassed by electrical and machinery product exports).[4] Rural non-state textile firms, including the small-scale private firms, have been growing rapidly at the expense of large state enterprises, especially during the mid-1980s and 1990s. The output of rural textile and clothing industry increased from over 37 billion yuan in 1991 (at 1990 prices) to 104 billion yuan in 1998 (see Table 5.2). The non-state sector out-performs the

Table 5.1 Exports of China's textiles and clothing (1985–2000)

Year	World textile and clothing exports (excluding fibres) ($ billion)	China's textile and clothing exports ($ billion)	China's share of world exports (%)
1985	93.4	2.4	2.6
1986	115.2	3.3	2.8
1987	152.7	11.3	7.4
1988	168.2	13.3	7.9
1989	180.3	15.4	8.5
1990	206.9	16.9	8.2
1991	221.3	20.2	9.1
1992	245.5	25.4	10.3
1993	238.4	27.3	11.4
1994	269.2	35.7	13.3
1995	303.5	38.2	12.6
1996	311.8	37.4	12.0
1997	335.8	45.9	13.7
1998	328.4	43.1	13.1
1999	323.0	43.3	13.4
2000	343.7	52.5	15.3

Source: UNCTAD *Economic Time Series (ETS) Database* (COMTRADE and UNSD Estimates).

Table 5.2 Basic economic data on China's textiles and clothing industry

	1991	1993	1995	1997	1998
I. Enterprises with independent accounting system at township level and above					
Textiles:					
No. of enterprises (000)	24.6	24.6	25.7	21.8	11.2
Employment (million)	7.56	6.8	6.7	5.96	3.93
Output value (billion yuan)	253.3	352.1	460.4	476	437.6
Output value (billion yuan at 1990 prices)	246.2	289.8	291.4	288.7	269.6
Output per worker (yuan at 1990 prices)	32,566	42,617	43,492	48,439	68,600
Clothing:					
No. of enterprises (000)	17.5	17.9	20	17.2	6.8
Employment (million)	1.72	1.64	1.75	1.62	1.27
Output value (billion yuan)	12.2	99.4	147	184.5	201.8
Output value (billion yuan at 1990 prices)	11.9	81.8	93.0	111.9	124.3
Output per worker (yuan at 1990 prices)	6,918	49,878	53,143	69,074	97,874
II. Township and village enterprises					
Textiles:					
No. of enterprises	29,348	31,530	29,326	24,839	21,226
Employment (million)	3.21	3.37	3.22	2.73	2.31
Output value (billion yuan)	84.91	184.9	348.13	291.81	263.99
Output value (billion yuan at 1990 prices)	82.5	152.2	220.3	177.0	162.7
Output per worker (yuan at 1990 prices)	25,700	45,163	68,416	64,835	70,433
Clothing:					
No. of enterprises	18,264	23,254	30,649	27,483	22,971
Employment (million)	1.30	1.57	2.34	2.27	2.14
Output value (billion yuan)	23.2	59.67	171.63	190.01	187.41
Output value (billion yuan at 1990 prices)	22.5	49.1	108.6	115.2	115.5
Output per worker (yuan at 1990 prices)	17,307	31,274	46,410	50,749	53,972
III. Village enterprises					
Textiles:					
No. of enterprises	16,994	18,886	17,551	14,879	12,714
Employment (million)	1.11	1.21	1.15	0.98	0.83
Output value (billion yuan)	29.59	64.72	125.97	102.13	92.40
Output value (billion yuan at 1990 prices)	28.8	53.3	79.7	61.9	56.9
Output per worker (yuan at 1990 prices)	25,945	44,049	69,304	63,163	68,554
Clothing:					
No. of enterprises	11,899	16,278	22,349	19,238	16,080
Employment (million)	0.62	0.79	1.23	1.14	1.07
Output value (billion yuan)	8.5	24.35	76.82	77.52	76.46
Output value (billion yuan at 1990 prices)	8.3	20.0	48.6	47.0	47.1
Output per worker (yuan at 1990 prices)	13,387	25,316	39,512	41,228	44,019

Table 5.2 Basic economic data on China's textiles and clothing industry (*Continued*)

	1991	1993	1995	1997	1998
IV. National total (I+III)					
Textiles:					
No. of enterprises	41,594	43,86	43,251	36,679	23,914
Employment (million)	8.67	8.01	7.85	6.94	4.76
Output value (billion yuan)	282.89	416.82	586.37	578.13	530.00
Output value (billion yuan at 1990 prices)	274.9	343.1	371.1	350.6	326.6
Output per worker (yuan at 1990 prices)	31,707	42,834	47,274	50,519	68,613
Clothing:					
No. of enterprises	29,399	34,178	42,349	36,438	22,880
Employment (million)	2.34	2.43	2.98	2.76	2.34
Output value (billion yuan)	20.7	123.75	223.82	262.02	278.26
Output value (billion yuan at 1990 prices)	20.1	101.8	141.7	158.9	171.4
Output per worker (yuan at 1990 prices)	8,589	41,893	47,550	57,572	73,248

Sources: Data for enterprises with independent systems come from *China Statistical Yearbook*, various issues and figures for TVEs come from *China's Township and Village Enterprises Yearbook*, various issues.

Notes:
1. The village enterprises' figures for 1997 and 1998 were estimated based on the average share of village enterprises as the total TVEs for 1991, 1992, 1994, 1995 and 1996.
2. Output value at 1990 price was deflated by general price index.

state sector due to lower labour costs, which make possible lower prices and greater flexibility in production and marketing. Higher labour costs in the state sector are due mainly to overstaffing.

China's state-owned textile industry has made efforts to reduce overcapacity and check overstaffing by shedding labour. From early 1998 to the end of 1999 China reduced the number of spindles in use by 9 million and redeployed 1.2 million workers to other sectors (Shi, 2001; *China's Textile Economy*, Vol. 1, 2001).

Table 5.2 shows that employment in textiles declined in enterprises under the independent accounting system (legal entities with fixed location, financial autonomy and authority to enter into contracts with other enterprises) and in town and village enterprises (TVEs). However, it increased in TVE clothing enterprises. It is likely that this trend will continue after accession. Output and employment data for the entire textile and clothing industry do not exist. We have, therefore, made these estimates in Table 5.2 on the basis of information available on enterprises with independent accounting system at township level and above, TVEs, and village enterprises. The national output and employment figures are estimated by aggregating data for enterprises under the independent accounting system and village enterprises.

These are lower-bound estimates since some township enterprises are not covered under the enterprises with independent accounting system. To that extent the national figures may be underestimated. An upper-bound estimate is

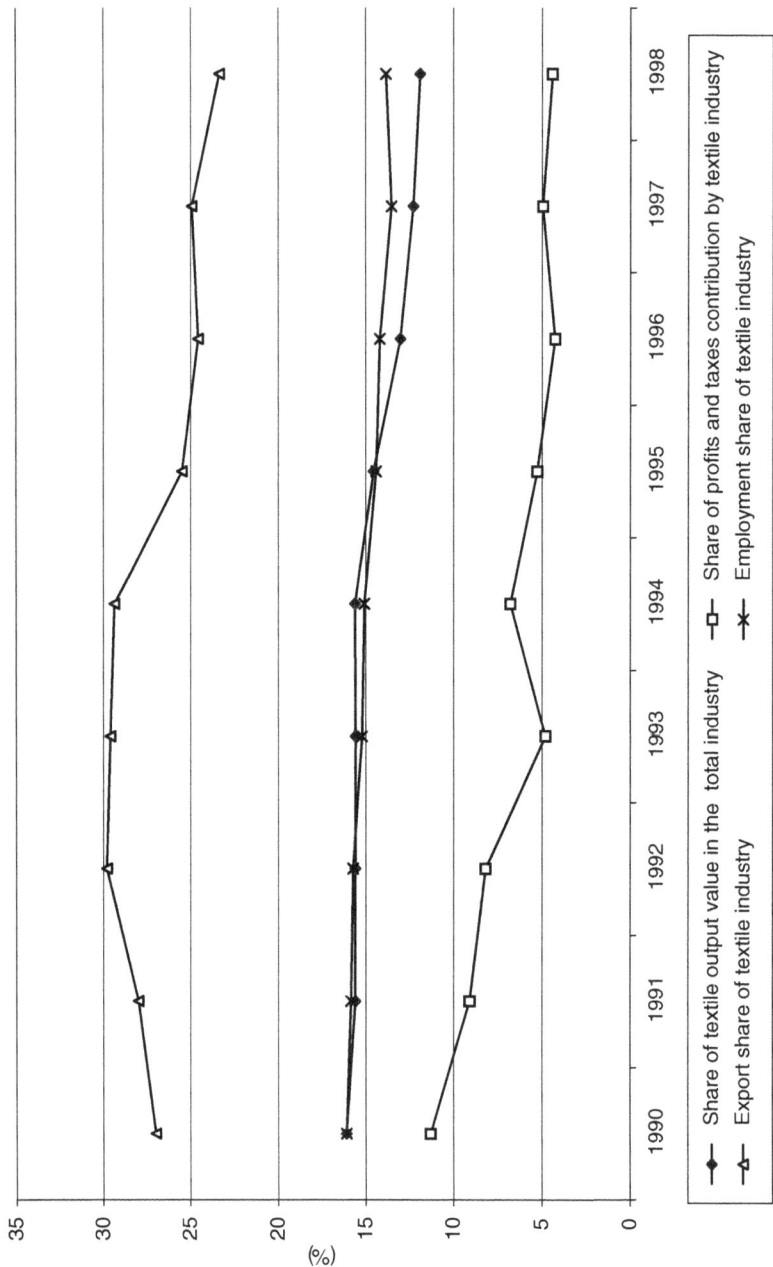

Figure 5.1 Shares of Chinese textile industry: Output, employment, exports and profits (1990–98)

Source: *Almanac of China's Textile Industry* (original in Chinese), various issues.

obtained by assuming that no TVEs are included under the independent accounting system. Unfortunately, we have no information on the size of TVEs that fall under this system. Therefore, no precise estimates can be made; the exact figure is likely to be somewhere between the upper and lower bounds.

China imports such textile inputs as cotton, textile fibres (China was the largest importer of textile fibres in 1995 with total imports of $5 billion) and textile machinery. Imports have increased of clothing, yarns and fabrics, textile machinery, and high-quality dying equipment. In 1995, the total textile machinery imports of $2.55 billion equalled the total value of textile machinery products made in China. These goods were imported despite the fact that they were subject to high import duties of up to 50 to 68 per cent.

After accession, textile imports, especially of textile machinery, will increase as global competition will necessitate technological modernization to raise labour productivity. Rising average incomes in China should raise demand for imported high-quality brand names, which are already increasingly being produced within China. While imports of final textile products (e.g. brand names) will displace domestic consumption, that of necessary material inputs will actually raise domestic production. During the past few years, the import/ export ratio in textiles and clothing (not including textile machinery) has been declining (see Table 5.3), which indicates improved balance of trade in textiles.

The textile sector underwent significant structural changes during the last two decades. The number of textile enterprises was reduced by more than half, from 24.6 thousand in 1991 to 11.2 thousand in 1998 (Table 5.2). The total employment in these enterprises declined from 7.6 million to nearly 4 million during the same period. In clothing, the number of enterprises declined from 17.5 thousand to nearly 7 thousand, and employment, from 1.7 million to 1.3 million. The number of TVEs also declined. This situation reflects the reorganization of enterprises in general and the closure of inefficient SOEs in particular. However, while employment declined in TVEs producing textiles it increased in those producing garments.

During the 1990s SOE profitability in textiles declined due not only to growing competition from non-state enterprises, but also due to the loosening of government control on wages in the wake of greater enterprise autonomy. Social burdens in the form of expenditures on workers' health, education and pensions were also reduced (Tables 5.4 and 5.5). On the basis of a sample of 700 SOEs during 1980–94, Zheng *et al.* (2001) estimate that the textile efficiency levels

Table 5.3 Import and export ratios for textiles and clothing

Year	Imports ($100 million	Exports ($100 million)	Import-export ratio
1995	158.2	358.8	0.44
1998	143.9	404.6	0.35
1999	139.2	412.7	0.34

Source: *Foreign Economic Statistical Yearbook (Zhongguo Duiwai Jingji Tongji Nianjian).*

Table 5.4 Selected efficiency indicators for textiles by ownership

	1990	1993	1995	1997	1999
I State/Non-State Enterprises†					
1 Ratio of value-added to gross industrial output (%)	21.5	27.0	19.5	23.5	24.7
2 Ratio of pre-tax profit to total capital (%)	9.8	3.6	8.5	2.5	2.7
3 Profit to total capital (%)	—	-0.2	-3.2	-1.9	2.8
4 Labour productivity (yuan per worker per year)	17,857	38,964	10,350	15,292	21,867
5 Ratio of profit to gross sales revenue (%)	1.54	-0.15	-0.97	-0.64	0.93
II State-owned Enterprises					
1 Ratio of value-added to gross industrial output (%)	21.5‡	26.0	17.9	22.6	26.9
2 Ratio of pre-tax profit to total capital (%)	11.0	1.7	0.5	-0.01	-3.7
3 Profit to total capital (%)	—	-2.3	-12.4	-13.4	-3.8
4 Labour productivity (yuan per worker per year)	17,857	31,419	—	—	15,325
5 Ratio of profit (loss) to gross sales revenue (%)	1.73	-2.0	-3.5	-4.7	-1.4
III Foreign-funded Enterprises					
1 Ratio of value-added to gross industrial output (%)	—	—	22.1	22.9	24.2
2 Ratio of pre-tax profit to total capital (%)	—	—	—	—	—
3 Profit to total capital (%)	—	—	—	—	—
4 Labour productivity (yuan per worker per year)	—	—	—	—	38,496
5 Ratio of profit to gross sales revenue (%)	—	—	—	—	—

Source: *China Statistical Yearbook*, various years. † Figures are for the enterprises with independent accounting system. ‡ Figure for 1991.

Note: The concept of 'pre-tax profit' appearing in the Chinese statistical yearbooks is different from that used in the Western literature. The pre-tax profit in China generally means firms' profit before paying corporate tax and sales tax. This explains why the figure of 'total profit' in the Chinese yearbooks is smaller than the figure of 'pre-tax profit'. In many cases pre-tax profit is positive but total profit is negative.

Table 5.5 Selected efficiency indicators for clothing by ownership

	1993	1995	1997	1999
I *State/Non-State Enterprises*[†]				
1 Ratio of value-added to gross industrial output (%)	32.7	23.6	25.1	28.3
2 Ratio of pre-tax profit to total capital (%)	8.9	15.5	16.7	12.2
3 Profit to total capital (%)	5.5	5.99	7.6	12.1
4 Labour productivity (yuan value-added per worker per year)	38,709	12,960	19,020	24,964
5 Ratio of profit to gross sales revenue (%)	3.5	1.8	2.4	3.3
II *State-owned Enterprises*				
1 Ratio of value-added to gross industrial output (%)	33.8	21.4	26.1	24.8
2 Ratio of pre-tax profit to total capital (%)	5.2	1.4	0.9	1.7
3 Profit to total capital	6.5	-2.8	-4.2	2.99
4 Labour productivity (yuan per worker per year)	33,599	–	–	24,964
5 Ratio of profit to gross sales revenue (%)	2.26	-1.00	-1.6	1.3
III *Foreign-funded Enterprises*				
1 Ratio of value-added to gross industrial output (%)	–	23.6	25.4	24.9
2 Ratio of pre-tax profit to total capital (%)	–	–	–	–
3 Profit to total capital (%)	–	–	–	–
4 Labour productivity (yuan per worker per year)	–	–	–	25,800
5 Ratio of profit to gross sales revenue (%)	–	–	–	2.9

Source: *China Statistical Yearbook*, Various years.

Note: [†] Figures are for the enterprises with independent accounting system.

were low: productivity growth was generally achieved through increase in capital investment rather than improvements in technical efficiency. The efficiency index for textile industry increased only marginally from 1.04 in 1980–81 to 1.17 in 1993–94.

The market shares for textiles are much higher for state-owned enterprises (SOEs) than for foreign-funded enterprises (FFEs), but the reverse is the case for clothing. The shares of SOEs for textiles, however, declined over time, whereas those of FFEs in textiles increased (see Table 5.6). As textiles require more sophisticated technology and greater investment than clothing, SOEs have traditionally been engaged in this sector more than in clothing. It is not certain that an increase in FFEs, with better technology and relatively higher labour productivity (due to higher capital–labour ratio in FFEs and overstaffing in SOEs) can compensate for employment losses resulting from the closure of domestic firms. However, most of the FFEs in textiles and clothing and other consumer goods belong to overseas Chinese from Hong Kong and Taiwan whose technological levels may not be much higher. (FFEs in the assembly of automobiles, discussed below, are different since the world's leading manufacturers have entered into joint ventures with Chinese firms.)

China's competitiveness in textiles and clothing has so far been maintained by shifting production from state-owned enterprises to non-state-owned enterprises including rural small enterprises, private enterprises, joint ventures and FFEs. TVEs play a very important role in China's textile and clothing exports (see Table 5.2). However, the growth of TVEs in China is very uneven across regions

Table 5.6 Sales and market shares of textiles and clothing by ownership

	Sales (billion yuan) (1993)	Market share (%)	Sales (billion yuan) (1995)	Market share (%)	Sales (billion yuan) (1997)	Market share (%)	Sales (billion yuan) (1999)	Market share (%)
Textiles								
Total sales	310.1		425.7		416.2		414.8	
State-owned	152.0	49.0	173.3	40.7	138.2	33.2	148.4	35.8
Foreign-funded	–	–	76.1	17.9	77.6	18.7	88.3	21.3
Non-state owned domestic	–	–	176.3	41.4	200.2	48.1	178.1	42.9
Clothing								
Total sales	81.8		134.6		160.2		184.7	
State-owned	8.1	9.9	9.1	6.7	8.5	5.3	13.5	7.3
Foreign-funded	–	–	68.4	50.8	71.8	44.9	90.9	49.2
Non-state owned domestic	–	–	57.1	42.4	79.7	49.8	80.3	43.5

Source: *China Statistical Yearbook,* various years.

Note: Market shares are percentages of total sales.

and provinces. Among the total output value in textile and clothing industry produced by TVEs in 1995, over 83 per cent came from only five provinces. Jiangsu and Zhejiang, the two provinces with a sizeable TVE production, account for 68 per cent of the national total output. Furthermore, as we noted in Chapter 3, overall TVE employment has remained more or less unchanged since 1996–97.

Does China still have a competitive advantage in textile and clothing sectors even after experiencing almost twenty years of rapid export growth? To answer this question, we need to examine where China's competitive advantage lies and whether there is still a potential for further growth.

As we noted in Chapter 2, many factors affect a country's competitive advantage in international trade: resource availability, unit labour cost, research and development, structural response to changes in international market and the exchange rate. China has a competitive edge in terms of materials for textile industry. It produces one-quarter of the world's cotton output and is the largest cotton producer in the world. It is also the largest producer of mulberry cocoons and silk materials, accounting for 70 per cent of the world output. The output of ramie fibre accounts for only 1 per cent of China's total fibre output but it accounts for 99 per cent of the world output. These factors, combined with an abundant rural labour force, will give China a head-start in the foreseeable future. China cannot meet domestically the total demand for chemical fibre materials; about 20 per cent of the demand is met through imports from abroad. China's ability to raise production of chemical fibre materials will be enhanced following accession.

China enjoys a labour cost advantage over many other developing countries. After India and Indonesia, it has the lowest unit labour cost in spinning and weaving (Table 5.7). UNCTAD (2002: 158) makes comparisons of hourly labour costs for 1998 between China and selected developing and developed countries and concludes that 'while China has labour cost advantage in clothing compared to most middle-income countries its competitive edge over India and Bangladesh, for example, is less clear-cut'. However, China's inland regions

Table 5.7 Labour cost comparisons in spinning and weaving in selected countries/ economies (1980–96) (US$ per hour)

	1980	*1984*	*1987*	*1990*	*1993*	*1996*
China	0.25	0.26	0.23	0.37	0.36	0.58
India	0.60	0.71	0.65	0.72	0.56	0.56
Rep. of Korea	0.78	1.89	1.77	3.22	3.66	5.56
Hong Kong (China)	1.91	1.65	1.93	3.05	3.85	4.90
Indonesia	0.22	0.23	0.20	0.25	0.43	0.52
Mexico	3.10	2.62	0.83	2.21	2.93	1.52

Source: Excerpted from *Almanac of China's Textile Industry* 1996. Figures for China and Indonesia for 1980 are taken from Shi (2001).

Note: Figures include social charges; based on the US dollar exchange rate on 7 May 1996. Data for 1980–89 and 1996 are for spring and 1990 and 1993 data are for summer periods.

and provinces, which supply a large proportion of textile materials, still enjoy abundant labour supply at a very low labour cost. Currently the eastern region is attracting labour migration from the hinterland, which involves dislocation and other social problems.

An alternative route is to take production and jobs to the interior. A combination of natural resources and cheap labour in the central and western regions and a sharing by the coastal enterprises of funds, technologies, marketing channels and experience will, in principle, enable China to continue to enjoy a dynamic comparative advantage in the world textile and clothing market after accession. In fact, this phenomenon may be similar to the 'flying-geese model' of trade and development according to which the more industrially advanced countries with higher value-added and capital-intensive industries pass on the older (mature) labour-intensive industries to less-developed and more labour-abundant countries where labour costs are much lower. A similar flying-geese pattern may emerge within China involving the relocation of production to the lower labour cost hinterland (see Chapter 7).

There is considerable controversy about the status of China's textile industry in terms of exports and employment in the post-accession period. Bach *et al.* (1996) argue that China will benefit substantially through the abolition of the Multi-Fibre Arrangement (MFA) quotas, which at present restrict its exports of textiles and clothing. This may not necessarily be so, at least in the short term, for several reasons. First, the share of export products under the quota restrictions is quite small. According to Yang Donghui, Secretary-General of the Chinese Federation of Textile Industry (CFTI), quota restrictions account for less than 27 per cent of the total textile and clothing exports. He noted that Chinese exports following accession were unlikely to increase significantly (*China Business Weekly*, 26 December 1999). Second, these restrictions will be lifted only gradually by 2005. Third, international competitiveness of the Chinese textile industry has been declining over time. A global competitiveness index for textiles estimated by GATT shows that for China it declined from 0.104 in 1989 to 0.014 in 1993. On the other hand, the index for Pakistan increased from 0.856 to 0.946, and for Indonesia, from 0.276 to 0.406. For clothing also the competitiveness index for China declined whereas it increased slightly for Indonesia (cited in Yu *et al.*, 2000). These estimates are consistent with more recent estimates of China's revealed comparative advantage (RCA) in textiles between 1992–93 and 1997–98 (Shafaeddin, 2002; Chapter 7, Table 7.1). Shafaeddin shows a deterioration of the RCA in textile yarn, non-knitted undergarments and woven cotton fabrics. Fourth, the inclusion of safeguard provisions to last till 2008 (as under the 1999 bilateral China–US agreement) are heavily biased against China and possible anti-dumping duties can discourage its textile exports even after the phasing out of MFA.[5] Finally, a global phenomenon of the supply of textiles exceeding demand is likely to worsen in the wake of the current economic recession.

Thus China may not be able to expand employment substantially through exports of textiles and garments. However, it may be able to do so on one condition – that it exploits differences in labour costs across regions by relocating production to low labour cost areas as discussed above. The coastal areas are already attracting a lot of low-cost labour from the hinterland to overcome local labour shortages, but freer labour mobility to these areas will be necessary.

The more optimistic estimates of Chinese exports and employment assume that (a) low labour costs will offer China a substantial comparative advantage, (b) a decline in the number of SOEs and an increase in non-state enterprises in textiles will improve competitiveness, and (c) employment through clothing exports, which are more significant, will more than compensate for any loss of employment in textiles. For example, Ianchovichina *et al.* (2000) (see Chapter 3, Table 3.1 and Table 5.8) estimate a decline in employment in textiles by 18 per cent between 1995 and 2005 but an increase in employment in clothing by 70 per cent during the same period. Others, like Wang (1999) and the Development Research Centre (DRC) (1998), are more optimistic about employment growth in textiles and clothing (see Table 5. 8). We believe that most of these estimates are exaggerated considering the declining comparative advantage of China in textiles noted above and the product–specific and general safeguard and anti-dumping clauses discussed in Chapter 1. The forecasts in Table 5.8 vary widely depending on the assumptions made. The results of simulations are often contradictory due to such unrealistic assumptions as equilibrium conditions in product and factor markets, and perfect factor mobility on which most of the general equilibrium simulation models are based.

Automobiles

Automobiles are quite different from textiles because they represent a sheltered domestic market. At present China does not export many automobiles. As we noted in Chapter 2, the highly protected nature of the industry limits competition. The industry consists of a few large SOEs and joint ventures of SOEs with foreign manufacturers (e.g. Volkswagen, Honda, General Motors, and Citroen). The latter are more efficient; their presence raises average efficiency of the industry despite lack of much domestic competition. Unlike textiles the automobile industry is relatively young; mass production in this industry started only in the mid-1980s. The average annual output of the industry remains quite low compared to the leading rival foreign firms. Labour productivity is also much lower compared to that of foreign manufacturers – only two to four vehicles per worker a year compared to 20 to 40 vehicles in the foreign industry (Yang, 1999). The industry is highly fragmented with small-scale firms having mushroomed in most provinces under protection by local governments.[6]

China's automotive industry has experienced a fundamental change in terms of output composition, technology and market structure since the government introduced the Automobile Industry Policy in 1994. Until the early 1990s, the Chinese industry produced mainly medium-sized trucks. Few automobiles or heavy trucks were produced at that time. In the late 1980s, production was

Table 5.8 Forecasts of employment, output, exports and imports of China's textiles and clothing

Author/study	Employment	Output	Exports	Imports
Wang (1999) (1995–2010) (% change)				
(i) Textiles	6.1	11.5	18.4	36.4
(ii) Clothing	38.7	43.7	66.7	111.6
Zhai and Li (2000) (1995–2010)				
(i) Textiles	2.8 million	$47 bn (26%)	$22 bn (64%)	$19 bn (86%)
(ii) Clothing	2.6 million	$63 bn (74%)	$59 bn (214%)	$1 bn (124%)
Zhang (2000) (1994–2005)				
Percentage change from base year	3.14	2.47	4.42	2.06
Ianchovichina et al. (2000) (1995–2005) (% change)				
(i) Textiles	–18.3	88		
(ii) Clothing	65.9	263.5		
UNCTAD (2002) (1997–2005) (% change)				
(i) Textiles	3.7	2		
(ii) Clothing	22.6	22.0		

Sources: Ianchovichina *et al.* (2000); UNCTAD (2002); Wang (1999); Zhai and Li (2000); Zhang (2000).

Notes: Ianchovichina *et al.* (2000) is a GTAP model making forecasts for 1995–2005; UNCTAD (2002) makes a 'comparison between the values resulting from the simulations of China's performance after its accession to WTO and the values for a hypothetical situation without China's accession' for 1997–2005 period; Wang (1999) uses a GTAP model focusing on the impact of the elimination of MFA quotas on China's exports during 1995–2010. He assumes Chinese additional tariff cuts of 40 per cent for industrial products on top of tariff schedules of October 1997. Zhai and Li (2000) use 41 sector, 10 households (five rural and five urban) recursive dynamic single-country model which incorporates China's two trade regimes, namely, ordinary trade and processing trade. It is based on 1995 SAM for China. They quantify the impact of the following four aspects of the accession: (a) tariff reductions in industrial sectors, (b) reduction of NTBs in industrial sectors, (c) agricultural trade liberalization, and (d) phasing out of MFA quota on textiles and clothing. Wang (1999) is a GTAP model focusing on the impact of the elimination of MFN quotas. Zhang (2000) constructs the model data base on the basis of China's 1992 input-output table. His simulations are based on trade-weighted average tariff reductions of 17.32 per cent in 1996 and 12.06 per cent in 1997.

switched from trucks to automobiles. In 1980, of the total automotive units produced in China, automobiles accounted for only 2.44 per cent, and trucks nearly 61 per cent. By 1999, the share of automobiles increased to 31 per cent whereas that of trucks declined to less than 32 per cent (see Fig. 5.2).

The automotive industry has made rapid progress since the early 1980s. From 1986 to 1999, the number of vehicles produced in China increased from 373,000 thousand to nearly 1,832,000; value-added, from 6.2 billion yuan to nearly

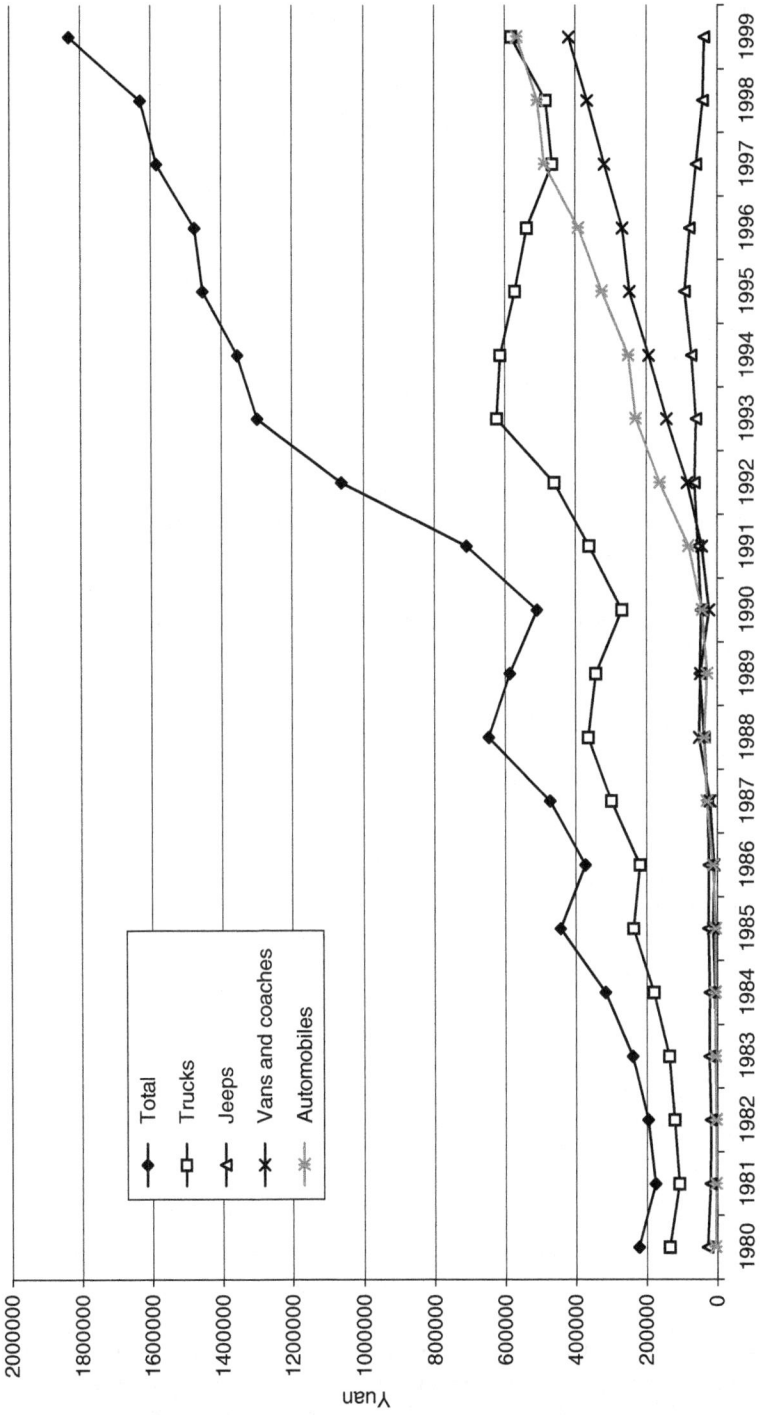

Figure 5.2 Composition of Chinese automotive production (1980–99)

Source: *China Automotive Industry Yearbook*, various issues.

Table 5.9 Imports and exports of Chinese automotive products (1980–99)

Year	Imports			Exports		
	Trucks and automobiles (no.)	Components value (million $)	Total value (million $)	Trucks and automobiles	Components value (million $)	Total value (million $)
1980	51,083	62.99	616.12	–	–	–
1985	353,992	288.48	2,936.89	–	–	–
1990	65,430	347.40	1,202.93	4,431	81.70	127.84
1995	158,115	854.69	2,575.49	17,747	376.09	721.38
1999	35,192	1,004.25	2,580.18	10,095	706.89	1,187.27

Source: *China Automotive Industry Yearbook* 2000 (in Chinese).

75 billion yuan, and employment, from 1.3 million to 1.8 million (see Table 5.9). The industry also generates *indirect* employment through such related activities as after-sales maintenance and repair services, gas stations and so on. Before the 1980s, demand for automobiles was met by imports as the industry produced only medium-sized trucks. In 1980, China produced 5,418 automobiles and imported 19,570, which was equivalent to 3.6 times the number of automobiles produced in China. From 1981 to 1990, China imported 351 thousand automobiles, that is, more than twice the number produced domestically.[7] By 1999, the number of automobiles produced in China reached 565.4 thousand with a total annual production capacity of more than a million.

In 1999, China exported a total number of 10,095 assembled vehicles, of which 3,868 were trucks and 326 automobiles; the remainder consisted of vans and other specialized vehicles (see Table 5.9). But exports of auto parts and components to the world market were much more significant, accounting for 78 per cent of China's total exports of automotive products (see Fig. 5.3).

The foreign affiliates of such automotive business groups as the Shanghai Automotive Industrial Group (SAIG) and Tianjin Automotive Industrial Group (TAIG), attached great importance to components manufacturing. Between 1992 and 1997 the share of components in output value increased from nearly 18 per cent to 27 per cent in SAIG and from 14 per cent to 30.5 per cent in TAIG. The localization rates measured in quantity were over 90 per cent in SAIG and TAIG.

Implications of the WTO entry for China's automotive industry

Prior to WTO membership China granted preferential tariff rates to automobile enterprises whose localization rates were high. The higher the localization the lower the preferential tariff. Preference was given when: (a) localization rate reached 40 per cent, 60 per cent, or 80 per cent on products (automobiles, coaches and vans) that incorporated imported technology on whole vehicles; (b) localization rate reached 50 per cent, 70 per cent, or 90 per cent on products

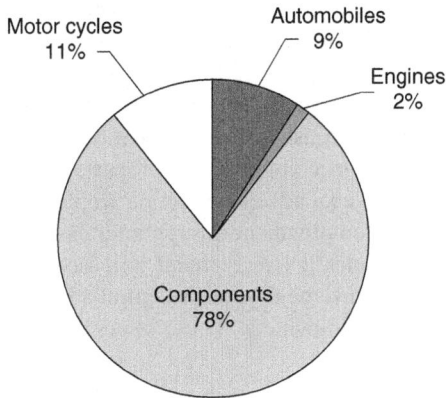

Figure 5.3 Composition of China's automotive exports (1999)

Source: *China Automotive Industry Yearbook* 2000.

Note: The figures include trucks, automobiles, auto parts and components, motor cycles and engines.

(trucks) incorporating imported technology, as well as on automobile (and motor cycle) assembly and key components.

In the granting of credit preference was given to enterprises with better export performance: those whose exports of whole vehicle products reached a certain specified percentage of the volume of their sales, and to automobile components manufacturing enterprises whose exports accounted for 10 per cent of their total annual sales.

China's WTO commitments for the automotive industry include the following:

- Reduction of tariffs on passenger cars to 25 per cent for all vehicles by 2006.
- Reduction of tariffs on auto parts to an average of 10 per cent by 2006.
- Reduction and gradual elimination of non-tariff barriers and increase of import quotas. Quotas will be eliminated in 2005. Meanwhile quotas will be expanded by 15 per cent annually to enable an increase in the imports of motor vehicles into China.
- Elimination of local-content requirements under which joint ventures and foreign firms will be free to source automobile parts and components domestically or from abroad.
- Lifting of measures which restricted the categories, types and models of vehicles to be produced, two years after accession.
- Raising of limits within which investments in automobile production could be approved at the provincial level.
- Granting trading and distribution rights to foreign enterprises including after sales and related services.

- Permitting foreign banks and non-bank financial institutions to finance purchase of automobiles by Chinese individuals.

A large tariff reduction after accession will create problems as the industry is currently heavily protected against foreign competition. Similarly, increases in import quotas will raise import competition. Not least, elimination of the local-content requirement will have an adverse effect on employment in China. As we noted in Chapter 1, indirect employment in supplier industries can be significant.

China's commitments under the Agreement will have implications for cost and quality, technology improvements, and structural adjustments in response to import competition and unemployment. These issues are discussed below.

Quality and cost considerations

Diseconomies of small scale in an industry where scale economies are significant, and much lower productivity at present mean that the unit cost of production of a Chinese automobile and its price are higher. An automobile made in China is 40–50 per cent more expensive than a similar model produced abroad (SETC, 1999, 2000).

The current market structure of the industry is oligopolistic as the bulk of marketing is in the hands of a few large state-owned firms. In 1998, the top five firms accounted for 62 per cent of the total market (Liu, 2001). However, the number of automobile firms declined from 283 in 1994 to 123 in 1998, with a subsequent substantial increase in average output per firm. Pressure for quality, efficiency and cost will be intensified after China's accession. Large joint-venture firms will strengthen their positions with the help of advanced foreign technology. Small high-cost firms will probably be squeezed out of the market.

It is interesting to note that the domestic industry succeeded in regaining market shares from foreign companies. The share of imported automobiles fell from 41 per cent of the total sales in 1994 to only 3.4 per cent in 1998 (Yang, 1999). One reason for this dramatic change, despite low economies of scale and lack of modern technology, seems to be the success of foreign automobiles assembled in China (e.g. Volkswagen and Peugeot) by joint ventures with Chinese SOEs. The sale of automobiles in domestic market depends on price, quality and technology. In an oligopolistic structure large automobile firms will reduce price to compete with smaller firms for market shares. Although the price of Chinese automobiles is higher, their quality and technology are not necessarily low considering that leading world producers of automobiles have joint ventures with Chinese firms. Home-made foreign automobiles such as Peugeot and Volkswagen are quite capable of competing with imported vehicles.

In the long run, the market shares will be maintained or expanded by raising further the productivity and technological levels and thus by reducing costs of production. Cost reduction by worker lay-offs will not be very significant since labour costs are already very low in China. Instead, overall cost reduction will require a lowering of materials and overhead costs. Direct and indirect labour costs account for a much smaller proportion of the overall cost of production than the cost of materials (see Mody and Wheeler, 1990, for illustrative comparative production costs of automobiles in Japan and the Republic of Korea).

Scale of production is one of the important factors influencing the unit cost of production. It is estimated that the unit cost will decline by nearly 30 per cent with an increase in production from 10,000 to 30,000 vehicles; it will drop by a further 9 per cent with an increase in production from 30,000 to 80,000 vehicles; a further drop of 5 per cent can be achieved if production rises from 80,000 to 150,000 vehicles. The cost of a *Xiali* brand automobile (produced jointly by Tianjin Motor Works and Datsun of Japan) can be reduced to below 30,000 yuan if production can be raised to 300,000 vehicles (*Chinese Economic Times*, 14 February, 2003).

The unit cost will also vary depending on the technology used. As the firms move from manual to semi-automatic to robotics technology, direct and indirect labour costs and labour to capital ratios will further decline. In the Chinese automotive industry cost reduction will depend on how fast it can exploit positive learning effects, automation and economies of scale. Currently, the average unit cost per vehicle is higher than that of foreign automobiles because of low learning effects, backward technology and limited economies of scale. Liu and Woo (2001: 153) note that from 1988 to 1998, China produced a total of only 2.5 million automobiles compared to an average annual output of 5.8 million automobiles produced by a leading foreign firm.

Some observers believe that China's automotive industry will be non-competitive after accession because of lower productivity and higher cost per vehicle noted above. While this may well be true, the cost estimates can be misleading because of the much lower labour costs and unutilized capacity in China, and exaggeration of total production costs which include costs of components (Liu, 2001). Adjusting for the above factors reduces the cost per vehicle from the oft-quoted $15,300 to $11,500. In the post-accession period, lowering of tariffs will mean a fall in prices of imported vehicles and a much keener competition in the domestic market.

The Chinese automobile producers such as Shanghai Volkswagen, Tianjin Auto and First Auto Works, have undertaken structural adjustment and cost reduction (Lardy, 2002). Shanghai Volkswagen, a profit-making producer, reduced costs in the 1990s by raising production levels and by making greater use of cheaper locally produced spare parts and components.[8] Lardy predicts that Shanghai Volkswagen will be able to reduce costs further and lower prices by about 15 per cent. The use of local components not only facilitates lowering of production costs but it also helps generate additional *indirect* employment (see below and Chapter 1).

Unemployment

The closing down of inefficient firms will add to unemployment. The use of new and more recent technology will further reduce the demand for labour, as we noted above. This phenomenon has already been at work. Two interesting developments are worth noting. First, between 1995 and 1999 total employment dropped by almost 146,000, representing 7.5 per cent of the sector's workforce, although the total sales value increased from 218 billion yuan to 312 billion yuan during the same period (an increase of 43 per cent). This is the result of an increase in efficiency involving the use of new labour-saving technology. Second, both sales and employment in SOEs and collectives declined in 1999 compared to 1995. SOEs accounted for 63 per cent of total sales and 77 per cent of total employment in 1995 and 37 per cent and 55 per cent respectively in 1999. On the other hand, joint ventures and other ownership categories (joint stock and private companies) show an upward trend. In 1995, both sales by joint ventures and other categories represented about 39 per cent of total sales; by 1999 the figure increased to 59 per cent (see Fig. 5.4). Employment shares rose from 13 per cent to 38 per cent during the same period (Table 5.10). These changes reflected a combination of efficiency gains, introduction of new technology, foreign investment, privatization, and the closure of some loss-making SOEs and collective firms. These trends will continue after the WTO entry, as the tariffs on imported automobiles and parts are lowered to 25 per cent by 2006.

Before WTO entry, the Chinese government's stringent clause concerning local content required joint ventures and foreign-funded firms to obtain spare parts and raw materials from within China under Article 31 of the Auto Industry Policy. This clause had a positive effect on employment and output in the spare parts and components industry as well as among suppliers of raw materials. Lower import tariffs were levied on manufacturers using a high proportion of locally made parts and components which induced firms to develop a local

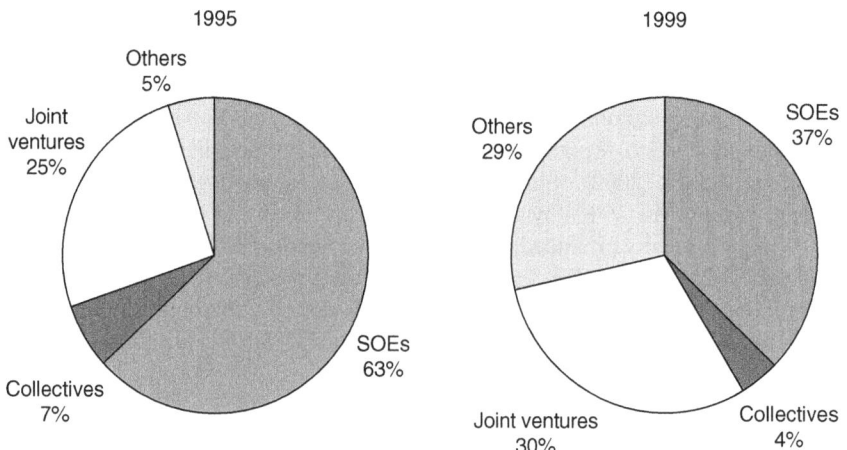

Figure 5.4 Shares of automotive sales by ownership

Source: *China Automotive Industry Yearbook*, Various issues.

Table 5.10 Sales and employment by ownership in the Chinese automotive industry (1995–99)

	SOEs		Collectives		Joint ventures		Others	
	Sales (million yuan)	Employment (no.) (000)	Sales (million yuan)	Employment (no.) (000)	Sales (million yuan)	Employment (no.) (000)	Sales (million yuan)	Employment (no.) (000)
1995	137,101	1,507.6	14,396	196.2	54,953	129.4	11,064	119.2
1997	149,666	1,441.8	20,924	229.3	72,120	163.4	20,787	143.7
1999	115,754	996.9	12,815	125.8	94,122	176.6	88,777	507.5

Source: *China Automotive Industry Yearbook* (in Chinese), various issues.

supply base for automobile components. In this connection Huang (2003) notes an aggressive drive by SAIG.[9] As several provinces were developing automotive industry, SAIG feared that suppliers in other provinces might divert their attention to assembly operations in other provinces.[10] Huang (2003: 268) concludes that 'for the Shanghai government, localization of components production boosted employment locally'.

The WTO Agreement eliminates local-content requirement, which can have adverse employment implications. However, a possible adverse effect can be neutralized if China expands its share of exports of spare parts and component, which have already been growing rapidly (see Table 5.9). It is not clear whether foreign joint ventures will actually switch from local to foreign suppliers of spare parts. Harwit (2001: 667) interviewed personnel of these joint ventures in summer 2000 who believe they would continue to build parts from supply networks in China. This may be due mainly to low cost of domestic suppliers, but quality considerations could well tilt decisions in favour of global (instead of local) outsourcing.

Table 5.11 presents forecasts of selected simulation studies regarding employment, output, exports and imports of automobiles. All the studies forecast a decline in employment of automobiles and a significant increase in their imports relative to their exports. Ianchovichina *et al.* (2000) estimate that employment of unskilled labour in automobiles will decline by 65.5 per cent between 1995 and 2005 whereas it would have increased by 8.4 per cent in the absence of accession. Employment of skilled labour is also estimated to decline by over 51 per cent during the same period. However, it would have increased by 53 per cent if there were no accession. DRC (1998) and Wang (1999) forecast less sharp decline in employment at 14.5 per cent and 24 per cent respectively.

Ianchovichina *et al.* (2000) and Wang (1999) forecast an increase in the exports of automobiles after accession despite a decline in output, presumably on the assumption of efficiency improvements (cost reduction) resulting from trade liberalization. But a massive estimate of exports by Ianchovichina *et al.* seems dubious and is due to a projection from a very low base figure in 1995.

Table 5.11 Forecasts of the employment impact of accession on Chinese automobiles

Author/study	Employment	Output	Exports	Imports
DRC (1998) (1995–2010)	−500,000 (−14.5%)	−81.2 (−15.1%)	−0.9 bn Y (−7.8%)	41.8 bn Y (105.1%)
Wang (1999) (1995–2010) (% change)	−23.5	−21.4	45	136
Ianchovichina et al. (2000) (1995–2005) (% change)	−65.5	−3.8	2522.6	550.7
Zhai and Li (2000) (1995–2010) (% change)	−15	−15	−8	105
UNCTAD (2002) (1997–2005) (% change)	−8.1	−11.1		

Sources: DRC (1998); Ianchovichina *et al.* (2000); UNCTAD (2002);Wang (1999); Zhai and Li (2000).

Notes: DRC (1998) assumes decline in tariff rates on automobiles from 129 per cent in 1995 to 54.5 per cent in 2010; Zhai and Li (2000) assume that average nominal tariff for industrial products will be lowered to 10 per cent in 2005, and on automobiles to 25 per cent, and that NTBs will be eliminated in eight-year phase-out period. Ianchovichina *et al.* (2000) assume 1997 tariff rates as baseline data.
Y = yuan.

Output decline is predicted on the assumption that cheaper imports induce consumers to substitute imported automobiles for domestic ones. But contrary to expectations, it is reported that automobiles made in China are selling better than imported ones. In August 2002 (first six months after accession) China imported a total of 51,890 automobiles, representing an increase of nearly 33 per cent over the same period in 2001. But the sale of domestic automobiles increased by about 40 per cent (*Shenzhen Business News*, 31 August 2002).

Whether consumers substitute imported automobiles for domestic ones will very much depend on whether and to what extent prices of domestic automobiles decline in the wake of global competition. As we noted above, cost of production of Volkswagen was reduced even prior to WTO entry. Furthermore, imports of intermediate inputs will also become cheaper after tariff reductions, which is most likely to reduce the domestic price of automobiles and create a greater incentive to export.

There will no doubt be more imported automobiles in the Chinese domestic market in the post-accession period. But foreign manufacturers will face competition from 'foreign makes' produced within China. They will not enjoy a comparative advantage in selling in the Chinese market vehicles produced and imported from abroad. Therefore, it is not certain that imported automobiles will capture a significant market share even when the tariff is lowered. As noted above, between 1994 and 1998 the Chinese joint ventures with foreign firms succeeded in regaining market share even though during this period import tariff rates on automobiles declined from 110–150 per cent to 80–100 per cent (see Yang, 1999).

Technology gap

The Chinese government encourages joint ventures to make foreign brands of automobiles in China in order to attract advanced technology. Domestic automobile firms will gradually gain experience through learning-by-doing. A huge domestic market and a gradual decrease in tariffs will give China's automobile firms some breathing space. The manufacture of auto parts and components for foreign brands will impose high-quality standards which will make it necessary to use modern technology. In this way the industry's technological gap with their international counterparts might be narrowed. This is what happened in the electrical and electronic sectors. However, it is not certain whether the same success can be achieved by the automotive industry. Indeed, there are limitations to the introduction of advanced foreign technologies through joint ventures. A foreign firm will be reluctant to transfer the most advanced technology if its share in the joint-venture firm does not allow it to exercise control.

A recent report notes that China's technological gap with developed countries in the manufacturing of conventional automobile powered by an engine is twenty years but the gap is only four to five years for producing electrical automobiles (*People's Daily*, 19 September 2001). This may give China some hope for competing with overseas automobile manufacturers (DRC, 1998). Following accession Chinese firms can export more labour-intensive products to the world market and import more intermediate and capital goods embodying higher technology at lower costs. But Korean and Japanese producers with superior technology, learning effects and economies of scale will be China's strong competitors in both the domestic and foreign markets.

National vs world brands

China has a long way to go before it can succeed in introducing a national brand in the international market. It faces a big challenge here. There is no evidence that its automotive industry has the resources and the technology capability to design and develop a new automobile which can compete in the global market in the near future. This will not, however, prevent the industry from being successful in producing good-quality *foreign* brands for the domestic and world markets.

China's automobile market is and will be dominated by the world brands. In 1998, of the total automobile sales, 91.7 per cent were domestically assembled foreign brands, and 3.4 per cent were imported. Home brand models accounted for less than 5 per cent, and were produced by joint ventures with large foreign firms. It is clear that the potential market for automobiles in China is very large. Zhai (2000) projects this demand to reach 2 million by 2005 and 4 million by 2010. It is estimated that in 2010 China's demand for automobiles will reach the level reached by Japan in the mid-1960s and by the Republic of Korea and Taiwan (China) in the mid-1980s, or 17 automobiles per 1,000 people. However, it will be a major challenge to meet this demand. China will need to reduce the price of its automobiles and remove restrictions on their purchase and to develop adequate road infrastructure.

Senior staff members of MOFTEC and SETC whom we met in April 2001 are optimistic about the industry's future considering the existence and growth of joint ventures with foreign firms with superior technology, marketing and access to global markets (see also Lardy, 2002; Liu and Woo, 2001). According to Liu and Woo (2001) increase in joint venture firms in the post-WTO entry period will enable them to successfully deter foreign entry by using what they term 'foreign-hit-foreign strategy' under which foreign makes produced in China can compete with those produced abroad. Lardy (2002: 113) concludes that 'China's entry into the World Trade Organization is likely to have only modest effects on the larger joint venture car producers'. He is led to this conclusion because of the gradual phasing of tariff reductions and the relatively high tariff (25 per cent) after 2006, a level which will still provide protection to domestic producers. Lardy (2002: 113) argues that foreign automobile firms in China have historically overestimated the size of the Chinese automobiles market.

We believe that the future is not so bright for China's automobile industry. However, the industry will not collapse. It can survive as long as the government chooses the right policy to attract manufacturing capability for producing automobiles to satisfy large domestic and global demand. Thus, much will depend on how fast the industry can reduce production costs to become globally competitive. Automobile imports into China following accession may not gain much price advantage if the pace of cost reduction within China is accelerated.

Household appliances

The Chinese household appliances sector has gone through three development stages. The first stage – from the late-1970s to the mid-1980s – represents initial market entry of domestic firms. During this stage foreign products were predominant. The second stage consisted of fast growth of domestic firms during the mid-1980s and mid-1990s with annual output growing at double digits. Since the mid-1990s, the sector has entered the third stage, which is characterized by a period of slow growth (perhaps coupled with the economic cycle), more competition, and greater pressures on profit margins. Many manufacturers of TV sets, VCDs, microwave ovens, air conditioners, washing machines and refrigerators, have experienced reduction in output and profits.

China has a large domestic market for household appliances in which Chinese firms (both state-owned and private) compete successfully with foreign firms. Production of household appliances did not start until the early 1980s. At that time the household appliances market was dominated by foreign firms. The 1990s witnessed an extraordinary expansion of Chinese domestic firms. Between 1996 and 1998 the market shares of domestic firms including SOEs increased at the expense of those of foreign-funded firms. Such foreign brands as Sony, Panasonic and Philips, which dominated the market before, have now been replaced by national brands (e.g. Changhong TV, Heier refrigerator, and Small Swan washing machine).

China's household appliances sector expanded rapidly from the mid-1980s to the mid-1990s (see Fig. 5.5). The domestic market is dominated by Chinese brands, which account for 95 per cent of the market for refrigerators, 83 per cent for washing machines, 74 per cent for air conditioners, 81 per cent for colour TVs, and 71 per cent for microwave ovens (OECD, 2002: 150). According to China Household Appliances Association, China produces 20 per cent of the total world production of which washing machines account for 25 per cent, microwave ovens 51 per cent, and domestic air conditioners 60 per cent (see *Beijing Evening News*, 27 August 2002). China has become the largest producer of TV sets, refrigerators, air conditioners, washing machines, electric fans, microwave ovens, vacuum cleaners and electric rice cookers.

How have Chinese firms succeeded in improving their market shares in the face of foreign competition? First, Chinese firms imported new technology from abroad which enabled good-quality production. Second, production costs are much lower in China than abroad, thanks partly to lower labour costs. Foreign firms are at a disadvantage because of higher costs of transporting such bulky goods as refrigerators and other household appliances.[11] Third, Chinese firms are adaptable to local demand and design. Local firms manufacture products according to Chinese consumer tastes and preferences. For instance, compared to Western consumers those in China (particularly in the colder northern region) prefer larger freezers and refrigerators in order to store more items for longer periods (Huang, 2003). Furthermore, for Chinese consumers the players have to be more robust for low-quality CDs and VCDs available in the market while Sony and Philips players are generally more sensitive. Thus the latter gradually lost their market to the Chinese counterparts. Consumer tastes and cultural factors are particularly important in such industries as household appliances (Porter, 1990). Fourth, products are sold at very low prices; labour cost of producing parts in China is much lower which drives foreign suppliers out of the market. Tariff protection encouraged the domestic production of many consumer items, which were formerly imported. Competition among Chinese firms is very fierce and many 'price wars' (TV price war, refrigerator price war and air conditioner price war), have been waged in the past. Firms must increase their economic efficiency if they are to survive these price wars. Unable to face competition, many small firms have been closed or merged with large firms.

Chinese firms have raised their market shares at the expense of foreign suppliers through price cutting. Changhong, the top manufacturer of TV sets (previously a military firm) started a price war in March 1996 by reducing the price of a colour TV set by 18 per cent. By the end of 1997, Changhong raised its market share in colour TV sets to 33 per cent, becoming the top firm in colour TV market. In April 1996, the market share of domestic brand was only 42.5 per cent, but by April 1997, the big four firms (Changhong, Panda, Hessi and TCL) accounted for 65 per cent of the market (see Mo, 1999). Finally, many large

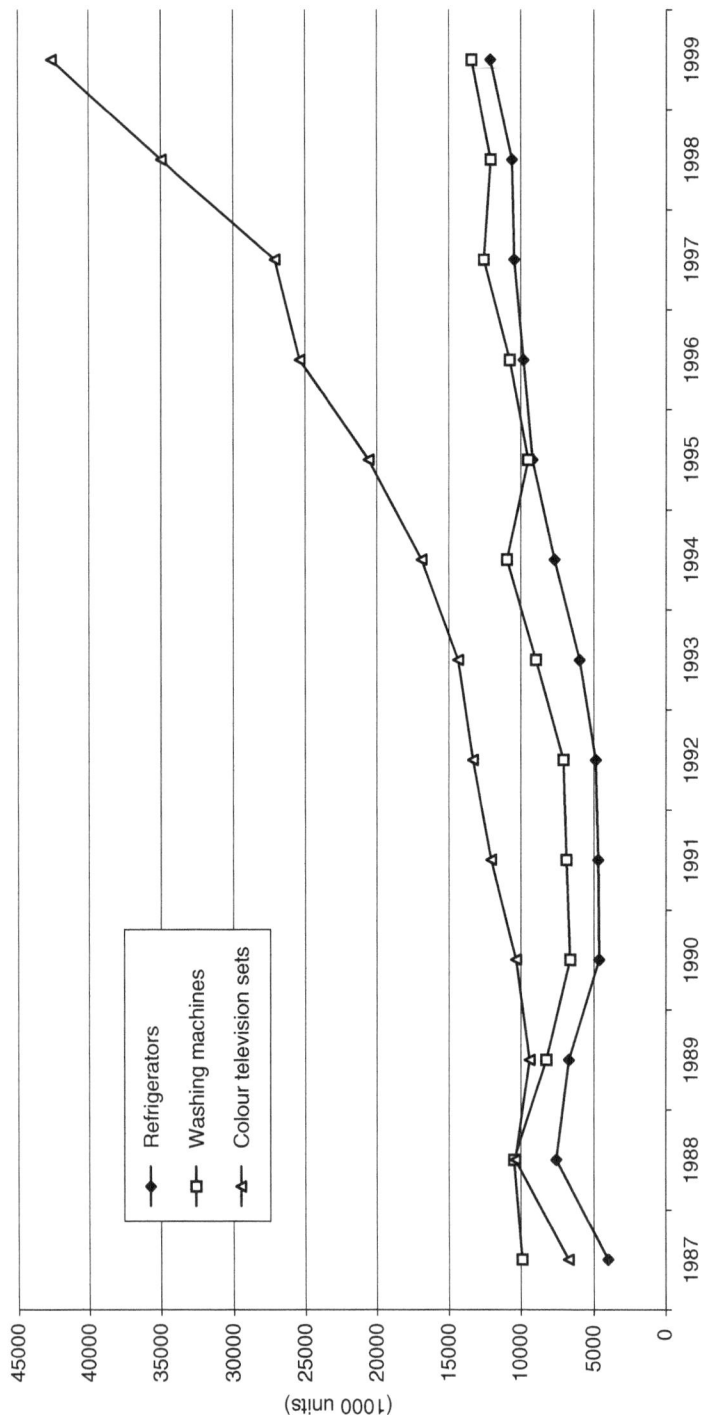

Figure 5.5 Output volumes of China's major household appliances (1987–99)

Source: *China Statistical Yearbook*, 2000.

firms set up national networks for after-sales service on which Chinese consumers rely when something goes wrong with their purchased appliances. It is also easier to obtain spare parts and components for domestic brands.

Exports and employment

Several Chinese firms have already entered American and European markets. After China's accession, they will further expand into these markets. Heier, the largest household appliances firm, has set up factories in Indonesia and the US, and has captured 20 per cent of the US market for small refrigerators.

The growth of domestic market for household appliances has slowed down since the second half of the 1990s due to urban market saturation and limited size of the rural market. Chinese firms have been forced to expand globally. Traditionally, the main exports included small electric fans and hair dryers. But recently air-conditioners and microwave ovens have also been exported not only to other developing countries but also to the US and European markets (Table 5.12). The Chinese exports of household appliances have been doing well since accession. In the first half of 2002, the Chinese domestic appliances sector exported goods worth $4.4 billion, which represented an increase of 28 per cent compared to the same period in 2001. Of the total production of 10.3 million microwave ovens, 8.3 million (or over 81 per cent) are exported (see *Industrial and Commercial Times*, 28 August 2002).

Reduction of tariffs on household appliances following accession will have a marginal effect on foreign firms in the Chinese market. Imported goods will not have much advantage over local suppliers as many famous brand goods are already made or assembled by Chinese firms in the form of Original Equipment Manufacture (OEM).[12] Chinese domestic firms will look for external markets for their excess production capacity as they gain experience in manufacturing and services through learning-by-doing. The total capacity for the production of major household appliances is almost double that of domestic demand. Lower

Table 5.12 Exports of China's household appliances (1999)

	Unit (million)	Value ($ million)
Electric fans	140.08	650.82
Air conditioners	2.02	489.01
Microwave ovens	5.82	356.43
Refrigerators	2.13	164
Washing machines	0.64	59.32
TV sets	12.98	803.12
Radios	127.78	299.19
Sound recording apparatus	161.52	2337.02

Sources: Data for electric fans, TV sets, radios and sound recording apparatus are taken from *China Foreign Economic Statistical Yearbook* 2000 (original in Chinese). Other data are from Yu (2000).

duties and access to international market may prevent at least some Chinese firms from extinction.

Apart from good product quality and low prices, two other factors explain better export performance of China's domestic household appliances. First, the demand for these products has been low in China's internal market in which price competition is very fierce. Many producers are aggressively beginning to explore export opportunities following accession. Second, the slowdown of the world economy may have had an effect on consumer spending. Western consumers have become more price sensitive and are looking for cheaper sources of supply. Many merchants are, therefore, outsourcing products from China. At the same time proprietors of many famous international brands are increasingly moving their production to China to take advantage of the large potential market and cheap labour costs. They are in a position to sell globally products made in China given their wide international sales network.

Although the penetration of household appliances in urban areas has gone up substantially, the average penetration rate in China is still quite low. Foreign firms are attracted by China's large market potential. However, these firms can no longer compete with local firms by shipping into China products manufactured abroad. Therefore, their production and marketing strategy has changed in favour of joint ventures with domestic enterprises to produce refrigerators and TV sets in China. Early in 2001 Toshiba, the Japanese producer of household appliances, decided to stop producing TV sets in Japan and to transfer all its production to China. In August 2001 the company decided to move washing machines to China to be assembled by Little Swan. Initially, Little Swan will assemble 500,000 washing machines annually. Its total annual output is expected to double by 2005.

China's domestic appliances sector provides *direct* employment to 200,000 (see *China Business Weekly*, 13 February 2001), but the *indirect* effect on employment could be many times higher. For instance, the Galanz group, the largest microwave oven maker, employs 11,000 people, but according to Yu Xiaochang (the company's Deputy Executive Director), Galanz provides indirect employment of 1 million jobs in such subsidiary operations as supply of spare parts and components and repair and maintenance services (see 21CN, 11 May 2001).[13] In 2000, sales of microwave ovens made by the Galanz Group accounted for 74 per cent of the domestic market and 35 per cent of the world market.

Table 5.13 shows employment figures for major household appliances but they represent only a part of total employment in the sector. The manufacturers of domestic appliances are under the control of different government departments. Some were the responsibility of the Ministry of Light Industry and others of the Ministry of Electronic Industry (although these two ministries have now been dismantled). Therefore, employment data from one source may not give a complete picture of the whole sector. A large number of jobs are also provided in the manufacture of such small devices as hair blowers, kettles, toasters, fruit juice makers, food processors and kitchen smoke extraction fans. Thus the estimates in Table 5.13 are understated since there are no detailed

Table 5.13 Employment in China's major household appliances (000)

	1991	1993	1995	1997	1999
Washing machines	40.8	36.6	38.5	40.2	34.6
Refrigerators	60.0	53.4	42.3	47.5	43.5
Electric fans	59.9	43.6	33.5	31.0	9.1
TV sets	–	173.4	167.9	150.7	133.1
Radios and auto recorders	–	139.2	115.3	92.5	83.7
Video recorders	–	–	9.8	13.6	17.3

Sources: Employment figures for washing machines, refrigerators and electric fans are from *China's Light Industry Yearbook*, various issues; Figures for TV sets, Radios and audio recorders and video recorders are from *China's Electronic Industry Yearbook*, various issues.

figures available for such appliances as air conditioners and microwave ovens, VCD and DVD players.

It is difficult to assess the employment prospects in the sector in the post-accession period. Although some efficient companies have increased their market share and employment, the sector as a whole has seen a reduction of employed workers. It is fair to say that the Chinese household appliances sector has made excellent progress in less than two decades. Therefore, there should be good prospects for creating additional employment if more exports can be expanded, in which case at least the present workforce will be maintained.

Household appliances vs automobiles

A comparison between the household appliances industry and automobile industry highlights some interesting points. Features common to both industries are the introduction of foreign technology and the assembly of products in China using imported parts and components. Both were successful in manufacturing goods in China and in reducing dramatically the demand for imports.

Differences between the two industries are also striking. In the household appliances sector Chinese firms have successfully created national brands, which dominate the entire sector. They have expanded further into foreign markets by successfully competing with foreign firms. In contrast, the automobile industry can only manage to assemble foreign brands to reduce importation. The degree of protection presents another sharp contrast between the two. The household appliances market was exposed to competition much earlier than the automobiles market. Protection of household appliances was much lower than that of automobiles. This may be due to the following reasons. First, in the late-1970s and early-1980s, tariffs on imported household appliances were quite high. But the demand for these goods was also very high. The possibility of making large profits induced many local authorities to support the setting up of many factories assembling household appliances. However, overcapacity created strong competition as a result of which consumers benefited through lower prices. A favourable market condition for the household appliances industry occurred much earlier than the automobile industry. In contrast, automotive industry limited market access and consumption. There are restrictions on the types of models and brands to be produced by enterprises. Second, the technology required for the automotive industry is much more complex and the size of investment much higher than that for the household appliances. Third, government policy may partly explain different situations of the two industries. Fourth, the automotive industry is much more capital- and technology intensive than the household appliances industry. Therefore, China will require more time to catch up with the industrialized countries, and even still longer to create its own brands of automobiles.

China's proven ability to manufacture household appliances for the world market suggests that it is also capable of making better automobiles in the future. The fact that China is already able to assemble world brands suggests that it is gradually moving up the technological ladder in the manufacturing sector.

One of the shortcomings in the Chinese automobile and household appliances industries is that the core technology and core parts are still being imported from abroad. It will, therefore, take time and resources for Chinese firms to be able to compete with international giants on an equal footing. In this context, China's accession to the WTO will offer Chinese firms good opportunities as well as big challenges.

Concluding remarks

We conclude that most of the forecasts of severe unemployment in China's major manufacturing sectors, particularly in automobiles in the wake of accession, are unwarranted. While it is true that major restructuring of many industries will be required, much of this process has already been underway for several years long before accession. It is true that manufacturing will not be a major sector for employment generation in the future because of its restructuring and technological modernization. But these factors would have reduced the growth of industrial employment even without accession. In particular industries the employment impact is likely to vary depending on the speed of restructuring and rationalization, growth in demand for its products and policies measures against China's products adopted by importing countries especially in the case of textiles. Most estimates of the employment impact on textiles are very optimistic and forecast a big increase in expansion of employment in textiles on the assumption of its labour intensity, decline in the share of SOEs and the phasing out of the Multi-Fibre Arrangement. We are less optimistic considering China's declining comparative advantage in textiles during the past few years and the possibility that importing countries (particularly the US) might invoke the product–specific safeguard clause and the anti-dumping clause against China which the WTO Agreement allows. However, China may be able to maintain its comparative advantage in textile exports if their production can be relocated and successfully implemented in the hinterland to take advantage of lower labour costs (Chapter 7).

In the case of automobiles most estimates forecast a big decline in employment. While we do foresee problems in the post-WTO period we think the adverse employment effects are exaggerated. Foreign participation in this industry is likely to increase even further after accession, thus bringing in superior marketing expertise, modern technology and scale benefits. These factors, combined with greater competition, should raise industrial efficiency. In the final analysis, the effect on employment will depend on the growth of domestic demand for automobiles, which is likely to grow with rising per capita incomes, availability of credit for the purchase of automobiles, improvement in distribution networks and after-sales services.

The household appliances industry may well be able to generate additional employment in the future if growth in domestic and foreign demand is maintained.

As we noted in Chapter 3, much of the additional employment is likely to be generated by the services sector, a subject which we discuss in Chapter 6.

6 Services

The services sector was neglected in most communist (socialist) countries, including China, prior to the economic reforms. Therefore, there has been tremendous scope for its expansion even before China's accession to the WTO. As we discussed in Chapter 3, a shift in labour force from agriculture to manufacturing has already been taking place during the past decades. Most observers predict a tremendous growth of employment in the services sector following accession. Due to the underemphasis or neglect of consumer services in socialist countries, the share of this sector in GDP is rather low. Also, producer services (e.g. sales, marketing, management, and consultancy services) were either underdeveloped or included under manufacturing. Similarly, business-related services such as finance and insurance are still quite small (see Figure. 6.1). Furthermore, the sector is quite heterogeneous, and many services are labour-intensive, non-tradeable and within proximity of consumers, features which lend themselves to greater labour absorption.

In this chapter we concentrate on three major service sectors: wholesale and retail distribution, banking and other financial services, and telecommunications. We examine past employment trends in these services as well as employment implications of the WTO Agreement, which, for the first time, opened up these and other tertiary sectors to domestic and foreign competition. But before we examine these issues, it is appropriate to briefly review the state of these services prior to the Agreement.

The state of services prior to WTO entry

Major services (e.g. wholesale and retail distribution, banking and other financial services, insurance, telecommunications, and railways) have until recently been under state monopoly. Market access to other Chinese services by foreign firms (e.g. professional services and tourism) has also been restricted. Prior to accession foreign consultancy firms were not allowed to provide management, legal, accounting or engineering services. But China gradually introduced deregulation, competition and market principles in a number of services even ahead of WTO membership, as we discuss below.

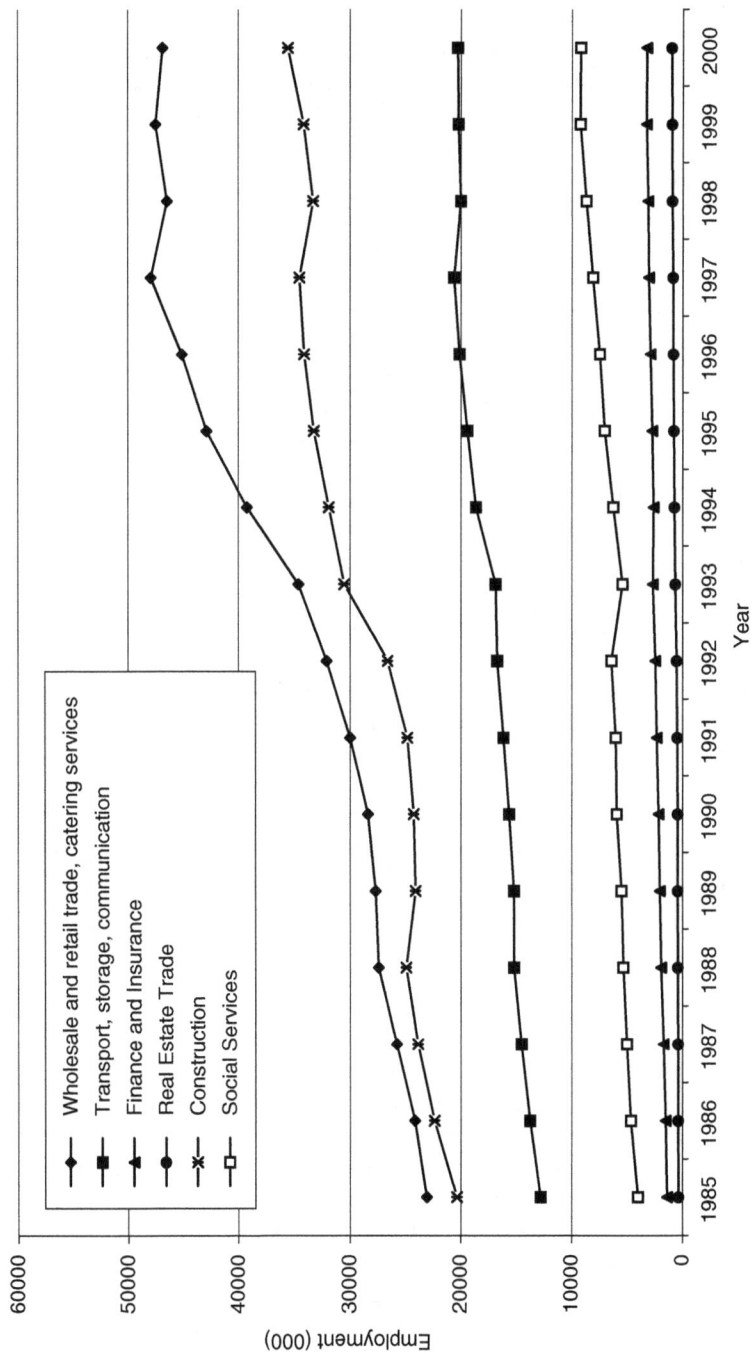

Figure 6.1 Employment trends in selected services in China (1985–2000)

Source: *China Labour Statistical Yearbook.*

Distribution

Prior to the economic reforms the distribution sector was a state monopoly with buying and selling of all goods in the hands of state-owned and collective companies. In wholesale and retail distribution, few foreign firms have been allowed so far even though the State Council regulations in 1992 allowed foreign firms the legal right to do so. Practical restrictions are imposed on such activities as wholesale and retailing, franchizing, and repair and maintenance services. Most foreign firms were required to undertake distribution through state-owned firms.

The distribution system consisted of a three-tier structure: the administrative planning level, a retail system of small shops, and a small number of department stores. Economic reforms gradually abolished this structure and replaced it by a market-oriented system under which price setting, buying and selling of goods and ownership of shops and stores were increasingly taken over by non-state enterprises. Only a few goods (e.g. foodgrains, cotton, coal and oil, and automobiles) were retained under the state planning system (OECD, 2002). The distribution sector was opened up for domestic competition: state-owned enterprises (SOEs), collectives and private enterprises vying for market shares. The market share of private enterprises rose from zero in 1978 to over 43 per cent in 1999, whereas that of SOEs declined from 54.6 per cent in 1978 to a little over 18 per cent (Table 6.1).

Over the years competition in retail distribution has intensified, especially between domestic and foreign enterprises with the opening of the sector to foreign retailing joint ventures (which were not allowed in wholesale distribution) in 1992 in specific areas and cities.[1] However, these joint ventures are mainly in large department stores and supermarkets which form only a small part of the total retail sector. The bulk of retailers are represented by medium and small speciality and family-run shops and bazaars in rural areas.

Banking and financial services [2]

Prior to 1994 there were four major specialized banks in China, namely, the Industrial and Commercial Bank, the Bank of China, China Construction Bank, and the Agricultural Bank of China. The sector subsequently saw the growth of commercial, policy banks and trust companies. In an effort to introduce market criteria and commercial banking principles, in early 1994 three policy banks were established: the State Development Bank of China, the Agricultural Development Bank of China, and the Export-Import Bank of China. At present, apart from the state-owned commercial banks and policy banks, there are two other categories of share-holding commercial banks (largely of a regional nature) and city commercial banks operating mainly in large urban areas. The latter grew out of the former urban credit cooperatives. There are also other financial institutions such as investment and trust companies (He, 2002). Joint ventures are at present limited in the banking and financial services, although

Table 6.1 Market shares in China's distribution sector by type of ownership (%)

Type of ownership	1978	1995	1999
State-owned enterprises	54.6	29.9	18.2
Collective enterprises	43.3	19.3	15.6
Private enterprises	0.0	2.5	43.2*
Family-run small shops	0.1	30.3	–
Others (including share-holding enterprises, joint ventures, and foreign-owned enterprises)	2.0	18.0	23.0

Source: *Market Statistics Yearbook of China* 1999.

Note: *Figure includes family-run small shops.

they are being allowed in order to enable domestic institutions to acquire international exposure and expertise.

Foreign banks have been allowed to open representative offices and commercial branches. But in order to protect domestic banks against too much competition, they were not allowed to deal in local currency except in Shanghai and Shenzhen on an experimental basis.[3] Business activities and geographical coverage of foreign banks were both limited as they dealt mainly with transnational corporations and joint ventures. As a result, in 1999 foreign banks were responsible for only about 2 per cent of total bank assets in China (OECD, 2002: 247–48).

The Chinese government adopted a number of policy measures in order to tackle the three most important problems facing the banking industry: non-performing loans, weak capital base and low profitability. It is estimated that in the late 1990s non-performing loans were as high as 50 per cent or more of total loans (OECD, 2002). The profitability of the four state-owned banks and ten shareholding banks declined in the late 1990s as is reflected in a fall in the average rates of return on total assets. Overlending by banks, especially to SOEs, has weakened their capital base. It is difficult to foresee how Chinese banks can face competition from major developed-country banks after accession without tackling these problems. To mitigate the problem of bad loans, in 1998 the government first issued a special bond of 270 billion yuan in order to recapitalize the four specialized commercial banks. The following year the government established asset management companies to take over bad loans of the four banks. Despite these efforts the problem of bad loans remains serious thanks to the expansion of lending to large inefficient SOEs which are not allowed to go bankrupt even though bankruptcy laws are now in place. Mounting losses suffered by these enterprises have raised the share of bad loans.[4] Banks continue to grant loans to loss-making enterprises (case of a 'soft-budget' constraint) to allow them to remain afloat since they provide massive employment and social welfare services. Thus banking reforms are tied up with other reforms, particularly of SOEs, which have not been as rapid as expected.

No legal framework exists to deal with non-performing loans, with the result that banks cannot be held responsible for their profits and losses. Neither do they lend on the basis of commercial criteria. Quite often branch offices of banks are forced by local governments to grant loans for even dubious and non-profitable projects.

The Chinese insurance and securities services also remain underdeveloped. China protected these sectors against foreign competition by forbidding foreign companies to do business in China. The Chinese insurance industry was a state monopoly prior to 1979. People Insurance Company of China (PICC) was the main insurance company which, as a division of the People's Bank of China, focused on property and transport insurance for SOEs. In 1985, China started liberalizing the insurance market by establishing a specialized agricultural insurance company (the Xinjiang Bingtuan Insurance Corporation) and two joint-stock composite insurance companies (the China-Pacific Insurance Company and the Ping An Insurance Company) (Probst, 2002). In 1992, the government permitted the first foreign insurance company (a part of the American International Group, AIG) into China. But its operations remained limited only to Shanghai. Lardy (2002: 71) notes that 'in 1999 the assets of foreign insurance companies accounted for less than 2 per cent of all insurance assets, and their premium income was only 1.3 per cent of total insurance premium income'.

China's securities market (stock exchange) remains small even though it has been growing. The government has continued to regulate this market for fear of a threat to China's overall financial stability following fluctuations in stock market prices. It has used the stock exchange market mainly to channel funds to SOEs. He (2002: 140) notes that many of the securities firms operating in China are in fact 'associates or subsidiaries of government agencies (especially fiscal departments, financial authorities or municipal authorities)'.

The above weaknesses of the banking and financial services suggest that this sector remains an infant industry. Many observers believe that reforms of the sector have not yet been implemented adequately to make the industry competitive following accession.

Telecommunications

The Chinese telecommunications industry has been a state monopoly since the early 1980s when several government circulars were issued to protect it. It was one of the most centrally planned and controlled sectors: market entry, pricing and business organization were regulated by the state through the Ministry of Posts and Telecommunications (MPT).

While foreign telecommunications equipment had to be imported, foreign telecommunications services were not allowed into China for reasons of state security. In May 1993, the MPT announced that 'no organization, enterprise or individual outside China may engage in the management of China's broadcasting networks, special wire or wireless services, or become a shareholder in a telecommunications business' (*Beijing Review*, 14–20 June 1993). However, in 1998, China Unicom, one of the two main telecommunications companies, needed capital and raised it by setting up what is called the China-China-Foreign joint ventures with 45 foreign companies. In preparation for WTO entry, in December 2000 China allowed AT & T, an American telecommunications company, to enter into a joint venture with Shanghai Telecom and Shanghai Information Investment. Since 1993, this is the first foreign company to enter China to provide telecommunication services.

The telecommunications industry made rapid progress under the state patronage. The MPT was allowed to retain 90 per cent of profit and foreign exchange earned. Banks granted loans on favourable terms to enable growth of the industry. The state also gave preferential tariff treatment for the import of telecommunications equipment; it allowed faster capital depreciation for the development of telecommunications infrastructure.

With the opening up of the economy, the demand for telephone and telecommunications services grew rapidly within China. Presumably to meet this rapid growth in demand and to prepare for accession, the Chinese government decided to abandon state monopoly of the sector, introducing competition into the telecommunications market. First, the government broke the monopoly of the erstwhile MPT by separating telecommunications (a rapidly growing and revenue generating part of it) into a separate Ministry of Information Industry (MII). Second, in 1993 the State Council deregulated the market for paging services by authorizing the licensing of new service providers.[5] Third, MII created China United Telecommunications Corporation (or Unicom) to compete with the MPT in the long-distance and international services market (Lu, 2000). Since then other telecom companies such as China Mobile, Jitong, and Netcom have also sprung up. Market shares of these companies show that competition in the telecommunications market remains limited with China Telecom and Unicom being the two main telecom companies (Table 6.2).

The Chinese telecommunications sector has grown phenomenally since the early 1980s. It has been exposed to domestic competition even though until recently it has been sheltered from foreign competition. It grew much faster than the Chinese planners had anticipated with switchboard capacity in 1995

Table 6.2 Market shares of Chinese telecom companies (first half of 2000)

	China Telecom	China Mobile	Unicom	Jitong	Netcom
Total telephone user base	68.1	25.8	6.0		
Long-distance optical cable	86.6		13.4		
Mobile phone subscription		81.2	18.8		
IP telephony	54.4		31.2	12.3	2.1

Source: *Zhongguo Jingji Shibao (China Economic Times)*, 20 October 2000.

Cited in Lu (2000).

exceeding 200 per cent above the Eighth Plan target. During the first half of the 1990s alone, China installed more than 73 million phone lines. This figure is higher than phone lines in all the developing countries excluding China (Lu, 2000). Since the mid-1990s the mobile telephone network has also expanded. By the end of 2001 China surpassed the United States, registering over 125 million subscribers. According to China's Minister of Information Industry (Wu Jichuan), by 2005 China will have achieved a penetration ratio of 40 per cent with the number of telephone subscribers (fixed line plus mobile) exceeding 500 million. The number of mobile phone subscribers will rise to 300 million by 2005, making China the world's largest mobile phone market (Wong and Wong, 2003). China's concessions under the WTO Agreement to open its domestic market to foreign competition are quite far reaching considering that until recently foreign entry was not permitted in banking, financial services and telecommunications. We discuss these concessions before considering past employment trends and future employment implications of accession.

China's commitments under the WTO Agreement[6]

One of the most far-reaching commitments under the WTO Agreement relate to the opening up of China's hitherto closed services sector. These commitments and obligations relate to several sub-sectors of services: banking, other financial services including insurance and securities, telecommunications, distribution, professional and business services, and tourism.

Wholesale and retail distribution

Until accession foreign companies could undertake distribution in China only through state-owned enterprises. However, the WTO Agreement has allowed foreign competition in this sector. Market access will be provided to foreign companies also in retail trade. On accession, two major urban centres, Zhengzhou (Henan) and Wuhan (Hubei) were opened to foreign retailers who entered into joint ventures with Chinese firms. All geographical restrictions on foreign retailing will be lifted within three years after accession. Foreign retailers will be allowed to engage in retailing of most products except tobacco and salt. In the first year after accession, retailing by foreign firms will not be allowed in books, magazines and newspapers. Within three years following accession, retailing of such products as pharmaceuticals, processed oils and pesticides will be allowed, and within five years, of chemical fertilizers.

All foreign-funded manufacturing enterprises (FFEs) will be allowed to distribute products manufactured within China. In franchizing, foreign enterprises will be free to operate in the Chinese market and China will negotiate bilaterally with WTO members regarding direct selling in the Chinese market.

Banking and financial services

Upon accession, foreign banks will be free to conduct foreign currency business without any geographical restrictions. They will also be allowed to do business in local currency and their geographical coverage for this purpose will be gradually expanded with the abolition of all restrictions five years after accession. The geographical restrictions for local currency business will be phased out gradually. Following accession, foreign banks are able to do business in local currency in four cities, namely, Shanghai, Shenzhen, Tianjin and Dalian. Within one year after accession the additional cities will be added to this list. Initially, foreign banks will be allowed to do business with Chinese *enterprises*, but within five years after accession foreign banking operations will be extended to Chinese *individuals* as well.

Foreign financial institutions (a foreign bank or financial company) with assets exceeding $10 billion will be permitted to establish a subsidiary in China. A foreign bank with assets exceeding $20 billion will be eligible to establish a branch in China.

The hitherto closed insurance sector is now open to foreign participation. Foreign non-life insurance companies are allowed to establish branches or joint ventures in China with majority ownership of 51 per cent. Wholly owned subsidiaries of foreign owned non-life insurance companies are permitted within two years after accession. Foreign life insurance companies are required to enter into joint ventures with Chinese enterprises with an investment of up to 50 per cent. Insurance companies are allowed to operate in a limited number of large cities; these geographical restrictions will be gradually lifted within three years of accession.

While China has agreed to open securities and fund management to foreign participation, some restrictions will continue to be imposed. For example, foreign fund management companies cannot own more than one-third of the shares. Foreign securities firms will be limited to doing business in B shares only, but not A shares, which generate higher income. There will be no geographical restrictions on foreign securities or fund management firms.

Telecommunications

Following accession, foreign firms in the telecommunications sector were allowed to establish joint ventures and provide services in the following cities: Beijing, Guangzhou and Shanghai. FDI in joint ventures will not exceed 30 per cent. Within one year after accession, this geographical area will be extended to Chengdu, Chongqing, Dalian, Fuzhou, Hangzhou, Nanjing and Ningbo, Qingdao, Shenyang, Shenzhen, Xiamen, Xi'an, Taiyuan and Wuhan. One year after accession foreign investment up to 49 per cent will be allowed and within two years, up to but not more than 50 per cent. The above geographical restrictions will be gradually lifted. The telecom services will include value-added services such as electronic mail, voice mail, online information and data base retrieval, and electronic data interchange, facsimile services and internet content and service providers. China will allow joint ventures with Chinese firms in mobile voice and data services.

Professional and business services

Foreign firms will be allowed in such professional activities as legal representation, accounting, auditing and book-keeping, and tax consultancy. Business partnerships and joint ventures will be permitted in medical and dental services including the setting up of clinics and hospitals as well as in software and data-processing services.

Tourism and related services

Foreign participation in hotels and restaurants will be allowed within five years of accession. Similarly, foreign tour operators and travel agencies will be allowed to provide services in main tourist places in China (namely, Beijing, Shanghai, Guangzhou, and Xi'an).

Employment trends in services

Before we examine the possible employment implications of accession in the future, it is useful to review and discuss past trends in employment growth in services. As we noted in Chapter 3, tertiary (services) employment growth has been more rapid than that in primary and secondary sectors, albeit from a low base. Figure 3.2 (Chapter 3) shows that since 1995 tertiary employment has overtaken manufacturing employment, which has flattened out. This has occurred despite the fact that most of the FDI inflows have been directed towards manufacturing. FDI in the services sector accounts for only about 3 per cent of the total. The service sector employment (in terms of both absolute numbers and share in total employment) has shown rapid growth. During the period 1990–99, the sector absorbed 71.6 million people, including the absorption of additional labour force and transfer of 48 million workers from other sectors (DRC, 2001).

During 1980–90 labour force in the tertiary sector grew annually by 7.9 per cent, whereas during 1990–2000 it grew by 5.2 per cent, compared to 5.9 per cent and 1.6 per cent respectively in the secondary sector (Rawski, 2002: Table 3). Also the employment elasticity of output was higher in services than in manufacturing. Figure 6.1 (page 117) presents employment trends in selected trade and business-related services and such traditional services as construction (often included with manufacturing in many developing countries) and social services. Distribution and catering services, transport and communications and construction are the major sub-sectors accounting for the bulk of employment growth during the period 1985–2000. Growth of employment in distribution (especially retail trade) and transport is estimated to be much higher than the official estimates suggest. Rawski and Mead (1998) show that farm employment is overestimated by a substantial amount and that employment in these services is underestimated. The so-called 'phantom' farmers (of the order of about 100 million) are believed to be engaged in non-farm employment in trade, transport and construction.[7]

Even on the basis of official figures, employment growth in distribution during 1980–99 was significant, recording an annual average rate of 6.4 per cent. The sector accounted for about 17 million new jobs during this period, of which more than half (about 10 million) were in private commercial enterprises and in self-employment (OECD, 2002: 302 and 304).

Employment in such business-related services as finance and insurance has remained quite low and almost constant. The underdeveloped nature of financial services has prevented the transformation of savings into investment thus hindering capital accumulation. Opening up of the financial sector should, in principle, lead to a growth of output and employment in the post-accession period (see below).

A comparison of tertiary employment growth between 1995 and 2000 by forms of ownership shows that SOE employment in information, consultancy and computer services declined substantially; so did employment in urban collectively-owned enterprises (COEs) (Fig. 6.2). In wholesale and retail distribution employment declined more significantly in SOEs than in COEs. In both 1995 and 2000 SOE and COE employment remained significant in banking, finance and insurance industry. SOEs remain the most important employer in posts and telecommunications; COEs and other forms of ownership account for very little employment in this sub-sector. Employment growth has occurred mainly in the 'others' category, which includes the private sector and joint-stock companies. The shares of private-sector employment increased significantly in consultancy services, wholesale and retail distribution and insurance, and to a lesser extent, banking and finance.

Both SOEs and urban collectives suffered from competition from the private sector. The most significant decline in SOE employment occurred in such labour-intensive tertiary industries as retail trade and construction. The share of retail sales of consumer goods by SOEs declined from 51 per cent in 1980 to 21 per cent in 1998 (Mai, 2000). However, the picture is different in large capital-intensive SOEs in such sectors as gas and electricity, telecommunications, large banks and insurance companies. These sectors remained protected, which explains why employment declined much less or even increased in some cases, e.g. posts and telecommunications, which accounted for 91 per cent of all workers in the industry in 2000, and electricity, gas and water, which accounted for 82 per cent.

In the process of economic development, labour first moves out of the primary into the secondary sector and then into the tertiary sector. When the degree of capital intensity in manufacturing is high (as in the Chinese case), shift may occur directly from the primary sector to traditional services. This may have

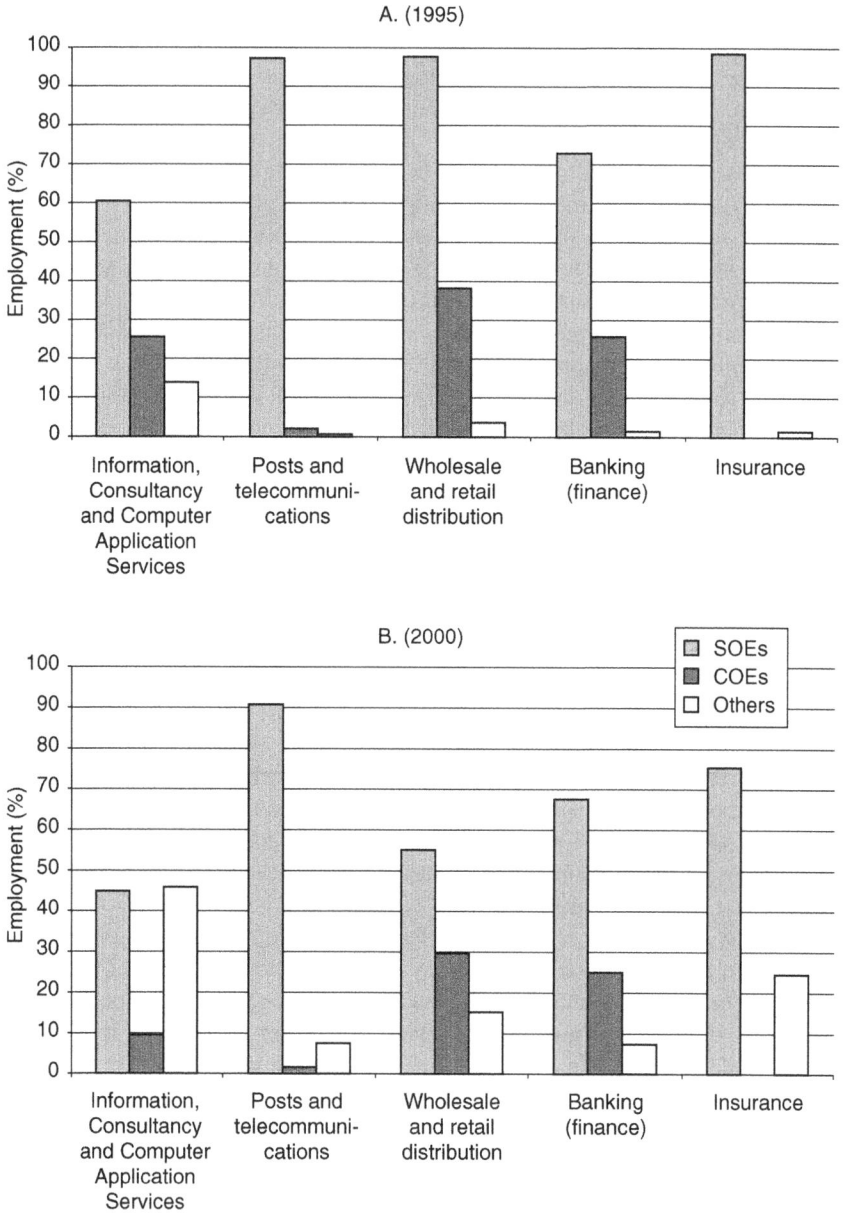

Figure 6.2 Employment in selected services in China by ownership categories (1995 and 2000)

Source: *China Statistical Yearbook.*
SOEs – State-owned Enterprises. COEs – Collectively-owned Enterprises.

been the case, particularly in China where these services were underdeveloped before the economic reforms due largely to governmental neglect. In 1999, the share of tertiary employment in China was about 27 per cent compared to about 60 per cent in most industrialized countries. Even in such developing countries as Egypt, Jamaica and Jordan the shares of tertiary employment were much higher (DRC, 2001). This gap between China and the rest of the world suggests that there is a potential for further employment expansion in the services sector.

Employment implications of the Agreement

Banks and financial services are assumed to be the most vulnerable sectors considering that these activities were completely closed to foreign participation prior to accession. As we noticed above, China has agreed to open up these sectors. Below we examine whether increased competition following accession will hurt employment expansion.

Forecasts of employment and output

Most forecasts of tertiary employment and output following China's accession to the WTO are positive despite an alarm about the vulnerability of financial and telecommunications sectors to global competition. For example, UNCTAD (2002), Zhai and Li (2000) of the DRC (China), and Wang (1999) forecast employment and output gains (Table 6.3). These forecasts are based on the assumption that volume of services will expand given their current low level and underdeveloped nature. On the other hand, Ianchovichina *et al.* (2000) forecast a significant decline in employment of unskilled workers despite an increase in output especially in business finance, trade, transport and utilities. But they forecast employment expansion of skilled workers, especially in business finance, as the nature and content of services becomes much more sophisticated with the entry of foreign firms. Anderson *et al.* (2002) forecast some decline in the employment of unskilled and skilled workers in the telecommunications services.

The above forecasts were made prior to accession on the basis of assumptions about the level of tariff and quota reductions, length of phase-in periods, the size of trade concessions and so on.[8] Conflicting and unrealistic assumptions are bound to give rather contradictory results which are presented here more as illustrations than as definitive predictions.

Having examined employment and output forecasts, we present below our arguments in favour of more optimistic employment implications for the three service sectors: distribution, banking and financial services and telecommunications.

Distribution

China has made significant concessions in offering market access to foreign firms in the distribution of wholesale and retail goods manufactured in China

Table 6.3 Employment and output forecasts for the Chinese services sector

	Output		Employment	
			Unskilled	Skilled
Ianchovichina et al. (2000) (1995–2005) (% change)				
Construction	149		49.7	119.9
Utilities	101.2		–30.3	–1.5
Trade and transport	114.4		–36.1	1.3
Business finance	105.1		–10.9	25.9
Government services	85.9		10.8	56.6
UNCTAD (2002) (1997–2005) (% change)				
Services	1.8		3.9	0.4
Wang (1999) (1995–2010) (% change)				
Housing and construction	0.6		0.5	
Services	1.5		1.1	
Zhang (2000) (1994–2005) (% change)				
Electricity and water	0.03		0.16	
Construction	–4.28		–4.55	
Transport	0.67		0.85	
Commerce	0.43		0.53	
Finance	0.80		1.22	
Services	1.72		2.06	
Administration	0.91		0.92	
Zhai and Li (2000) (1995–2010)				
	(%)	(bn yuan)	(%)	(000)
Construction	1.2	33.1	2.2	928
Infrastructure	0.2	2.8	1.1	416
Commerce	1.8	45.4	3.3	2,615
Services	–0.1	–3.5	0.1	49
Anderson et al. (2002) (2002–2007) (% change)				
Construction	0.9		1.0	
Trade and transport	0.0		0.0	
Commercial services	–2.0		–2.0	
Communications	–0.6		–1.0	
Other services	–1.7		–2.0	

Source: Anderson *et al.* (2002); Ianchovichina *et al.* (2000); Wang (1999); Zhai and Li (2000); Zhang (2000); UNCTAD (2002).

and abroad (see above). In the context of the China–US bilateral agreement (which has been incorporated in the China–WTO Agreement), the then US Trade Representative, Charlene Barshefsky noted that in the liberalization of its distribution system China's commitment was broader than that made by any other WTO member (cited in Lardy, 2002: 80). It is, therefore, likely that China's large and small enterprises will face fierce competition from foreign firms following accession. This may well be true, but will it lead to a substantial loss of employment? It is generally believed that increase in competition will lead to the elimination of small retail shops. The forecasts in Table 6.3 (with the exception of those by Ianchovichina *et al.*) do not suggest this, however. Zhai and Li (2000) of the Development Research Centre (DRC) of the State Council of China forecast an increase in employment of 2.6 million unskilled workers during the period 1995–2010. Furthermore, the experience of OECD countries suggests that liberalization of retail trade has only a limited negative effect on employment. This is because large retail stores (which often displace small retail shops) continue to need a minimum amount of labour to remain open at all times, and also because liberalization leads to a growth of new types of retailing and specialized stores. During the past decades employment in the distribution sector has continued to grow in almost every OECD country despite substantial liberalization and productivity gains (Pilat, 1997).

Following accession FDI is likely to increase in China's distribution sector, which will contribute to employment generation. There should be a net employment gain even after allowing for the disappearance of some small and inefficient retailers unless foreign enterprises substantially increase their market shares, which is unlikely. Combined with this, a growth of variety and quantity of goods circulation in the economy following trade expansion, will also be favourable to employment growth. Furthermore, there is a favourable prospect for China to enjoy better access to the distribution channels abroad.

Competition in China's domestic wholesale and retail markets was already quite keen on the eve of China's entry to the WTO. This is true especially in large cities with higher incomes and population density. Growth of foreign trading companies is likely to be limited to selected regions and market segments. Superior management and operating techniques and worldwide networks of foreign companies should induce joint ventures with Chinese firms and ensure restructuring and modernization through learning-by-doing.

Banking and financial services

Some Chinese scholars (Lin, 2001b; Wu, 2000) believe that growth of foreign banks will take deposits away from Chinese banks, thereby reducing the latter's profitability and employment. A decline in the business transactions of Chinese banks following foreign banks' entry into the Chinese market may lead to lay-offs since the Chinese banks are already overstaffed. Retrenchment of staff is seen as the only way to maintain profitability of these banks in the face of foreign competition. While Lin recognizes the possibility of foreign banks taking over deposits from the Chinese banks, he argues that this may not actually happen since a new banking rule requires depositors to disclose their real names, which they may not do because of a large amount of ill-gotten money. Thus competition for deposits between foreign banks and Chinese state banks will be only for *new* savings rather than for savings already deposited with the state banks.

Western literature raises similar fears to those noted above. OECD (2002: 256) notes that 'the possibility that foreign banks, even with a limited share of the market, will have serious adverse impacts on the financial performances of Chinese banks cannot be ruled out'. It notes further that whether it actually occurs will depend on the overall development of the banking system in China. Nolan (2001a) argues that China awaits a serious challenge from foreign competition since there are wide gaps between Chinese domestic and foreign financial institutions in respect of capital, assets and profitability. The scale of foreign companies in terms of assets and employment is many times larger than that of Chinese companies in commercial and investment banks and insurance companies. This will put the latter at a particular disadvantage. The top four Chinese banks rank very high in terms of employment but their productivity is very low. The Industrial and Commercial Bank of China (ICBC) and the Agricultural Bank of China (ABC), each employ half a million persons. Nolan (2001a: 187) concludes that 'China has huge advantages as a late-comer, with access to massive pools of global capital and technology' but 'at the level of the large firm it faces greater challenges than have confronted any previous late-comer country'.

There is no doubt that banking and other financial services will be subjected to competition. It is also well known that China's banking industry suffers from several weaknesses which were brought to light particularly after the 1997 Asian financial crisis: high ratio of non-performing loans to total loans, ineffective supervision of the banking industry and high ratio of short-term debt to total reserves. The high share of non-performing loans is due to lending to SOEs on the basis of political rather than commercial criteria. China's top four state banks have equity-to-asset ratios, which range from a little over 2 per cent to 5 per cent, that is, well below the Bank of International Settlements (BIS) international standard of 8 per cent. However, the closure of Hainan Development Bank, China Venturetech Corporation and Guangdong International Trust and Investment Corporation in 1998 following the Asian crisis, suggests that China is serious about reforming the debt-ridden banking system. Banking reforms include recapitalizing banks, curbing rampant growth of finance companies with irregular practices, and the tightening of bank supervision and control (Bhalla, 2001).

There are other factors which, at least in the near future, may yield some positive employment in Chinese banks and other financial institutions. As Lardy (2002) argues, it is not certain that foreign banks' domestic currency market will grow much (some Chinese scholars have predicted that it will grow by as much as 15 per cent). Volume of loans (which included both foreign and local currency loans, the latter being quite limited at present) by foreign banks declined following the 1997 Asian currency crisis. Furthermore, foreign banks may not find creditworthy borrowers in the near future. The total assets of these banks are only about 1.5 per cent of China's total financial assets, which is extremely small. Even if foreign banks increase their market shares in China, domestic banks are also likely to become more sophisticated and financially sound over time. Therefore, it is quite possible that they will recapture the lost ground from foreign banks.

Compared to the Chinese banks foreign banks are at a disadvantage in lending to Chinese enterprises. Their business is limited in scope because of various government restrictions which have not yet been lifted. These banks suffer from a poor deposit base, lack of inter-bank market and retail networks, which will require some time to develop (Bhattasali and Kawai, 2001). Chinese banks enjoy comparative advantages in terms of better knowledge of local market and business, proximity and close ties to customers and government, and easy access to local currency. Therefore, it is unlikely that foreign banks will increase their lending substantially to domestic enterprises following accession. Thus competition between the two types of banks may be less severe than is often assumed.

China's insurance industry is heralded as 'the largest insurance market in the world' (Shen, 2000). By 2004 the insurance market is expected to double to $30 billion, as is predicted by the Chinese regulatory authorities. There are several reasons to expect a rapid and significant expansion of this market. First, awareness of insurance is growing among the Chinese people. Second, privatization and subsequent growth of private enterprises is already making insurance services grow. Third, worker retrenchments in SOEs and a drop in social benefits have indirectly generated additional demand for insurance services, particularly those related to property and life.

The government had opened up the industry to domestic and limited foreign competition on the eve of its accession to the WTO in order to improve its efficiency. The number of domestic and foreign companies has gradually increased. Although the market share of foreign insurance companies is quite small in terms of absolute amount, their business is quite substantial. Following accession, an overall growth of insurance business is likely to accompany an increase in the number of both domestic and foreign companies, which should, in principle, have a favourable effect on employment.

The opening up of China's domestic market in services to foreign participation will have a number of positive and negative employment effects some of which may be immediate while others are more long term. First, increased competition should, in principle, lead to greater allocative efficiency. This should ensure an increase in the volume of business transactions in such sectors as financial services, securities and insurance in which a considerable growth potential remains to be exploited. The presence of foreign financial institutions may also help promote the development of domestic financial institutions. Second, there should be greater direct and indirect positive employment effects of foreign investment and expenditure through backward and forward linkages and through multiplier effects. Third, additional employment will be generated through the establishment of joint ventures, the promotion of Chinese supplier networks and a growth of new firms. China's accession to the WTO should open up opportunities for the development of small and medium-sized Chinese banks, which may facilitate growth of small and medium enterprises thus generating additional employment. But the negative employment effects can also occur through the displacement of inefficient Chinese firms, global instead of local sourcing of spare parts and components and an increase in the import of intermediate inputs.

Telecommunications

Implications of the opening up of China's telecommunications sector are less serious than those of market access to foreign banking and financial firms. This may be due partly to the national security considerations. For example, China has tried to control the transmission of internet information, especially of dissident movements like Falun Gong. On the one hand, China needs advanced telecommunications technology for socioeconomic development. On the other hand, it fears that too much exposure to foreign competition through internet providers and other information services may compromise its national security and political stability. This is a dilemma which the Chinese authorities currently face.

In general, growth of telecommunications installations in developing countries in the past has been as high if not higher than in industrialized countries. This may be explained by the scope of leapfrogging by late-comer countries especially since they are less saddled with the old infrastructure which would need to be scrapped to introduce newer technology. The advance in electronics technology has reduced the cost of installations, especially in rural areas where satellite technology is much cheaper.

Measuring the direct and indirect employment impact of the telecommunications services and manufacturing equipment is a complex matter considering the uncertainties of the rate of technological innovations, productivity gains, strategies of transnational corporations (TNCs) which supply telecommunications equipment, and their possible relocation to China to service domestic and global markets following accession. While an increase in telecommunications investment and improvement in services will contribute to employment growth through increase in output and incomes, in principle, they may also displace some labour indirectly. But such labour displacement is likely to be more than offset by other jobs created directly and indirectly.

The WTO Agreement is unlikely to have any major adverse effect on employment considering the existence of growth potential of the sector noted above. If anything, employment is likely to grow with the expansion of market demand and volume of business especially in mobile telecommunications. Hoong (2001: 46) notes that 'as a result of Chinese consumers' high propensity to own mobile phones the market is still expected to grow by more than 20% annually over the next decade'. Although China is a poor country with very low

GDP per capita, it has already surpassed the US in terms of the number of mobile subscribers even though mobile subscriptions and phone calls are more expensive in China than elsewhere. However, it is true that the number of mobile phone subscribers per 1,000 inhabitants is the lowest in China among the Southeast Asian countries (at 34 compared to 38 in the Philippines and Thailand, 107 in Malaysia and 504 in the Republic of Korea) (Table 6.4). Therefore, there is a clear growth potential in China in this sector.

In fixed telephone density (telephone lines per 100 inhabitants), although the gap between the low-income countries (like China) and the middle-income countries has declined, the density of middle-income countries was still 42 per cent higher between 1987 and 1998 (Lu, 2000). In 1999, China's telephone density was at the same level as that in Thailand, but much lower than that in Japan, the Republic of Korea, Malaysia and Singapore (Table 6.4). This suggests that China has a growth potential also in fixed telephone density.

The internet services in China are, at present, very underdeveloped compared to those in other Southeast Asian countries with the exception of the Philippines and Thailand. This is understandable considering the sensitivity and fear of the Chinese government about national security noted above. Notwithstanding this the internet services are likely to expand, as is suggested by a rapid growth of internet cafés in China's major cities.

During 1995–99, China invested nearly $73 billion in telecommunications, which was higher than the combined total investments by Indonesia, the Republic of Korea, Malaysia, the Philippines and Thailand (Table 6.4). Although growth in telecommunications services is likely to taper off after a period of phenomenal growth noted above, expansion in different types of services should provide market for both foreign and domestic firms. This is all the more so since foreign firms are required to establish joint ventures with domestic firms. DeWoskin (2001: 637) notes that 'slow (transfer) rates and high costs suggest a huge opportunity for profitable market entry when the sector liberalizes'. Market expansion should bolster domestic industry and thus generate additional employment in addition to what will be directly generated by foreign investment.[9]

China Mobile and Unicom are the two Chinese companies enjoying access to both domestic and international capital markets. Domestic competition for the past two decades has prepared them as major players in the Chinese market. Therefore, they may be able to withstand foreign competition mainly through joint ventures with foreign giants, which will give them access to capital and modern technology. In this sector initially foreign competition may be somewhat restricted since during the first year of accession only 30 per cent foreign investment is allowed in joint ventures with Chinese telecom firms in a selected number of major Chinese cities.

Concluding remarks

In general liberalization of services and market access to foreign firms in the services sector is likely to lead to an overall growth in the volume of services and

Table 6.4 Telecommunication indicators for China and selected Southeast Asian countries (1999)

Indicator	China	Indonesia	Japan	Korea, Rep. of	Malaysia	Philippines	Singapore	Thailand
Telephone lines per 100 inhabitants	8.6	2.9	55.7	43.8	20.3	3.9	48.2	8.6
Mobile phone subscribers per 1,000 inhabitants	34.2	10.6	449.4	504.4	137.0	38.3	463.0	38.4
Internet users per 1,000 inhabitants*	7.0	4.3	213.9	233.6	68.7	6.7	270.0	13.15
Internet hosts per 100,000 inhabitants	5.7	10.1	2,084.1	991.8	270.0	16.6	4,209.0	66.0
Personal computers per 1,000 inhabitants	12.2	9.1	286.9	183.3	68.7	16.9	482.6	22.7
Television sets per 1,000 inhabitants**	286.7	135.7	712.7	356.1	172.8	109.7	322.2	240.5
5-year investment in telecommunications ($ million) (1995–99)	72,841.8	6,000.2	165,583.5	22,784.9	7,716.8	6,635.3	2,532.8	2,025.7

Source: International Telecommunication Union (ITU) STARS data base.
*estimates. ** = for 1998.

thereby in employment. Prior to China's accession this sector was closed to both domestic and foreign enterprises. Most of the services were state monopolies. Therefore, trade liberalization in services should lead to a growth of domestic private enterprises. This is particularly so since both foreign and domestic enterprises can now apply for trading rights to which they were not allowed before 1999.

However, China will face major challenges in competition after foreign companies enjoy access to its domestic market for banking, insurance and telecommunications services. China's tertiary sector is, at present, under-developed compared to other developing as well as industrialized countries. This situation provides both an opportunity and a threat: an opportunity because there will be plenty of scope for an expansion of all types of services; a threat because hitherto protected services are inefficient and their low productivity makes them vulnerable to shocks through global competition following accession.

The Chinese tertiary sector is quite heterogeneous. It consists of both non-tradeables, such as personal services where service providers have to be close to final consumers, and major industry-linked tradeable services like banking, insurance, telecommunications and professional services. In principle, in keeping with its dynamic comparative advantage discussed earlier, China should be able to generate both additional output and employment through the expansion of labour-intensive services (construction and consultancy) and their export.

7 China and the 'flying-geese' (FG) theory

The flying-geese (FG) theory of trade and development originated in and has been applied to Southeast Asia and the Pacific. Its original formulation by Akamatsu (1935) occurred at a time when Japan itself was a labour-intensive economy, and when trade was seen as a major mode of technology transfer. At this time transnational corporations (TNCs) played a limited role. Akamatsu developed the theory on the basis of experience of the evolution of Japanese consumer goods industries (e.g. cotton textiles) during the pre-war period. On the basis of empirical data, he showed a flying-geese pattern of industrial upgrading (or catch-up industrialization) through the following three stages: imports, domestic production, and subsequent export of manufactured goods to the less developed countries.[1] This sequential pattern emerged in Japan, thanks to the exceptionally high savings ratio and effective technological assimilation and progress. With growing labour shortage a gradual shift took place from consumer goods to capital goods which assumed the role of a leading sector in economic development.

The 'flying-geese' theory

The development of the Akamatsu (FG) theory has some parallel with Vernon's product cycle theory which examines how the life cycle of products in developed countries affects firm competitiveness and industrial production. But the two are different in so far as Akamatsu was concerned with the leading sectors and the development of less developed countries, whereas Vernon's theory is focused on firm behaviour in developed countries (Bernard and Ravenhill, 1995).[2]

The FG theory implies that the more industrialized countries have lost their comparative advantage in mature labour-intensive industries. According to the changing comparative advantage in trade these countries with higher value-added and capital-intensive industries transfer older (mature) labour-intensive industries to less-developed and more labour-abundant countries where labour costs are much lower (Dowling and Cheang, 2000; Kojima, 2000; Ozawa, 2001). The leader geese (Japan, for example) gradually lose their comparative advantage in labour-intensive industries which give way to capital goods production and export. This regional division of labour can be both horizontal (entire industry or product may be transferred) and vertical (only some operations and sub-processes as assembly may be transferred).

The theory assumes a rather orderly tier-system under which the US transferred older industries to Japan which in turn transferred them to the ASEAN and to China. This is possible only when countries are at different stages of development so that factor endowments and costs vary across countries. One can group countries involved in this process into four tiers: (a) Japan and the US, (b) Canada and Asian NIEs, (c) ASEAN and (d) China and India, and other newly emerging economies with surplus labour. The regional flying-geese model of development as applied to Southeast Asia explained the pattern of industrialization through Japanese trade and foreign direct investment (FDI) and the relocation of its labour-intensive production to the newly industrializing countries (NICs), that is, ASEAN, China and so on. In the 1980s appreciation of the Japanese yen and rising labour costs forced Japanese firms to relocate un-competitive production processes and industries to lower-cost countries in the region. Japanese FDI in East and Southeast Asian countries expanded significantly and Japanese firms started out-sourcing parts and components from these lower-cost countries.[3] Japanese firms may have relocated to the NIEs and ASEAN-4 to avoid ever-increasing cost burden of domestic production and profit squeeze rather than being particularly attracted by the promising local markets (Ozawa, 2001: 484–85). Ozawa maintains that 'an orderly transplantation of only comparatively disadvantaged industrial activities was switched to a distortional, premature and disorderly transfer of still comparatively advantaged activities from Japan'. One reason for the outward FDI flows from Japan was 'tariff jumping' which is no longer a valid reason under conditions of trade liberalization, WTO rules and globalization.

The FG theory has evolved over time. Since the original Akamatsu formulation subsequent versions of the theory developed by Kojima (1973, 1985, 2000) emphasized the role of FDI as an agent of technology transfer and of TNCs as benevolent agents cooperating with governments of the follower countries. The theory is based on the assumption of cooperation between leaders and followers. Kojima (2000) shows how FDI can be pro-trade and anti-trade, and that pro-trade FDI can promote comparative advantage of both the leader and the followers, which may explain the complementary and harmonious relationship between them. The leader invests in a follower country in an industry in which it has comparative disadvantage. This enables follower country to gain comparative advantage in the given industry, whereas in the lead country, capital goods industry is promoted with a dynamic comparative advantage. Thus pro-trade FDI leads to a 'virtual circle of regional growth' through beneficial enlargement of production and trade. Kojima's refinement of the Akamatsu version of the FG theory can be summarized in terms of the following components:

• Diversification and rationalization of industries in the catch-up process of industrialization.
• Introduction of pro-trade FDI to promote industrialization of the Southeast Asian region.

- Presentation of a theory of 'agreed specialization' under which industrial and trade structures in each country converge and intra-industry trade becomes important for regional integration. This prevents trade conflicts and competition.

It is paradoxical that the process of catch-up industrialization by which the FG theory is characterized, itself leads to similarities of industrial structure and exports of the leaders and followers thus breeding competition. Kojima (2000: 394) notes that the above situation 'creates many problems such as over-production, fierce competition, dumping and protectionism in the importing countries'. This catch-up process is likely to lead to similarities in industrial structures between developing countries. Complementarity in trade occurs when countries produce and specialize in different products for exchange. With changing comparative advantage growing similarities in industrial structures will promote competition, particularly within a group of countries such as the NICs, which are gradually catching up with each other. For example, this has been evidenced by the fierce competition among these economies in the computer industry.

The transfer of labour-intensive products and exports from the lead goose can indeed lead to competition for local producers in the follower countries, especially since these products are likely to be cheaper and more modern. The immediate result of trade between lead goose and follower goose can be displacement and impoverishment of traditional producers (Rowthorn, 1996). However, in the medium term the follower country, with transfer of technology from the leader, acquiring of modern tastes and government support, the follower country can become competitive and even drive out imports from the leader. As Rowthorn (1996: 10) notes, 'the result may be impoverishment for those who work in this industry in the leading country and the wheel will thus turn full circle'.

As we will argue below, in China many provinces compete with each other for unskilled and skilled labour, raw materials, markets and FDI. Cooperative relationship between provinces is promoted mainly through state intervention and at times, even coercion. Can such promotion of cooperation be exploited to China's advantage in maintaining or raising its global competitiveness in the wake of the WTO entry? This is one of the main questions that we address in this chapter.

The negative effects of FDI and TNCs in the host countries are by now quite well known and can be real. The non-harmonious effects between countries are not recognized in the recent versions of the FG theory although the original Akamatsu version recognized them. Japan's FDI in the Asian region (to the NIEs, the ASEAN and China) led to a 'triangular trade' in capital goods, components, and other inputs, which culminated into trade deficits of these countries with Japan. These deficits are claimed to have emerged due to the absence of reverse trade flows (Bernard and Ravenhill, 1995: 200). However, this claim is not borne out by facts. Shinohara (1996) shows that reverse flow of trade, especially in machinery, took place from the ASEAN countries to Japan.

These exports consisted not only of machinery parts imported from Japan but also of parts made wholly in such ASEAN countries as Thailand. Japan concentrated its FDI in machinery industry[4] which may explain these reverse flows of machinery exports to the lead goose (Japan) described as a 'boomerang effect'. Such an effect can lead to an industrial hollowing out of advanced countries since it is confined not only to light consumer goods industries but also to such other industries as shipbuilding and iron and steel.

Some critics of the FG theory (e.g. Bernard and Ravenhill, 1995) have argued that it does not fully explain the Southeast Asian development since the follower countries (e.g. the Republic of Korea and Taiwan) have not fully adopted the Japanese model of development. These countries are much more dependent on imported technology and have thus lacked comparable (to Japan) innovative capacity. Bernard and Ravenhill (1995: 189) conclude that 'the argument that a "Japanese model" has been generalized throughout East Asia is partial at best and difficult to sustain'.

Neither does the FG theory explain the present weak financial position of Japan. For example, Ozawa (2001) argues that it does not properly investigate the Japanese institutional set-up (state-directed bank-based financing of industry, the dualistic industrial development, and labour-management system of job primacy over efficiency) and deepening financial morass. The above institutional arrangements are no longer suitable for future growth.

Empirical tests of the theory

Most of the empirical tests of the FG theory employ the index of revealed comparative advantage (RCA) in particular commodities and sectors over time to determine shifts in comparative advantage, trade patterns and structural adjustments in individual industries, regions and countries (e.g. Chen, 1992; Chow and Kellman, 1993; Dowling and Cheang, 2000; Fukasuka, 1992; Rana, 1990; Rao and Das, 1995; and Yamazawa *et al.*, 1991). Indices of revealed comparative advantage (RCA) (Panchamukhi, 1992) and intra-industry trade (IIT) are estimated (Fukusaku, 1992; Rao and Das, 1995) generally using 2–3 digit SITC classification of industries. Strong empirical evidence is available supporting shifts in comparative advantage from Japan to other Asian countries (e.g. Watanabe and Kajiwara, 1983). However, shifts in comparative advantage from the NICs to other less developed Asian economies is less clear-cut. While Fukusaka (1992), Rana (1990) and Yamazawa *et al.* (1991) provide evidence supporting this shift, Chow and Kellman (1993), Cline (1984), and Lutz and Kihl (1990) do not.

As we discussed in Chapter 2, the RCA index is based on the market share principle. In the context of a developing country such as China suffering from market distortions, the market shares are not a perfect index of comparative advantage. It assumes that markets function perfectly well in all countries, which is not the case. In developing countries institutional factors account for market failures which require selective responses. However, in the absence of better indices and relevant data, most authors use this index to measure comparative advantage so that the greater the RCA the greater the comparative advantage and competitiveness of a particular country in exporting a particular product in the world market. Of course, one can argue that the market share is an outcome of competitiveness rather than its cause. The dynamic comparative advantage may simply be the result of faster growth of productivity relative to a given country's competitors. The problem of causation is often difficult to sort out. Lall (2001b: 1508) notes rightly that competitiveness is not easy to measure because 'the concept remains multifaceted and always needs simplifications and judgements'. He shows how the World Economic Forum (WEF) competitiveness index suffers from fuzziness and confusion due to lack of robust data and analytical foundation (see Chapter 2).

There are other limitations of the RCA method. Its application to actual trade data may reflect not only the changing comparative advantage of exporting countries but also the demand conditions in importing countries. Furthermore, the RCA index is likely to be influenced by a host of factors other than trade, e.g. pre-trade relative prices, and government macroeconomic policies in exporting and importing countries (see Fukasaku, 1992).

Fukasaku (1992) computed RCA for 151 categories of commodities at 3-digit SITC level for eleven Pacific-Asian economies excluding China for 1979 and 1988. A correlation was made between the RCA vector and vector of changes in product categories for a source country whose competitiveness has declined. A negative correlation suggested that the pattern of comparative advantage between two countries actually shifted in line with the flying-geese model. The estimation of RCA and IIT for four types of manufactured product groups (see below) supported two main conclusions. First, inter-industry trade specialization increased significantly during the 1980s. Second, the level of intra-industry trade between pairs of Asian Pacific countries increased thanks to similarities in demand and production structures and low transportation costs between two trading partners.

Chen (1992) computed RCAs for Japan, Asian NICs and ASEAN-4 (Thailand, Philippines, Singapore and Indonesia) for 1970, 1976, 1980 and 1985. He considered four types of product categories, viz:

1   *Unskilled labour-intensive products*, e.g. footwear, textiles, clothing, toys.
2   *Natural resource-intensive products*, e.g. leather and wood manufacture, precious stones, construction materials and metal processing.
3   *Technology-intensive products*, e.g. metal-working machinery, manufacture of explosives, electrical and non-electrical machinery, and telecommunications equipment.
4   *Human capital-intensive products*, e.g. household electric equipment, paper and paperboard, clocks and watches, and musical instruments.

Chen's findings support the FG theory in trade in unskilled labour-intensive goods, skill-intensive and technology-intensive goods. We showed in Chapter 2 that in China between 1980 and 2000 the comparative advantage in exports shifted from resource-intensive primary products towards labour-intensive manufactures. The RCAs for the export of primary processed goods, which are mostly resource-intensive, declined during this period and those for labour-intensive manufactured goods increased (see Table 2.6).

The novelty of the Chen approach is to introduce different stages of the technology cycle in different sub-sectors of particular industries explaining comparative advantage and specialization. Chen argues that this type of technology-based specialization is more like a parading 'battalion of soldiers' (involving different patterns) rather than flying geese.

Dowling and Cheang (2000) estimate the rank correlation coefficients for the RCA vectors for the four newly industrialized economies (NIEs) (Hong Kong, the Republic of Korea, Singapore, and Taiwan) and the ASEAN-4 (Indonesia, Malaysia, the Philippines and Thailand) for 1970, 1985 and 1995 in order to assess changes in comparative advantage. A negative or low coefficient indicates substantial structural changes whereas a positive and large coefficient suggests absence of a change in a country's competitive position. The authors use trade and FDI data from such industries as electronics and chemicals to show that industries enjoying increasing comparative advantage also attract the largest share of FDI. They show that comparative advantage has shifted from Japan to the NIEs and then to the ASEAN-4. Thus their conclusion is that the FG theory was applicable during the 1970–95 period.

Having briefly reviewed the theory and its empirical testing, our next task is to examine whether and how the theory applies to China.

Applicability of the theory to China

There are two ways in which the 'flying-geese' theory can apply to China. First, as we noted above, China's low labour cost advantage, *inter alia*, attracted FDI from Japan and other industrialized countries within the Asia-Pacific region. There is no doubt that a substantial increase in intra-regional trade in the Southeast Asian region is the consequence of China's open-door policy since 1978. China's exports to such countries as Singapore and Japan consist not only of unskilled labour-intensive goods in which it currently enjoys a comparative advantage, but increasingly of skill-intensive goods such as clocks and watches and machinery. After accession, China is expected to attract massive FDI inflows especially in such sectors as banking, telecommunications and insurance industries which are being opened up to foreigners.

Second, the 'flying-geese' theory can apply to China not as a follower goose but as a leading goose, so that with the rising labour costs China may lose its current comparative advantage in trade in unskilled labour-intensive products which could be shifted to such lower labour cost countries in the Asian region as Bangladesh, Indonesia and Vietnam. Outflows of FDI from China could also occur along with a shift of production. To some extent this is already taking place, especially in terms of outflows of Chinese FDI to other countries in the region and elsewhere. World Bank (1997: 26) notes that 'in 1995 China's outward investment accounted for about 2 per cent of global capital flows, making it the eighth largest supplier among all countries and the largest outward investor among developing countries'. The past few years have witnessed a dramatic increase in the number of Chinese TNCs and their affiliates abroad. The foreign affiliates are currently estimated at over 6,000 (Cai, 1999). Large FDI outflows are destined for neighbouring economies including Hong Kong. One of the motivations for outward investment in manufacturing in the past was to circumvent trade barriers (e.g. the establishment of textiles and clothing firms in South Asia and Africa). This market-seeking factor will be much less important in the post-accession period than profit-seeking (through higher returns) and technology-seeking to maintain or raise competitiveness. Domestic competition and saturation of the domestic market (existence of large excess capacity in China is now well known) may also explain FDI outflows for market seeking abroad. In the past, especially before 1994 when the yuan was overvalued, high domestic costs induced FDI outflows from China. These outflows reached record levels in 1992 and 1993, totalling $4 billion and $4.4 billion respectively (Cai, 1999). This situation was similar to that of Japan during the overvaluation of the yen.

It is also possible that after accession foreign investors will have a lower incentive to invest in China in several businesses whose goods could be supplied to China from other cheaper production sites in the region. Rising production costs in China may move TNCs production bases away from it. This will be particularly so in conditions of political instability. Furthermore, reduced state intervention and greater transparency in the distribution process may diminish the role of local partners. Thus joint ventures with foreign partners may gradually disappear (see Nolan, 2001a). However, this is more likely to happen in manufacturing than in services which have been opened to foreign investment only after accession. As we noted in Chapter 6, under the WTO Agreement initially joint ventures will be permitted only in such services as insurance and telecommunications.

There have been indications in the past that many Chinese TNCs relocated their production facilities from the coastal areas (where production costs are rising) to lower-cost hinterland in China rather than moving abroad (Zhan, 1995). It is not clear whether China's comparative advantage due to low labour costs and cheap transportation will disappear in the foreseeable future. As we discussed in Chapter 3, China is unlikely to lose this advantage quickly given its substantial labour surpluses in both agriculture and industry, which are unlikely to dry up in the short run.

However, some empirical estimates show that China's comparative advantage in such labour-intensive exports as textiles and clothing have been declining during the 1990s. Table 7.1 gives estimates of RCAs in textile and clothing products for 1992–93 and 1997–98, and changes in RCA over time on the basis of the formula noted in Chapter 2. The ratio of less than 1 shows a decline in comparative advantage whereas the ratio of higher than 1 shows an improvement.

Table 7.1 Indices of China's revealed comparative advantage in textiles and clothing (1992–93 to 1997–98)

Textiles				Clothing			
Item	R_1	R_2	R_1/R_2	Item	R_1	R_2	R_1/R_2
652 Cotton fabrics, woven	4.08	5.23	0.78	845 Outer garment knit non-elastic	4.77	4.22	1.13
658 Textile articles	5.31	7.17	0.74	843 Women's outerwear non-knitted	4.61	6.49	0.71
653 Woven man-made fabric	2.42	2.14	1.13	842 Men's outerwear non-knitted	5.43	6.78	0.80
651 Textile yarn	1.86	2.27	0.82	846 Undergarments knitted	4.93	4.36	1.13
654 Other woven textile fabric	2.76	3.89	0.71	844 Undergarments, non-knitted	4.85	7.70	0.63
655 Knitted etc. fabric	2.02	2.73	0.74	831 Travel goods, handbags, etc.	8.86	8.60	1.03
				848 Headgear, non-textile clothing	7.53	6.72	1.12
				847 Textiles clothing accessories	5.17	3.80	1.36

Source: Shafaeddin (2002). Based on UNCTAD data base.

Note: R_1 is RCA for 1997–98, R_2, RCA for 1992–93.

In textiles, China's comparative advantage declined in woven cotton fabrics, textile articles, textile yarn, and knitted fabrics, whereas it improved slightly in woven man-made fabrics. In clothing, its comparative advantage improved except in cases of men's and women's outerwear (non-knitted) and undergarments.

It is possible that the decline in China's comparative advantage in textiles will continue into the post-WTO period when other neighbouring countries such as Bangladesh, Indonesia, Pakistan, and Vietnam exploit their comparative advantage of lower labour costs. As we noted in Chapter 5 (Table 5.7), the unit labour costs in Chinese cotton weaving and spinning in the 1990s were generally higher relative to those in other Asian countries for which data are available. These labour costs are likely to be even higher in the post-WTO period, which may shift comparative advantage further away from China.

In the long run, China may move into the position of second-tier NICs such as Malaysia and Thailand. It will thus look for less developed and more labour-abundant neighbours like Vietnam and Bangladesh to relocate production processes there.

Applicability of the FG theory within China

There seems to be a parallel between the application of the FG theory to Japan and the Chinese policy of the coastal areas helping the hinterland. In both cases, the policy was state driven. The Japanese import-substitution-cum-export promotion drive after the Second World War was sponsored by the state and inspired by the infant-industry argument (see Ozawa, 2001). Once export industries started losing competitiveness (as a result partly of the appreciation of the yen) they were transferred to lower-cost Asian developing countries through FDI there. These goods transferred abroad were imported back home. The Chinese experience of cooperation between the coastal areas and the hinterland is explicitly based on a government policy of *dirigisme* like the Japanese. It also represents a relationship of learning and catching up (or teacher–learner relation) under which the less-developed hinterland receives financial and technical assistance from the eastern coastal regions. Similar to the Japanese experience, motivation for the coastal areas to provide such assistance and transfer production there will arise from the rising costs of production (especially labour costs) due to congestion and labour shortages in the coastal areas. Labour costs in the coastal areas are much higher than those in the interior, for example, the central and western regions. They are well above the average figure in the eastern region and much below the average in central and western regions. In the case of garment making, a labour-intensive activity, the annual labour cost per worker in the western region is one-third of that in the eastern region (Table 7.2). Labour share in total cost is significantly higher in the western region, where labour plays an important role due to its less skilled nature and low productivity of its export sector. Zhang and Felmington (2002) show that in this region productivity of the non-export sector is higher than that of the export sector. They also show that exports have a positive growth effect on the central and eastern region but not on the western region.

Table 7.2 Labour costs in manufacturing in Chinese regions (for 14 large cities)

Region/industry	Annual labour cost per worker (yuan)	Labour share in total cost (%)
Overall	9,645	12.5
East	11,218	11.4
Central	7,630	15.3
West	6,144	18.1
Garments	7,380	11.9
East	7,927	11.9
Central	5,914	10.5
West	2,658	19.7
Transport equipment	13,819	11.5
East	15,443	10.7
Central	7,161	10.4
West	9,317	41.6
Electrical machinery and equipment	11,037	11.2
East	12,416	10.7
Central	6,618	20.3
West	3,292	18.9

Source: Chen *et al.* (1999: 121–23).

Note: East includes the following provinces and regions: Beijing, Tianjin, Hebei, Liaoning, Shanghai, Jiangsu, Zhejiang, Shandong, Fujian, Guangdong, Guangxi and Hainan. The Central region consists of Inner Mongolia, Shanxi, Heilongjiang, Jilin, Anhui, Jiangxi, henan, Hubei and Hunan. The West includes Guizhou, Sichuan, Gansu, Yunnan, Tibet, Shaanxi, Qinghai, Ningxia and Xinjiang.

China's recent accession to the WTO will provide an impetus for export competitiveness which will in turn drive high-cost export production from the coastal areas to the lower-cost hinterland. This hypothesis is based on the assumption that it is more economical and less socially disruptive to shift investment and production to sources of labour surplus (the interior provinces) than for people to move away from home. For several years now growing labour shortages and increasing labour demand in the coastal areas have attracted immigrants from the hinterland. According to the Population Census 2000 about 22 million net migrants (those who move within provinces as well as across provinces) in 2000 worked in 12 coastal provinces (cited in Fu and Balasubramanyam, 2002) While such migration may enable the coastal areas to maintain competitiveness and rapid growth, it deprives the interior less-developed regions of relatively more efficient workers who decide to migrate. This internal brain drain may be partly responsible for the latter's relatively slower growth. It is also likely to widen the income gaps between poor (non-coastal) and rich (coastal) regions. The Fu and Balasubramanyam estimates show that a 1 per cent increase in the share of migrants in the population of the hinterland raises the per capita income gap by 0.1 per cent. Of course, the extent of these income gaps will depend, *inter alia*, on the extent to which remittances by migrants have a positive equalizing influence on incomes. Furthermore, a 1 per cent increase in FDI in the coastal regions relative to the hinterland is estimated to raise the income gap by 0.12 per cent. Fu and Balasubramanyam (2002) show a high rank correlation of 0.77 between immigration from the hinterland and FDI in the coastal regions (see Table 7.3). This result suggests that FDI in export-oriented labour-intensive industries in the coastal provinces/ regions has attracted the bulk of labour. Guangdong, which is the main recipient of FDI, attracted 12 million out of a total of 22 million immigrants in 2000, that is, nearly 55 per cent of the total.

The above estimates confirm our argument that migration to coastal areas is a less efficient or inferior strategy to that of relocating investment and production in the hinterland to create local employment. Deng's policies under which growth was pursued in the coastal areas at the cost of equity (that is, letting the rich get richer first) gave a clear head-start to these areas. In fact, the share of total investments going to the coastal eastern region increased and that of the western region declined during five-year plans since the economic reforms began. In the

Table 7.3 Immigration and FDI in the Chinese coastal regions

Province	Immigrant		Realized FDI by 1999	
	Number (000)	*Rank*	*Amount ($million)*	*Rank*
Beijing	1,240	7	12,715	7
Tianjin	390	10	12,109	8
Hebei	850	8	6,118	11
Liaoning	530	9	12,800	6
Shanghai	2,020	2	25,180	4
Jiangsu	1,990	3	37,305	2
Zhejiang	1,830	4	9,575	9
Fujian	1,380	6	30,078	3
Shandong	1,530	5	18,138	5
Guangdong	13,000	1	86,911	1
Guangxi	−2,620	12	6,418	10
Hainan	160	11	5,799	12
Total	22,300		263,146	
Rank correlation coefficient		0.77		

Sources: Fu and Balasubramanyam (2002).

Note: Data on immigrants are from the Population Census 2000, whereas that on FDI from MOFTEC.

first three years of the Ninth Five-year Plan (1996–98) share of investment in the western region (15.6 per cent) was lower than its share (18.8 per cent) during the First Plan (1953–57). The highest investment shares of the western region were recorded before the start of economic reforms. Since then the shares of investments of the coastal eastern region have risen substantially (see Table 7.4).

In theory, trade externalities may be assumed to occur when trade expands in the coastal areas leading to growth of overall economic activity spilling over into the hinterland (Brun *et al.*, 2002). But studies (e.g. Fu and Balasubramanyam, 2002) have shown that, in practice, spill-overs from the coastal areas to the hinterland have been limited.

Spreading the fruits of growth to the interior provinces was one of the declared objectives of the regional development policies, which has not been achieved so far. Dengist policies were explicitly or implicitly based on the expectations of a trickle-down growth model, which was popular for several years. There are anecdotes as well as empirical studies (see below) showing how local governments introduced trade barriers preventing such externalities from being realized. These barriers may have also hindered the diffusion of technological and managerial knowledge from the coastal to non-coastal areas despite government's efforts to promote technical cooperation between the two. Some studies (e.g. Moreno and Trehan, 1997) explain lack of such diffusion by locational and geographical factors. Distance and cultural differences (in confidence, trust, common knowledge) will raise costs of transportation and monitoring, whereas proximity will lower them. As the western region is quite far from the eastern region, it may not have benefited from trickle-down or spillovers as much as the closer regions and provinces. Others (e.g. Batisse, 2002; Poncet, 2002a) underline the importance of cities and urbanization in enhancing the importance of spillovers.

Table 7.4 Share of investment in China's three regions in economic plans (1953–98)

Region	1953–57 (First)	1958–62 (Second)	1963–65 Adjustment period	1966–70 (Third)	1971–75 (Fourth)
Eastern	36.9	38.4	34.9	26.9	35.5
Central	28.8	34.0	32.7	29.8	29.9
Western	18.8	22.0	25.6	34.0	24.5

Region	1976–80 (Fifth)	1981–85 (Sixth)	1986–90 (Seventh)	1991–95 (Eighth)	1996–98 (Three years of the Ninth)
Eastern	42.2	47.7	51.7	54.2	52.5
Central	30.1	29.3	24.4	23.5	23.2
Western	19.9	17.2	15.8	14.7	15.6

Source: *China's Investment in Fixed Assets, Annual Statistics* (1950–95).

The catch-up strategy based on learning is not new. History provides many examples of this: the US catching up with Great Britain, Japan catching up with the US and the East Asian countries catching up with Japan and so on. However, what is rather unique about the Japanese and East Asian experience in the application of the FG theory is a deliberate attempt on the part of both leaders and followers to cooperate for regional growth. This was made possible by multi-layered interactions between countries and regions at different stages of development. This again is the logic of the Chinese official policy of enforcing cooperation between the coastal areas and the hinterland. (The government is naturally worried about growing regional income inequalities which are likely to be exacerbated after the WTO accession as discussed in Chapter 3.) The Western Development Strategy launched by the Chinese government in 1999 gives further impetus to this cooperation. This strategy is aimed at narrowing income disparities between the coastal and non-coastal provinces. The main measures adopted to achieve this objective are: infrastructure development by the central government, preferential policies such as tax concessions to attract to the hinterland domestic investment by the coastal provinces and FDI by foreign investors, and the participation of more developed coastal provinces in the development of the western region.

Empirical evidence of FG application to China

We believe that in the short and medium terms, the FG theory may apply regionally within China. Our main concern in this chapter is to ascertain quantitatively, notwithstanding data limitations, the extent to which the Chinese coastal areas will shift production towards the hinterland where production costs (especially labour costs) are much lower. The Chinese coastal areas have developed much faster than the hinterland, bringing about differences in their comparative advantages for producing for export and for domestic consumption. Thus, the coastal areas with increasing labour shortages and more capital-intensive production may shift labour-intensive production processes to the non-coastal areas. However, labour costs are only one of the factors determining the location of production and investment. The non-coastal areas lack infrastructure which may deter FDI and production shifting there.

In principle, the FG theory could apply to the Chinese coastal (the lead geese) and non-coastal areas (the follower geese) on the following conditions:

- If trade between coastal and non-coastal areas increases over time.
- If according to the principle of comparative advantage coastal areas exported to the interior areas capital-intensive and high-tech goods in which they enjoyed comparative advantage in exchange for labour-intensive and resource-intensive goods from the hinterland.
- If labour-intensive production is relocated from the coastal to non-coastal areas.
- If FDI going into labour-intensive industries in the less developed hinterland increased over time.

• If financial and technical cooperation existed between the coastal and non-coastal areas promising eventual narrowing of income gaps between the two areas.

Our next task is to empirically examine whether in China all the above conditions, or at least some of them, are fulfilled. Data limitations do not allow us to undertake any rigorous empirical tests. Therefore, as second-best solution we discuss below whatever partial evidence exists in support of or against the above hypotheses.

Inter-provincial trade

We need to examine the changing comparative advantages of the coastal and non-coastal regions to test whether the FG theory applies within China. This can be done in various ways. First, one can compare inter-provincial trade and production over time to see whether this trade has increased. Second, a proxy variable may be used to test the theory indirectly. Thus we may examine how exports and FDI of foreign firms in labour-intensive industries in the coastal provinces changed relative to those of domestic firms in the non-coastal provinces. Third, estimates can be made of the revealed comparative advantage (RCA) in trade for the Chinese provinces by using the RCA formula mentioned in Chapter 2 in which country i is replaced by province i. The provinces may be grouped into three regions: central (non-coastal), west (non-coastal) and east (coastal).

Inter-industry trade between the coastal and non-coastal provinces could be estimated by the following trade index. Index of inter-industry trade between coastal and non-coastal areas:

$$T_{ik} = X_{ik} + M_{ik} \tag{1}$$

Where T_{ik} is trade of a coastal province i with a non-coastal province j in industry k, X_{ik} is total export of province i in industry k, and M_{ik} is total imports of province i in industry k.

Intra-industry trade of province i in industry k (IITik) will be equal to the value of total trade, that is, $X_{ik} + M_{ik}$, minus net exports or imports (or $X_{ik} - M_{ik}$). Total intra-industry trade is usually expressed as a percentage of total trade of a given industry, so that when either X_{ik} or M_{ik} is zero, there is no intra-industry trade. Alternatively, all trade will be intra-industry trade when $X_{ik} = M_{ik}$.

In the absence of any borders within the country it is hard to find any cross-province or inter-border trade data for coastal provinces' trade with the hinterland not only for China but also for many other countries.[5] Such data are rarely collected. Some attempts (e.g. Naughton, 2000; Poncet, 2002b) have been made to use the Chinese provincial input-output tables to assess changes in the extent and importance of inter-provincial trade. Using the provincial input-output data for 1987 and 1992, Naughton comes to the conclusion that growth in inter-provincial trade between 1987 and 1992 exceeded that of provincial GDP and foreign trade. He also concludes that intra-industry trade in manufactures was more important than inter-industry trade. Inter-provincial trade is noted to be significant for all provinces regardless of the location or stage of development. Naughton (2000: 17–18) notes that for the '14 inland provinces for which we have good data, domestic inflows were 43% of GDP and outflows were 55%, only slightly lower than the 11 coastal provinces at 58% for inflows and 63% for outflows'. On the basis of these results he comes to the conclusion that 'national economic integration of China was increasing'. However, one needs to be aware that the data for 1987 and 1992 are not strictly comparable (differences in the sample of provinces and the coverage of trade flows), which may introduce a margin of error.

Using the provincial input-output data for 1992 and 1997, Poncet (2002b) comes to the opposite conclusion, namely, that China is fragmented. She shows that the intensity of inter-provincial flows has declined during this period. This is demonstrated by the greater proportion of local goods being consumed by a province than those from other provinces. The local governments with much greater autonomy under the decentralization policy imposed trade restrictions (e.g. ban of imports from another province, tariffs and dumping charges) in order to protect local economic activity, generate local employment and promote social stability. Poncet notes that this economic and trade fragmentation in China 'contrasts with results obtained on other economies (Canada, USA, European Union, OECD)'.

Trade and economic fragmentation militates against the efforts of the Chinese authorities to integrate into the global economy following its entry into WTO. Free access of foreign goods into the Chinese domestic market is unlikely to be ensured as long as provinces restrict domestic trade. Furthermore, inter-provincial trade restrictions represent a case of conflict rather than cooperation between provinces on which the flying-geese theory is based.

There is no conclusive evidence that trade between provinces is particularly restricted despite anecdotes and some empirical studies discussed above. In principle, inter-provincial trade flows should have increased over time with increases in investments in the transportation and communications infrastructure and the opening up of the provincial economies in the 1990s. However, the subject remains controversial for several plausible reasons. First, detailed empirical data are either not easily accessible (or available) or are not robust enough which may explain conflicting results in the literature. Naughton (2000: 31) concludes that 'there is a great deal we don't know about inter-provincial trade and specialization and national integration in China'. In principle, the integrating effects of improved transportation infrastructure can be offset by the disintegrating effects of increased local protection and regional barriers. But there is no real reason to believe that local protection was much greater in the 1990s (for which Poncet shows fragmentation) than in the 1980s (for which Naughton shows integration). On the contrary as Naughton (2000) argues, the reasons for local protection (e.g. local employment generation and subsidies to inefficient local firms) have diminished in importance as a result of capacity expansion, growing competition, limited resources available for protection, and the central government policy of SOE restructuring and lay-offs. Furthermore, although certain cases of local protection may be real (e.g. in the case of automobiles), by 2001 the central government had banned illegal fees and other types of local protection to automobile industry as well as all other regional blockades (Lardy, 2002: 150). Finally, although the central government's policy of urging the coastal areas to provide technical and financial assistance to the less developed hinterland may not have been as successful as expected, in principle it should have raised trade and investment flows between provinces.

Revealed comparative advantage

A priori, the RCA indices for labour-intensive products should improve over time for the non-coastal areas enjoying lower labour and transportation costs. For the same products RCI indices for the coastal areas should decline over time as the costs of production rise with increasing labour shortages. It is also interesting to examine how the RCA indices for particular sectors have changed for the coastal versus non-coastal provinces. RCA greater than unity indicates comparative advantage; RCA less than unity shows comparative disadvantage. In Table 7.5 we present estimates of sectoral RCA indices for the Chinese provinces for 1990 and 1998, which show a number of features. First, neither the coastal provinces nor the hinterland has any comparative advantage in such capital-intensive exports as machinery and equipment. This is to be expected. Second, in 1998 with the exception of Hainan, Hebei and Shandong, the coastal provinces did not enjoy any comparative advantage in primary resource-based products which in general tend to be labour intensive. These three provinces also enjoyed comparative advantage in these products in 1990 with the RCAs greater than unity for Guangxi and Zhejiang. However, these two provinces lost their comparative advantage in 1998. On the other hand, quite a large number of non-coastal provinces in 1998 (14) enjoyed comparative advantage in the export of primary products. Third, in the case of exports of manufactures, which are generally labour-intensive, both the coastal and non-coastal provinces show a comparative advantage since the RCA indices for most provinces are greater than unity. However, the indices are generally much higher for the non-coastal provinces. It would seem that while non-coastal provinces enjoy a comparative advantage in the export of labour-intensive manufactures, the coastal provinces may enjoy relatively greater comparative advantage in less labour-intensive manufactures. Lack of disaggregated data does not permit us to sub-divide the manufactured exports into labour-intensive and capital-intensive categories.

The relocation of labour-intensive production to the non-coastal provinces

There is evidence that China's production and export structure is becoming more and more compatible with its comparative advantage with the implementation of

Table 7.5 RCA indices of exports of the coastal and non-coastal provinces

Province	1990			1998		
	Primary products	Manufactured materials & finished goods	Machinery & equipment	Primary products	Manufactured materials & finished goods	Machinery & equipment
Coastal Provinces						
Shanghai	0.44	2.40	0.28	0.31	1.93	0.75
Beijing	0.49	2.42	0.23	0.84	1.27	0.75
Tianjin	0.92	1.87	0.26	0.48	1.32	1.10
Guangdong	0.71	1.87	0.56	0.28	2.16	0.66
Zhejiang	1.13	2.07	0.17	0.63	2.31	0.35
Liaoning	2.94	0.66	0.12	1.16	1.25	0.76
Jiangsu	0.87	2.12	0.19	0.35	1.96	0.68
Fujian	0.72	2.19	0.26	0.71	2.04	0.39
Shandong	1.97	1.38	0.10	1.33	2.07	0.28
Hainan	1.33	1.76	0.09	1.57	1.82	0.12
Hebei	2.61	0.99	0.05	1.32	1.54	0.26
Guangxi	1.77	1.24	0.11	0.98	2.42	0.18
Non-coastal Provinces						
Heilongjiang	2.17	1.12	0.21	4.05	1.22	0.16
Xinjiang	2.18	1.29	0.05	0.39	3.04	0.09
Jilin	2.77	0.67	0.10	2.67	1.67	0.21
Hubei	0.94	2.07	0.19	0.71	2.35	0.30
Inner Mongolia	1.97	1.30	0.14	2.10	2.11	0.06
Qinghai	1.39	1.76	0.15	1.89	1.98	0.02
Shanxi	1.89	1.34	0.09	3.97	1.15	0.04
Ningxia	1.62	1.29	0.37	1.23	2.31	0.03
Hunan	1.15	1.60	0.18	1.06	2.11	0.16
Anhui	1.68	1.49	0.12	1.01	2.24	0.23
Henan	1.53	1.75	0.15	1.16	2.30	0.14
Sichuan	1.51	1.47	0.23	1.36	1.42	0.47
Yunnan	1.31	1.47	0.26	2.04	1.14	0.23
Jiangxi	1.18	1.70	0.13	1.95	2.16	0.08
Shaanxi	1.00	1.83	0.30	0.82	2.12	0.51
Gansu	1.33	1.42	0.21	1.25	2.14	0.19
Guizhou	1.69	1.01	0.28	3.03	0.91	0.15

Source: Estimates are based on data from *China's Customs General Administration.*

reforms and liberalization policies. China's comparative advantage in labour-intensive production lies mainly in the non-coastal areas where labour costs are lower. The comparative advantage of the coastal provinces lies increasingly in less labour-intensive and high-tech production for exports. Anecdotal evidence (in daily press in China, e.g. *Xinhua News*) suggests that the central government has in fact closed down many textile and garment factories in the coastal areas because they were inefficient due to the rising labour costs there.[6] The government may have reopened at least some of these factories in the interior provinces to take advantage of lower labour costs. Indeed this is suggested by changes between 1988 and 1998 in the coastal provinces in respect of output value of textile industry under the central government, physical output of cotton fabrics, number of cotton spindles and physical output of garments (Table 7.6). With the exception of output value of textile industry, all the shares for the coastal provinces have declined between 1988 and 1998. The results suggest that labour-intensive production of cotton fabrics and garments may have shifted to the hinterland. An increase in the share of output value of textile industry may be explained by the fact that textile industry, especially the segment using chemical fibres, is capital-intensive in which the coastal provinces enjoy a comparative advantage.

Many observers (e.g. Fewsmith, 2001b; Shafaeddin, 2002) believe that China will lose competitiveness in labour-intensive products in the post-WTO accession period. Their premise, *inter alia*, is based on the assumption that labour costs are

Table 7.6 The textile and clothing industry in China's coastal provinces (1988–98)

Item	1988 Value/ quantity & percentage	1994 Value/ quantity & percentage	1996 Value/ quantity & percentage	1998 Value/ quantity & percentage
No. of cotton spindles (10,000 pieces)	1,505 (57.8)	2,364 (56.8)	2,392 (57.3)	1,918 (52.7)
Cotton dyeing & printing capacity (100 million metres)	62 (55.8)	92 (62.2)	97 (64.2)	51 (42.8)
Output of garments (10,000 pieces)	166,669 (73.7)	671,112 (85.8)	1,118,170 (88.0)	695,468 (46.3)
Output of cotton fabrics (100 million metres)	–	128 (60.7)	127 (61.0)	113 (46.9)
Output of silk goods (10,000 metres)	130,850 (81.7)	273,270 (87.3)	465,955 (92.6)	348,028 (54.5)
Output value of textile industry under the central government (100 mill. yuan at 1990 prices)	–	1,909 (69.1)	5,307 (80.3)	5,765 (84.2)

Source: *Almanac of China's Textile Industry,* various issues.

Note: Coastal provinces include Beijing, Fujian, Guangxi, Hainan, Guangdong, Jiangsu, Zhejiang, Shanghai, Tianjin, Shandong, Hebei, and Liaoning.

rising in China, that China's hitherto protected state-owned enterprises (SOEs) are inefficient, and that global competition from more successful competitors from abroad will reduce relative competitive advantage of China in several industries (see above). As we noted in Chapter 3, the hinterland provinces provide low-cost labour for the manufacture of export products in the coastal areas. China can maintain its comparative advantage in labour-intensive production and exports by relocating production to these non-coastal areas (see Chapter 5 for an elaboration of this argument in the context of competitiveness of China's textiles and clothing industry). This alternative to migration from the non-coastal areas has many advantages: less social disruption, generation of output, incomes and employment within the non-coastal areas, lower regional inequalities and the overall development of the hinterland.

During a visit to China in March–April 2001, the authors held discussions with the senior staff members of the Ministry of Foreign Trade and Economic Cooperation (MOFTEC) who believed in the feasibility of investment and production moving from the coastal to non-coastal areas especially after China's accession to WTO when competitive production for export will become even more important. The MOFTEC staff noted the tremendous increase in labour costs in such coastal areas as Fujian and Jiangsu. In the coastal areas, insurance of employees is required. Jobs can be transferred to the hinterland through the relocation of investment and production if timely delivery of products can be ensured. This may in future reduce rural-to-urban migration.

The feasibility of relocating production and investment is further enhanced by the recent reinforcement of the government policy towards the hinterland enshrined in the Western Development Strategy (WDS) and exhortation to the coastal cities to support the hinterland regions financially and technically. The application of the FG theory within China between its regions will depend, *inter alia*, on how successful the central government is in transferring resources from the coastal to the non-coastal areas. Kueh (1996: 165) gives some empirical evidence of fiscal transfers from the open coastal provinces (OCPs) to the hinterland during the 1980s. He concludes that China's strategy of seeking foreign capital may be interpreted as a means of assisting in the industrialization of the Chinese hinterland by diverting the major proportion of hard foreign currency returns earned in the coastal region towards the less inhabited interior provinces. We argue that this may also be interpreted as a strategy to maintain China's comparative-cost advantage in exports of labour-intensive activities despite rising production costs in the coastal areas.

The relocation of foreign direct investment

The following FDI index can be used to test the FG model:

$$I(k) = I_{ik}/I_k \tag{2}$$

where I_{ik} is FDI in industry i in host country k, and I_k is total FDI in host country k. The ratio will lie between 0 and 1: the higher the ratio the greater the investment comparative advantage of a country in a given industry. It is clear that coastal provinces are providing technical and financial assistance and investment to the non-coastal provinces under the government's policy of inducing cooperation between advanced and less advanced regions. However, many studies (e.g. Brun *et al.*, 2002; Fu and Balasubramanyam, 2002) note that linkages between these two regions are rather limited. The government policy of cooperation between the coastal areas and the hinterland did not work too well because of the lack of any clear-cut incentive and the underdeveloped nature of infrastructure in the hinterland. Another reason for weak linkages is that most of the export-oriented FDI is in the form of processing trade (see Chapter 8, Table 8.2) with few backward linkages with the hinterland. The Western Development Strategy and its focus on infrastructure development in the western region may help to promote these linkages.

We examine three sets of FDI indices to determine whether relocation of FDI to hinterland has taken place. These are:

- ratio of provincial FDI to total FDI in China;
- FDI provincial ratio adjusted for GDP ratio so that the FDI index weighted by GDP is: $(FDI_p/FDI_e)/(GDP_p/GDP_e)$; and
- FDI per capita in each province over time.

The uneven regional distribution of FDI in China is now well known. It is depicted in Figure 7.1 which compares the shares of FDI of the coastal and non-coastal provinces and the east, central and west regions for 1992–99. The shares of FDI have remained more or less constant for the coastal and non-coastal regions although individual provinces recorded absolute variations. For example, the shares of such coastal provinces as Fujian, Guangdong and Liaoning, which attract the bulk of FDI, declined between 1992 and 1999. The FDI shares improved only marginally in the non-coastal provinces.

There is an indication of a shift of FDI away from Guangdong province which attracted the largest share for a long time. Does this suggest that some FDI may have shifted to the non-coastal provinces? Although the evidence is not conclusive, there is some suggestion that this may well be true since FDI shares of such other coastal provinces as Fujian and Liaoning remained constant in the early and mid-1990s (Bhalla, 1998).

The regional disparities may be due to uneven rates of growth of the coastal and non-coastal provinces and the government policies which are biased in favour of the coastal regions. A disaggregation of the FDI by regions shows that in the 1990s, FDI was much lower in the non-coastal areas compared to the coastal areas. This is not surprising considering the backward infrastructure, landlocked nature, and lack of purchasing power of people in these areas.

During the 1980s the coastal and non-coastal provinces registered similar growth rates. However, in the 1990s the real per capita GDP of the non-coastal

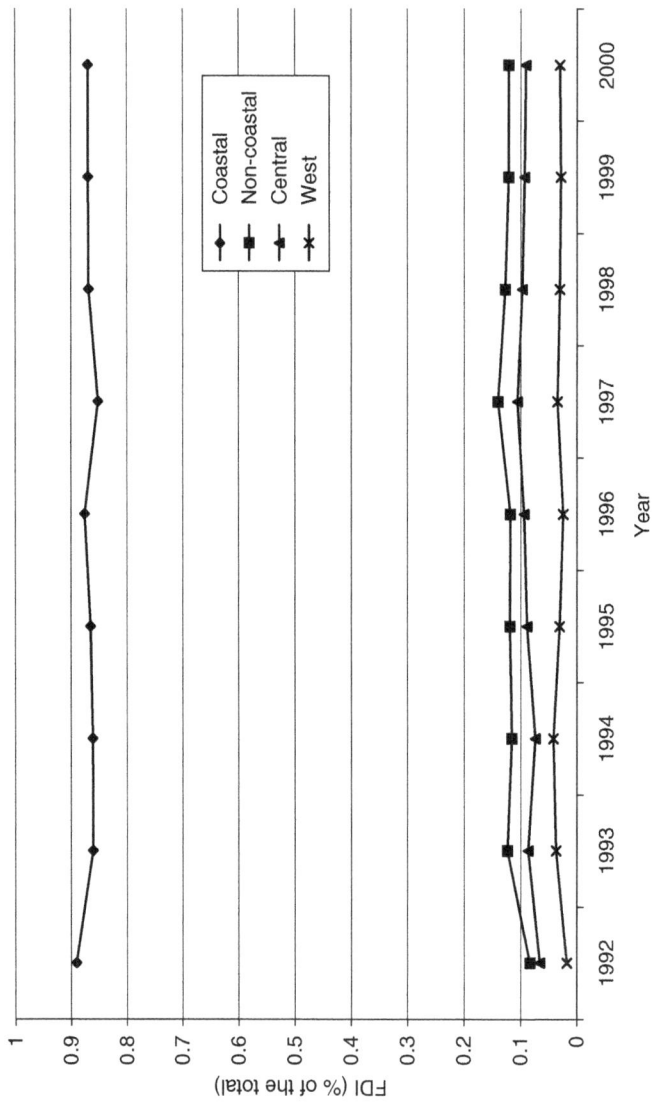

Figure 7.1 Changes in FDI by region (1992–2000)

Source: Based on data from *China Foreign Economic Statistical Yearbook.*

provinces grew much more slowly. Greater attractiveness of the coastal provinces for FDI may have been due to their faster growth as well as to their better links with overseas Chinese investors from Hong Kong and Taiwan.

FDI ratios adjusted for GDP ratios are given in Table 7.7, which shows that these ratios for many coastal provinces declined between 1995 and 2000. This is

Table 7.7 GDP adjusted FDI ratios for China's coastal and non-coastal provinces

Province	1992	1995	1998	2000
Coastal Areas				
Shanghai	1.04	1.83	1.68	1.52
Beijing	1.19	1.20	1.86	1.49
Tianjin	0.63	2.57	2.72	1.56
Guangdong	3.74	2.95	2.61	2.56
Zhejiang	0.41	0.55	0.45	0.58
Liaoning	0.80	0.79	0.97	0.96
Jiangsu	1.65	1.57	1.59	1.64
Fujian	4.35	2.91	2.21	1.92
Shandong	1.07	0.81	0.53	0.76
Hainan	6.02	4.54	2.81	1.82
Hebei	0.21	0.30	0.58	0.29
Guangxi	0.67	0.65	0.80	0.56
Non-coastal Provinces				
Heilongjiang	0.20	0.35	0.32	0.20
Xinjiang	0.13*	0.10	0.03	0.03
Jilin	0.29	0.55	0.45	0.40
Hubei	0.45	0.41	0.45	0.48
Inner Mongolia	0.03	0.09	0.13	0.16
Qinghai	0.02	0.01	0.04**	0
Shanxi	0.23	0.09	0.28	0.30
Ningxia	0.10	0.03	0.14	0.14
Hunan	0.31	0.35	0.45	0.40
Anhui	0.15	0.37	0.17	0.23
Henan	0.10	0.25	0.24	0.24
Sichuan	0.15	0.24	0.28	0.27
Yunnan	0.09	0.13	0.14	0.14
Jiangxi	0.41	0.37	0.43	0.25
Shaanxi	0.20	0.50	0.37	0.38
Gansu	0.002	0.18	0.08	0.14
Guizhou	0.14	0.14	0.09	0.05

Sources: For FDI data, *China's Foreign Economic Statistical Yearbook*; for provincial population data till 1998, *Comprehensive Statistical Data and Materials on 50 Years of New China*; for GDP data, *China Statistical Yearbook*.
* = 1993. ** = 1999.

true also of many non-coastal provinces. FDI per capita estimates are more appropriate than the total FDI in each province because they eliminate the effect of inter-provincial size differences. These estimates, given in Table 7.8, show that the FDI per capita has been rising between 1992 and 2000 in many non-

Table 7.8 FDI per capita for China's coastal and non-coastal provinces (1992–2000) ($)

Province	1992	1995	1998	2000
Coastal Areas				
Shanghai	37.3	222.3	275.8	188.8
Beijing	31.1	92.3	177.3	121.8
Tianjin	12.2	169.9	233.3	116.5
Guangdong	54.9	149.9	168.9	130.5
Zhejiang	5.4	28.8	29.6	34.5
Liaoning	12.4	35.2	53.5	48.2
Jiangsu	21.1	73.5	92.3	86.4
Fujian	46.2	127.6	129.2	98.9
Shandong	11.2	30.0	24.8	32.7
Hainan	67.4	151.3	97.8	54.7
Hebei	1.7	8.4	21.7	10.1
Guangxi	4.1	14.7	18.9	11.7
Non-coastal Provinces				
Heilongjiang	1.9	12.2	13.9	8.1
Xinjiang	3.3*	3.3	1.2	1.0
Jilin	2.7	15.6	15.7	12.3
Hubei	3.6	10.8	16.5	15.6
Inner Mongolia	0.2	2.3	3.9	4.4
Qinghai	0.14	0.3	0.5**	0.9***
Shanxi	1.8	2.1	7.7	6.8
Ningxia	0.7	0.8	3.5	3.1
Hunan	2.1	7.6	12.6	10.5
Anhui	0.8	8.0	4.5	5.3
Henan	0.6	5.2	6.6	6.1
Sichuan	1.3	6.6	7.1	6.0
Yunnan	0.6	2.4	3.5	3.0
Jiangxi	2.5	7.1	11.1	5.5
Shaanxi	1.3	9.2	8.3	8.0
Gansu	0.01	2.6	1.53	2.4
Guizhou	0.6	1.6	1.2	0.7
National Average	9.4	31.0	36.4	32.2

Sources: For FDI data, *China's Foreign Economic Statistical Yearbook*; for provincial population data till 1998, *Comprehensive Statistical Data and Materials on 50 Years of New China*; for data for 2000 *China Statistical Yearbook*.
* = 1993. ** = 1997. *** = 1999.

coastal areas, particularly Heilongjiang, Henan, Hubei, Hunan, Jiangxi and Yunnan. In two coastal provinces (namely Hainan and Shandong) FDI per capita declined between 1995 and 2000 suggesting that the capacity of some of these provinces to absorb additional FDI may have been saturated.

8   China's possible response to global competition

Our analysis suggests that the employment impact on China of accession to WTO will be mixed. The degree of domestic and foreign competition varies from industry to industry. Many Chinese industries are already globally integrated and competitive, e.g., electronics, textiles and clothing and household appliances. These industries will continue to be competitive in the global market although controversy surrounds the future of textiles and clothing. Industries enjoying protected domestic market (e.g. automobiles) will face fierce global competition once tariff reductions are implemented. Such industries will have to accelerate the process of restructuring to attain competitiveness. At least initially, they are likely to incur substantial transition costs. Inefficient firms in these industries will most likely disappear with possible adverse employment effects.

SOE ownership in industry is already declining. Following accession joint ventures between Chinese non-state firms and foreign firms will become predominant. At present joint ventures in the automobile sector are restricted to SOEs. The process of industrial restructuring in general and SOEs reforms in particular, has already been underway for a number of years. WTO accession provides a timely external pressure for furthering this process which has met with opposition within China because of the heavy social costs involved. Rising unemployment in SOEs will become worse due to the process of technological modernization and bankruptcies. Future employment growth within the manufacturing sector is likely to occur in the dynamic non-state and private domestic enterprises, joint ventures and foreign firms. State enterprises will increasingly lose their importance as providers of jobs. However, the manufacturing sector is unlikely to be a major employment-generating sector as we discussed in Chapter 5. Instead employment expansion following accession is more likely to be in the tertiary sector. Although competition for China's banking, insurance and telecommunication industries will become keener, an overall expansion of the present underdeveloped tertiary sector may generate both additional output and employment.

While there is consensus that accession will contribute to GDP growth, its contribution to employment growth is the subject of major controversy. Optimistic and pessimistic estimates of employment prospects abound depending on the assumptions one makes about growth, export prospects, demand, employment elasticity and so on. The current world economic recession does not augur well for China's future prospects of economic growth and export promotion. It is also worrying that the employment potential of Chinese industrial growth was very limited prior to accession because of the low employment elasticity of output and high degree of capital intensity (see Chapter 3).

Labour displaced from SOEs and inefficient non-state firms will need to be reabsorbed in other sectors. Private sector (whose contribution to output and employment has been underestimated in the past), and various types of services (e.g. retailing, distribution, tourism, leisure and other services) will be the major sources of additional employment following accession. There may also be some scope for employment growth in labour-intensive agricultural activities such as vegetables, fruits, and cut flowers, in which China will enjoy a comparative advantage. China does not have a resource advantage in such land-intensive staple crops as foodgrains, feed grains, sugar and oilseeds. Therefore, it will be necessary to reallocate resources within the primary sector from the land-intensive to labour-intensive crops.

However, it is not certain that a decline in SOE employment will be more than offset by an increase in employment in the private sector including foreign enterprises. While multinational investments are known to generate additional employment in host countries, such employment is often not substantial given the capital-intensive and technology-intensive nature of their operations.

Most estimates of the employment impact of accession consider only *direct* employment which is unlikely to increase significantly in view of the necessity to technologically upgrade China's industry. Much of the additional employment is likely to occur *indirectly* through inter-industry and intra-industry linkages. But substantial increase in direct and indirect employment may not occur in the short run considering the magnitude of required industrial restructuring and economic transformation involving labour retrenchment and the existence of a backlog of unemployed on the eve of China's WTO entry. Trade liberalization following accession will intensify competition for Chinese enterprises in the domestic and export markets. Many inefficient enterprises, especially SOEs may, therefore, disappear. Abolition of local-content requirement will adversely affect employment growth. This has led many to believe that China might take drastic corrective measures (regardless of its commitments under the WTO Agreement) in the event of major unemployment crisis. What could China's possible response be to this probable situation?

China's possible response

Sceptical observers believe that China will suffer serious social instability and hardship as a result of accession to the WTO. They further argue that China will be forced to respond to vested interests, growing social hardships and worsening unemployment. It is generally believed that Chinese SOEs will suffer from insolvency, firm closures and unemployment in the absence of protection in the post-accession period. An article in *The Economist* (15 September 2001: 49) draws a gloomy picture. It states: 'It is impossible to honour the kind of promises China has made without upsetting a lot of people whose livelihoods will be undermined or whose privileges will be whittled away by the country's increasing exposure to foreign competition.' Some Chinese scholars also feel that China has given away too much, that the Chinese leadership has taken a gamble in joining the WTO, and that in doing so China will allow foreign multinationals to take over China's market and turn the country into a subsidiary of foreign companies (see Han, 2000). They interpret China's WTO membership to be a sell-out and a way for the US to gain control of the Chinese economy and to speed up its Westernization. Han presents an alarming picture of China's WTO membership resulting in rising unemployment because of the closure of un-competitive enterprises, consumer choice in favour of cheaper imported goods, and the domination of the Chinese domestic market by foreign multinational enterprises. He quotes anti-globalization views in the West to support his criticism of the government's decision to join the WTO. The fact is that anti-globalization supporters in the West are concerned with job losses as a result of freer trade. This kind of job threat will come precisely from such developing countries as China.

In principle, if trade liberalization and resulting global competition hurts employment, China may respond in several ways: (a) non-compliance of the WTO accord or re-negotiation of the accord; (b) devaluation of the currency to make imports more expensive in order to discourage import competition and protect employment; and (c) shifting of production from tradeables to non-treadables. These three options are discussed below.

Non-compliance

Western scholars and policy-makers (e.g. Fewsmith, 2001a) express fears about China's commitment to honour the WTO Agreement if social and economic conditions in China become really harsh as a result of accession. After noting some positive indicators of China's preparations for the accession (namely cutbacks in SOE employment, consolidation of the automobile industry, and promotion of competition in the telecommunications sector) Fewsmith (2001a: 590) notes:

> Despite these and other preparations, there will inevitably be cases of non-compliance. Some will be because China simply cannot change its political economy rapidly enough before WTO provisions come fully into effect within five years of accession; others will be because of fights to preserve entrenched interests often with government backing (at one level or another), and still others will happen if it is believed that compliance will incur social disorder.

Will China renege on its commitment to WTO rules? To answer this question, we need to analyze what benefits China can derive from this possible action.

Unless the social or/and economic conditions unexpectedly become very bad, it is unlikely that the Chinese government will renege since the cost of breaking WTO rules can be quite high in terms of penalties, downgrading of credit rating and dwindling of FDI inflows. Also China is aware of the legal retaliation mechanisms to which other WTO members can resort in case of China's non-compliance. Furthermore, it has undertaken serious adjustment measures (shedding SOE labour and promoting competition in telecommunications) well ahead of accession. The United States government is offering legal and technical assistance to China to ensure its compliance with WTO obligations. Charlene Barshefsky, the then US Trade Representative, noted that President Clinton requested the US Congress to provide special resources from the national budget to support what will be 'the largest monitoring and enforcement effort for any agreement ever' (cited in Nolan, 2001a: 207).[1] Specific commitments and timetables for the implementation of the US–China Agreement are very detailed, which should facilitate compliance. Finally, the Protocol of China's Accession explicitly provides for periodic review of China's implementation of the Protocol provisions. Under the 'Transitional Review Mechanism' the General Council of the WTO and its subsidiary bodies are called upon to review, within one year after accession, the implementation by China of the WTO Agreement and the related provisions of the Protocol. China has agreed to supply relevant information for this purpose (Protocol of Accession, 2001, Article 18). Therefore, we do not agree with Fewsmith (2001a: 590) that 'there will inevitably be cases of non-compliance'. The Chinese government has taken serious actions well before joining the WTO as we noted above. It is difficult to envisage a situation in which China would renege on the WTO Agreement, especially after as long as 15 years of painstaking efforts to secure accession.

One way to judge whether China will honour its commitments under the WTO Agreement is to examine China's past record in honouring its obligations under bilateral and multilateral agreements. Scholars (Feinerman and Chang) at the Georgetown University Law Centre (Washington DC) have compiled a record of China's compliance with recent international obligations which shows that China's record, though rather mixed, is no worse than that of many other developing countries (cited in Rosen, 1999b). Based on the Feinerman-Chang data Rosen (1999b) makes a generally favourable assessment of China's record (see Table 8.1). Lardy (2002: 141) comes to a somewhat similar conclusion when he states: 'By and large China complies, but it frequently takes time and effort to do so...'.

China has honoured its 1992 bilateral agreement with the United States on market access. Under this agreement, China was expected to (a) reduce non-tariff barriers, and (b) make its trading system more transparent. The agreement called upon China to phase out over a five-year period, 90 per cent of quotas and licensing requirements on its imports. China lifted these restrictions according to schedule. It also made the trading system more transparent by periodically publishing trade laws and regulations (Lardy, 2002: 136–40). However, while

Table 8.1 Chinese compliance with multilateral agreements

Area of agreement	History and degree of compliance	Score
Environment	Appears to meet core obligations of each agreement. Full implementation is limited by regional inconsistency and poor technical skills.	Fair
Intellectual property	China enacted the first copyright law in 1991. Violators of the law are punished; counterfeit goods have been seized; compensation for infringement of copyright generally paid although below the international norm.	Good
Non-proliferation	China acceded to Non-proliferation Treaty in 1992. Chinese compliance is noted to be fairly comprehensive although China exported specialized nuclear equipment to the Islamic Republic of Iran, and Pakistan. As of 1999, China has discontinued nuclear exports to Iran and has promised to terminate those to Pakistan.	Fair
Private agreements	Private commercial agreements are not fully enforced. Outcomes of venture capital disputes in the past have been quite mixed.	Poor to Fair

Source: Abridged and modified version of Table 4 in Rosen (1999b).

transparency has improved, scope for further improvement still remains. Foreign business firms (especially from the US) have complained about difficulties in understanding which rules and regulations applied to their businesses. Lardy (2002) cites several other examples of partial (but not full) compliance by China of such other agreements as 1992 bilateral agreement with the US to modify Chinese legal structure to conform with WIPO requirements and the 1995 agreement on the closure of Chinese factories producing pirated goods.

Another positive indicator of China's good intentions to honour its commitments is that it implemented some of its obligations ahead of schedule, e.g. implementation of tariff reductions, and commitment to the Information Technology Agreement (ITA), and telecommunication services. But one may argue that these commitments are more indicative of China's enlightened self-interest than of its intention to honour its multilateral obligations.

Critics see the autonomy of provincial and local governments as a possible hindrance to the implementation of the WTO Agreement. They argue that local governments in the past have hindered interregional trade flows in order to protect their own industries and trade. Therefore, there is no guarantee that they will allow imports from abroad to move freely across local boundaries. There is no conclusive evidence that interregional trade has been blocked to a significant degree (see Chapter 7). While it is true that some local governments have imposed trade barriers, their power and autonomy is exaggerated.[2]

There is no doubt that joining the WTO presents a big challenge to Chinese companies as well as the government. Although China has already started the process of SOE restructuring, it may take longer to complete the task underway than the phase-in period of five to six years under the Protocol of Accession. China's major trading partners such as the US believe that the phase-in period for China should be shorter considering the large size of the Chinese economy, rapid growth of its GDP and rapid export expansion. Special safeguard provisions have also been applied to China till 2008 because of the non-market nature of its economy. In particular, this applies to textiles and clothing exports as noted above.

Some implications of WTO accession can be very severe, especially for the financial sectors. There are reasons to be alarmed about the difficulties facing Chinese companies and society. But the majority of the Chinese people still believe that China stands a good chance of success, and that it has accumulated valuable experience during the reform process over the last two decades. Therefore, it is more ready now to take up new challenges than ever before. Besides, China reserves the right to take measures to protect vulnerable sectors, which are allowed under the WTO rules.

However, there are practical hurdles such as a revision of the legal system to comply with WTO rules, which may take longer than expected. In the final analysis, compliance with the WTO Agreement is a part of a general problem of law enforcement in a developing country like China. The decentralized nature of China's administrative and regulatory system, inadequate flows of information between different levels of administration, local protection, and lack of checks and balances on law enforcement, all these factors can be stumbling blocks (OECD, 2002).[3] We believe that China would be careful not to renege on a major multilateral agreement for which it has fought so hard for so long and for which it made rather unique concessions as discussed in Chapter 1.

Devaluation

Some Western scholars and organizations believe that in future China may be forced to devalue its currency in order to discourage imports and protect employment in inefficient non-competitive industries. For example, UNCTAD (2000: IV–V) noted: 'if accession to WTO necessitates a devaluation of its currency to protect some of the country's less competitive industrial enterprises (particularly those still under state ownership) against an unexpected surge in imports, other countries of the region are likely to be affected in consequence'. Arguments are also presented in favour of devaluation for raising China's exports rather than for protecting employment. Since the Asian crisis in 1997, there has been a serious debate about the pros and cons of China devaluing its currency. Immediately after the Asian crisis, the Chinese leaders consistently sent signals that the Chinese currency would not be devalued. Despite this reassurance, however, the financial media speculated on such devaluation. Leggett (1998) stated that 'fear of a yuan devaluation has continued to roil global financial markets, and has hung heavy on confidence domestically'.[4] As the Southeast Asian governments (Indonesia, Malaysia and Thailand) failed to prevent the slide of their currencies many observers saw little chance of China being able to maintain the stability of its currency in the face of financial turmoil. Such a view was supported by the fact that China showed symptoms of a financial crisis: high ratio of non-performing loans to total loans, ineffective supervision of the banking industry, and high ratio of short-term debt to total reserves. China shared these vulnerability indicators with the affected Southeast Asian economies such as Indonesia, the Republic of Korea and Thailand. Many considered the overall health of China's banking and financial system as even shakier than that of the Republic of Korea and Thailand. For example, the ratio of non-performing loans in China is higher than the ratios in these two countries before the crisis.[5]

Many observers expected China to devalue the yuan immediately after the 1997 Asian crisis in order to remain competitive with the Southeast Asian economies. However, China's situation was quite different from that of these economies. Its short-term debt was much less acute, it had trade surplus rather than deficit, it accumulated large foreign reserves and its currency was not convertible on capital account (see below). So the conditions for currency depreciation did not exist. China did not devalue its currency not only for *political* reasons (international prestige and goodwill on the eve of WTO entry) but also *economic* ones (China's price and quality competitiveness despite robustness of the yuan due to massive capital inflows and large trade surplus). China did not consider devaluation as an option for expanding exports as this would have most likely triggered competitive devaluations by the neighbouring economies, thus prolonging the crisis.

We believe that devaluation is not a suitable option for China to protect its less competitive industrial enterprises. It is a double-edged sword; while it will make imports more expensive and thus discourage import competition, it will make exports cheaper unless of course, other countries do not set in motion competitive devaluations. But increase in the cost of imports can raise the cost of production of export goods since such production is quite import intensive. China's export volume contains over 50 per cent of processed goods involving labour-intensive assembly in which it will continue to enjoy comparative advantage in the foreseeable future. Table 8.2 shows that processed exports shot up from $12.9 billion (or 27 per cent) in 1988 to nearly $138 billion (or 55 per cent) in 2000. In the processing of goods (e.g. clothing and footwear), foreign firms provide to the Chinese TVEs and other non-state firms components and imported inputs for production. They agree to purchase the output produced with these inputs for sale abroad. Lardy (1998: 211–12) notes that 'because there is no foreign equity position for the firms engaged in the assembly activity, these exports do not get reported as joint venture exports'. He estimates that these joint venture exports combined with processing exports amount to about two-thirds of China's total exports. This is a significant proportion of China's total exports whose competitiveness would be adversely affected if China were to devalue. On the other hand, in the absence of such devaluation the lowering of tariffs would reduce the cost of imported processing materials after accession.

Table 8.2 China's processed and non-processed exports (1986–2000)

Year	Total exports	Non-processed exports		Processed exports	
	Value ($ billion)	Value ($ billion)	(%)	Value ($ billion)	(%)
1986	30.9	25.3	81.1	5.6	18.1
1987	39.4	29.6	75.2	9.0	22.8
1988	47.5	36.6	77.0	14.0	29.6
1989	52.5	31.6	60.1	19.8	37.6
1990	62.1	35.4	57.1	25.4	40.9
1991	71.8	38.12	53.0	32.4	45.0
1992	84.9	43.68	51.4	39.6	46.6
1993	91.7	43.20	47.1	44.2	48.2
1994	121.0	61.56	50.9	57.0	47.1
1995	148.8	71.37	48.0	73.7	49.5
1996	151.1	62.84	41.6	84.3	55.8
1997	182.8	77.97	42.7	99.7	54.52
1998	183.8	79.3	43.1	104.5	57.0
1999	194.9	84.0	43.1	110.9	57.0
2000	249.2	111.5	44.7	137.7	55.0

Source: Lardy (2002); Yang (2000); *China's Customs Statistics Yearbook.*

China relies heavily on the exemption of import tariffs on material inputs required for export production. This is a method for stimulating exports, which discriminates against industries relying more on domestic inputs. This partial and selective liberalization will be replaced by comprehensive liberalization after accession, which will reduce the cost of domestic inputs to exporters. This may shift production towards exports relying more on domestic rather than imported inputs (Ianchovichina *et al.*, 2000). Such a shift should have a favourable *indirect* effect on employment.

China has foreign reserves of $212.2 billion and the current account is in surplus. China's foreign debt level is maintained at a healthy level and it is mainly a medium- and long-term debt. China's accession to the WTO and the hosting of 2008 Olympic Games in Beijing will stimulate more FDI inflows into China. Although the reduction of import tariffs will encourage imports, easy access to the world market will promote exports. Vast pools of cheap labour are expected to maintain the competitiveness of Chinese labour-intensive manufactures. China's domestic inflation rate is still quite low, due to overcapacity and oversupply and strong competition in the domestic market. These factors do not put any pressure on China to devalue. On the other hand, the recent weakness of the Japanese yen (in December 2001 it fell by 7 per cent, to 132 yen to the dollar – see *The Economist*, 2002) is putting pressures on the Asian currencies including the Chinese yuan. China and the Republic of Korea have warned Japan that the Yen devaluation runs the risk of triggering competitive devaluations and causing economic instability in the rest of Southeast Asia.

Exchange rate policy

In principle devaluation can be used as an exchange-rate policy instrument to ensure export competitiveness in world markets. As an open export-oriented economy, it is important for China to sustain competitiveness and to recover quickly from any external shocks like the ones from the 1977 Asian crisis. Some authors have argued that China's devaluation in 1994 made it more competitive than the Southeast Asian economies, which largely explained China's success in the export markets. We showed in Chapter 2 that Chinese currency depreciated over the years and that its depreciation coincided with export expansion. Figures 2.1 and 2.2 in Chapter 2 show that the Chinese yuan was quite overvalued in the mid-1980s but has been depreciating gradually since then. However, although China has benefited from this devaluation making it more competitive than the Southeast Asian economies, the effect may not have been as strong as is usually assumed. The adverse effect of China's devaluation on Southeast Asian exports and its positive effect on China's exports may have been much weaker than is often claimed considering that the market exchange rate, at which the bulk of Chinese exports were already being traded, did not change (see Bhalla and Nachane, 2001).

As China is a major trading partner of the Japanese and Southeast Asian economies, continued slow growth and recession in these economies after the 1997 crisis, therefore, slowed down its export growth. However, while China's exports to the Republic of Korea and Japan fell immediately after the crisis, those to Australia, Russia, the European Union and the United States continued to grow appreciably, which suggests that its exports remained price competitive despite the depreciation and realignment of Asian currencies.

Apart from China's price competitiveness, there are several other reasons why Chinese goods were not driven out of export markets in the wake of the Asian crisis. First, the tight monetary policies and restructuring of the affected Southeast Asian economies hurt their exports. Second, since exports of the Southeast Asian economies are very import intensive, currency appreciation in these economies made imports of inputs more expensive, which did not make exports that much cheaper. Third, Southeast Asian exports faced difficulties in securing letters of credit through local banks, and in securing containers to ship their exports (see Bhalla, 2001). Finally, China avoided the adverse effects of the Asian crisis because the yuan is not convertible on capital account. While Chinese importers can buy foreign currencies for their overseas purchases, exporters have to exchange all their foreign exchange earnings into yuan. Approved foreign enterprises are allowed to purchase yuan to make direct investment in China but foreign fund managers are not allowed to buy or sell local currencies to fund investments in China's stock market. As Chinese corporations and banks are not allowed to borrow or lend capital abroad without government approval, its currency is much less vulnerable to changes in investor sentiments or speculative attacks.

In the long run, the effect of WTO entry on China's exports will depend on the strength of the income and price effects on demand for its exports. The *income* effect will be positive and stronger after WTO entry as it will enable increase in trade, investment and financial flows with the rest of the world. The *substitution* effect will involve some loss of exports as a result of a loss of market shares to competitors. It may also take the form of some erosion of special benefits to China through ties with Hong Kong (see Bergston, 2000). China's exports are unlikely to be adversely affected to the extent that China produces export goods which are not competitive with those of the other Southeast Asian economies. China's export volume contains over 50 per cent of processed goods (see Table 8.2) involving labour-intensive assembly in which it will continue to enjoy comparative advantage in the foreseeable future.

Currently China adopts a fixed exchange rate to the dollar. A general expectation is that China will be induced to float the exchange rate after its accession to the WTO. A number of alternative scenarios will include floating the currency, fixing the exchange rate within a broad band, or making the currency fully convertible. These decisions are for the future and will depend on whether China's currency is overvalued, undervalued, or more or less in equilibrium. China's official pronouncements have been in favour of full convertibility of the currency. However, the 1997 Asian crisis must have dampened China's resolve in favour of capital account convertibility (CAC).[6] It appears that China is leaning towards a two-track system under which during the first stage, the currency will be allowed to float, to a limited extent, by widening its trading band. This will allow currency fluctuations in response to supply and demand conditions in the world market. In early 2001, China was expected to widen the trading band against the dollar by 3 to 5 per cent of a daily reference rate on either side (Holland, 2000). The second track is the eventual CAC of the currency, which is fraught with greater difficulties. During the past few years, the Governor of the People's Bank of China has stated its long-term goal of full CAC without setting any definite timetable.

The government is likely to continue regulating bank deposit rates. It is also likely to keep these rates low in order to allow the banks to earn a wide margin between their borrowing and lending rates as long as the reforms and restructuring of state-owned enterprises (SOEs) and the banking sector are not fully implemented so that the problem of non-performing loans and loss making is solved.

As an alternative to full CAC at once, say within five years, a more likely scenario for China is to follow the Taiwanese system of the Qualified Foreign Institutional Investor, which allows financial markets to be opened gradually to foreigners while controlling the magnitude of flows, thus preventing massive capital outflows which involve a serious destabilizing effect.

The logic of a possible devaluation in the post-WTO phase is based on the following assumptions. First, WTO rules require China to open its domestic market to foreign goods and services. Some observers (e.g. UNCTAD noted above) believe that China's inefficient SOEs will fail to face global competition. China's balance of trade will deteriorate if exports do not expand rapidly (which is a big if in conditions of slow growth in such trading partners as Japan, the United States and the European Union). That may even lead to a deficit in trade balance (experience of such countries as Mexico on the eve of joining NAFTA suggests such a possibility). Other things being equal, this may call for a depreciation of the exchange rate, or devaluation.[7] However, China continues to enjoy a large current account surplus which reduces the need for devaluation.

Production shift from tradeables to non-tradeables

China has a large and expanding domestic market to fall back on when world export markets shrink. It is quite possible that the failure to expand exports rapidly will induce the Chinese policy-makers to shift production from tradeables to non-tradeables and to domestic market. We noted in Chapter 5 that there has been a rapid expansion of the domestic market for automobiles and household appliances. Even in the case of textiles and clothing, the domestic market is expanding for such higher-value-added goods as designer clothes and brand names with rising per capita incomes. Massive government expenditure can boost domestic demand even if the Chinese economy slows down, which is likely during a global economic slowdown. Indeed, during the past few years China has maintained its high growth rate at around 7 per cent precisely through such measures.

For a large economy such as China's, the export sector is not as important as for smaller, more open economies. Large economies are likely to have lower trade ratios than small ones for several reasons: large size of domestic market enabling economies of scale, less dependence on imports of minerals and raw materials which are locally available, and natural protection to domestic producers against foreign competition because of relatively higher transport costs (Perkins and Syrquin, 1989).

China's export-to-GDP ratio is exaggerated for several reasons. First, China's exchange rate based GDP relative to exports could be underestimated because of the divergence of domestic prices from world prices. Therefore, it would be more realistic to use the purchasing power parity measure of GDP rather than that based on the official rate of exchange. This measure will raise the level of GDP thus bringing down the ratios. Maddison's estimates based on GDP in terms of purchasing power parity show that Chinese exports rose from 1.7 per cent of GDP in 1978 to 4.3 per cent in 1995. These estimates are well below the official Chinese and World Bank estimates (see Maddison, 1998). Estimating export-GDP ratios for Chinese provinces for 1994, Bramall (2000) arrives at a Chinese share of exports in GDP at 4.9 per cent. His provincial estimates of export shares show that Guangdong is the only province with over 20 per cent share; other coastal and non-coastal provinces have export shares ranging from 6 to 9 per cent in Beijing, Fujian, Shanghai and Tianjin, and 0.9 per cent to

4.4 per cent in other provinces. In per capita terms also China's exports look much less impressive than those of Hong Kong, the Republic of Korea, Singapore, Taiwan and Thailand. In 2000, China's per capita exports were $197 compared to $1,114 for Thailand, $3,665 for the Republic of Korea, and $6,744 for Taiwan, $28,837 for Hong Kong and $34.468 for Singapore (UNCTAD, 2001; ADB, 2002).[8]

As we discussed above, a very high proportion of China's exports are in the form of processed goods (see Table 8.2); if we use the value-added export figure, the export contribution to China's GDP would be very different. Also, China's prices of non-traded goods (particularly services) relative to those of tradeables are artificially low. Therefore, the contribution of the service sector to total GDP is relatively smaller than it would otherwise be. Although price liberalization has taken place in recent years it has not gone far enough. While divergence of Chinese and world prices has narrowed, it has not been eliminated.

Notes

1 The road to WTO membership

1 The former Chinese leaders, Jiang Zemin and Zhu Rongji, respectively, President of PRC and Premier, asked Cao Jianming (former President of East China Political and Legal College, Shanghai) to undertake a cost-benefit analysis of China's entry to the WTO before giving the green light to the negotiators. It is reported that Cao strongly advocated China's bid for WTO membership arguing that the net benefits would outweigh the costs (cited in Lai, 2001).

2 In 1986, this bill was vetoed by the President of the United States.

3 The Ministry of Foreign Trade and Economic Cooperation (MOFTEC) grants trading rights to enterprises which meet certain criteria. Trade corporations (domestic and foreign) are allowed to trade in most products except a few which are handled only by what are called 'designated' trading corporations.

4 Compared to 137 cases for China during 1995–99, those for two other large-sized countries, namely, India and Brazil, were 38 and 41 respectively (Finger *et al.*, 2000). Chinese estimates show that by the end of 1998, 23 countries had filed 327 anti-dumping cases against China (Lai, 2001). Lai quotes these estimates from a paper by Cao Jianming prepared for the Chinese government entitled '*Reasons for China's Admission to the WTO*' published in *Huaxia Zhoubao* (Huaxia Weekly), 8 January 2000.

5 In 1997, Australia decided to stop considering China as a non-market economy for the purposes of determining dumping margins. This decision was taken recognizing that over 90 per cent of commodity prices in China are now market determined (see Yang, 1999: 528).

6 This product–specific safeguard clause is different from the WTO Agreement on Safeguards under which it is much more difficult to introduce restrictions on imports. The WTO Agreement on Safeguards requires an aggrieved member to prove that serious injury to the domestic industry would occur as a result of excessive imports from a country, whereas product–specific safeguards applied against China refer to a milder term of 'market disruption'. For a discussion of the differences between WTO Safeguard Mechanism and the product–specific safeguards, see Lardy (2002: 81–86).

2 Trade liberalization, competition and employment

1 The Lydall study attempted to estimate the employment effects of liberalization by the developed countries of imports from developing countries of twelve selected groups of manufactured goods. It concluded that primary (initial and linkage) effects depended on the stage of development of a country, measured by GDP per capita. The total primary effect of trade expansion will lead to an increase in employment of more than two workers in developing countries with a GDP of $500 per capita (at 1963

prices) and more than 4.6 workers in countries with a GDP per capita of $100. The multiplier effect as a result of increased foreign exchange earnings was estimated to raise employment between two and fives times the primary increases. Although these are rough orders of magnitude, they underline the importance of secondary effects. The study concluded that 'very great gains in employment in developing countries could follow from a greater degree of liberalisation' (p. 16).

2 Zhang *et al.* (1998) state that 'protectionism often failed because efficiency gains from exchange significantly exceeded the net benefits of erecting trade barriers'. Barriers imposed by local governments included sales quota for local stores to sell locally made goods, prohibition of non-local manufacturers and traders from opening shops, and forcing local enterprises to purchase goods and inputs from local producers and suppliers. Added to these, transport bottlenecks in China create barriers across regions.

3 The IMD has also developed a competitiveness index, which is much less rigorous than the WEF index. It is not discussed here. For a discussion of this index, see IMD (2000), and for a brief assessment, Lall (2001b).

4 The CCI is made up of 64 variables of which 49 represent business environment and 15 company operations and strategy.

5 In China inflation did indeed occur during the reform period especially in 1988–89. Low interest rate policy and relaxation of credit control, *inter alia*, were responsible for inflationary pressures. However, with market liberalization and price stabilization inflation rate declined in the 1990s. Price reforms should contribute to greater allocative efficiency and low inflation in the long run when industrial structure becomes more competitive.

3 The impact of accession on employment

1 For a review of other unofficial estimates of urban unemployment, see Solinger (2001).

2 Referring to the early 1990s, Solinger (1999) cites figures of rural migrants between 50 and 60 million.

3 A national survey, which collected twenty-year employment histories from 1,199 households, shows that urban employment of rural migrants has continued well into the late 1990s despite slackening of growth in labour demand (cited in Rawski, 2002: 9).

4 Earlier official estimates show that by the end of 1999 cumulative figure of laid-off workers was nearly 25 million, or nearly 21 per cent of 'staff and workers' at risk and a little over 13 per cent of the urban labour force. Prior to 1998 only annual net lay-offs were reported in official statistics (see Appleton *et al.*, 2002).

5 Empirical estimates of total factor productivity in SOEs, collectives and TVEs vary a great deal as they are sensitive to the price deflators used for inputs and outputs. For a review of this literature, see Huang *et al.* (1999).

6 For a recent analysis of the determinants and consequences of SOE lay-offs, see Appleton *et al.* (2002).

7 Rawski (1999) divides Chinese unemployment into three categories: (a) cyclical unemployment depending on export boom or decline in foreign sales, (b) transition unemployment which is unrelated to labour demand and supply conditions, and (c) structural unemployment resulting from heavy industry built in the northeast under the plan system.

8 The Chinese policy-makers believe that a major hurdle in the re-employment of *xiagang* workers is their 'aristocratic mentality' which prevents them from accepting jobs that are available in the non-state sector (see Gu, 1999; Yang, 1998).

9 Fan *et al.* (1998: 37) note that in '1993 the bonus payment accounted for more than 22 per cent of the total wage bill in coal mining and oil extraction even though the two sectors have suffered consistent losses'. If losses are attributed to such exogenous

factors as price and foreign exchange controls, SOEs (the agent) can successfully negotiate hidden or open financial support with the principal (their supervisory government bodies).

10 We are grateful to Professor John Gilbert of the Economics Department, Utah State University, for clarifying this point.

11 The Xu-Chang model divides each Chinese sector into a 'planned' segment and a 'market' segment with separate prices to reflect the mixed and transitional nature of the Chinese economy. Inputs in each sector include skilled and unskilled labour, capital and intermediate products (see Xu and Chang, 2000).

12 For example, forecasts made by Zhang *et al.* (1998) of the employment impact of unilateral tariff reductions used the tariff rate that prevailed in 1993 (see Lardy, 2002).

13 Employment estimates for these sectors are as follows: textiles, 2,825 thousand; clothing, 2,610 thousand; food processing 168 thousand; construction 928 thousand; and service sector 2,664 thousand (*Economic Daily*, 11 July 2001).

14 Cited in *China Daily*, 7 February, 2002.

15 Rural households are estimated to suffer income losses of about 1.5 per cent whereas income of urban households is estimated to increase by 4 to 5 per cent.

4 Agriculture

1 China's current urbanization rate is quite low – 31 per cent, which is 15 percentage points lower than the world average. It is estimated that the urbanization rate will rise to 60 per cent in two decades, or an annual rate of increase of 1.5 per cent. China is planning to set up twenty new cities annually during the next twenty years, which will help improve the urbanization of rural areas. The number of rural residents working in cities increased by 7.8 million in the year 2000.

2 According to the Tenth Five-Year Plan (2001–2005) township enterprises will provide 10 million jobs for surplus rural labour during the plan period. By 2005 the number of employees in township enterprises is expected to reach 135 million (Ministry of Agriculture communiqué, 21 August 2001).

3 The original figures in Chinese currency were converted into US dollars at the rate of $1 = 8.27 yuan.

4 A recent study by Morgan Stanley shows that total factor productivity in China's agricultural sector has been growing at about 4 per cent per annum, that is, at about the same rate as the non-rural sector, suggesting a new surge in rural development in the coming years.

5 The Ministry of Agriculture of China has prepared six plans for agricultural development, covering production of quality grain, animal husbandry, horticulture, processing of farm produce, fisheries and state farms. The aim of these plans is to boost agricultural industries so as to improve the competitiveness of China's agriculture in the global market.

5 Industry

1 In 1999 China's industrial sector absorbed 23 per cent of total employment compared to about 50 per cent in agriculture and 27 per cent in services (OECD, 2002: 128).

2 Despite China's rapid industrial growth for over two decades none of China's industrial enterprises has entered Morgan Stanley's list of world's top 250 'competitive edge' companies. There are only five Chinese companies listed in the Fortune 500 (see Nolan, 2001a, 2002).

3 The most common form of quantitative restrictions is the bilaterally negotiated quota (e.g. between China and the US), which is determined through negotiations of the total amount of textile products and categories to be traded. This quota is expected to be revised in the coming years.

4 Before the mid-1970s, China's textile industry served mainly the domestic market. The annual total export of textiles then was $1 billion. Since the normalization of the US–China relationship in 1979, China's export of textile products and clothing increased very significantly and exports to the US market shot up to $550 million in 1979, $1.04 billion in 1980, $1.83 billion in 1981 and $2.22 billion in 1982. This dramatic increase in exports caused concerns in the US, which led to the imposition of quota restrictions on textile and clothing imports from China. The first agreement on imports of textile products from China was signed in September 1980. Under the agreement the US applied quota restrictions on eight textile products and put a ceiling on annual growth rates of the quotas at 5–6 per cent. The product volume subject to quota restriction was 14 per cent in 1981 and 33 per cent in 1982.

5 Yang and Zhong (1998: 19) note that a special safeguard provision expected to be included in the protocol of China's accession to the WTO (which was eventually included) 'may prove to be more discouraging than the MFA in the past'. This is because under the MFA restrictions were imposed on all major exporters whereas the safeguard provision singles out China

6 With the exception of Qinghai and Tibet, the two high-altitude provinces, all other provinces have firms producing automobiles. In 1998, there were 115 automobile firms in China with an average output volume of only 14,000 vehicles per firm, which is extremely small compared to Japan, the Republic of Korea and Brazil. High protection rates in the 1980s and 1990s encouraged local governments to go into automobile production, which was protected through a regional import substitution strategy (see Huang, 2003).

7 In March 1989, the State Council issued industry policy guidelines, in which the automobile industry was listed as the government's priority for investment. The government supported six automobile manufacturing bases, including the First Automobile Factory, Second Automobile Factory, and auto manufacturers in Shanghai, Tianjin, Beijing and Guangzhou.

8 In 1987, only 2 per cent of the value of the Volkswagen Santana was accounted for by such local parts as tyres, radios and antennae, whereas in 1997 nearly 93 per cent of all components were produced in China (Thun, 2001).

9 In the early stages of automobile assembly (as in China), local-content requirements are confined to simple mechanical components (e.g. starters, batteries, radiators and seats). However, the domestic market for complicated and skill-intensive parts and components grows more rapidly in later stages of growth of the industry. In Mexico and the Republic of Korea (which are more advanced producers of automobiles than China) thew local content is known to exceed 80 per cent (Abrenica, 1998).

10 In China uncertainties about regular supplies of high-quality components provided a strong incentives for automotive corporations in favour of backward integration. SAIG used to obtain these components from Guizhou prior to the setting up of its local base for components supply. High-quality requirements could not explain the decision for backward integration because Volkswagen had imposed high technical standards which Guizhou suppliers had successfully met. For a detailed discussion of the motivations for setting up a local components base in the automotive industry, see Huang (2003).

11 Despite this disadvantage, however, TNCs still accounted for 28 per cent of the market shares for refrigerators in China, which is quite significant (see Huang, 2003).

12 OEM is contracted production or manufacturing of goods under which the product does not bear the name of the manufacturer. Instead it has brand names attractive to buyers.

13 Internet paper, (www.21CN.com).

6 Services

1 The city of Shanghai had eight-four foreign joint ventures with Chinese enterprises and with total annual sales in Shanghai of 10 billion yuan, representing about 8 per cent of total sales (OECD, 2002: 306).
2 For a detailed discussion of the Chinese banking industry and its problems, see Bhalla (2001), Lardy (1998) and Wong (2001).
3 At the end of 1999, 177 foreign banking institutions operated in 23 Chinese cities and Hainan province. Of this total, 25 foreign banks (19 in Shanghai and 6 in Shenzhen) were allowed to do business in local currency (see Wong, 2001).
4 There is no agreement on the precise magnitude of bad loans in China. OECD (2002) cites a figure of over 50 per cent of all bank loans by state-owned banks in China. The Chinese official estimates are much lower than this figure. It is estimated that 'problem loans' form about 20 to 25 per cent of all loans a third of which (about 8 to 9 per cent) are non-performing loans of the commercial banks (see Wong, 2001).
5 For a detailed discussion of China's telecom industry, see DeWoskin (2001), Lu (2000), Nolan (2001a), and Wong and Wong (2003).
6 This section is based on the Protocol of Accession of China to the WTO, Annex 9, Lardy (2002) and OECD (2002).
7 Rawski and Mead (1998) show that standard figures of farm employment used by Chinese and non-Chinese scholars are highly exaggerated. Their calculations show that the margin of error might be as high as 100 million of what they call 'phantom' farmers. These farmers have moved to such non-farming activities as construction, and trade and transport where they remain unrecorded. They defend their argument by noting the Rural Survey Team of China's State Statistics Bureau (SSB) estimate of 8.6 per cent of farm workers shifting to non-farm occupations in 1993 and only 1.7 per cent returning to farming, which indicates a net outflow from farming of nearly 7 per cent. They note also that labour input per mu of cultivated or sown area declined significantly during the 1980s.
8 Wang (1999) notes that many of the assumptions on which forecasts are based are oversimplified and that the forecasts are not realistic predictions.
9 Pyramid Research forecasts growth of China's telecommunications infrastructure as follows: increase of main business lines from 38 million in 2000 to 74 million in 2004; of residential lines from 93 million to nearly 149 million; and of internet hosts from 55 thousand to 0.5 million during the same period (cited in DeWoskin, 2001).

7 China and the 'flying-geese' (FG) theory

1 The Akamatsu model is designed to explain the process of 'catch-up' industrialization in late-comer developing economies. He presents two patterns of this process. The first, the basic pattern, refers to a single industry growing through three successive stages of import substitution, domestic production and export. The second, variant pattern, refers to a diversification of industries and their transformation from simple consumer goods to capital goods and from simple to more sophisticated products.
2 Life cycle of a product or an industry goes through a number of stages: (a) introduction of a new product via imports, (b) substitution of domestic products for imports when domestic demand grows, (c) exports of products when domestic demand slackens, (d) slowdown of production in the face of growing competition and maturing of industry or products, and (e) relocation of industry outside the country when wages and other costs of production become very high and the country loses its comparative advantage in the product or industry. There is increasing pressure at this stage to recycle comparative advantage by investing in the industry in a late-comer developing country with lower production costs (Dowling and Cheang, 2000).

3 Ozawa (2001) notes that the Japanese FDI in the Southeast Asian region may have been quite excessive, driven by the rising production costs caused by its overvalued currency. The Japanese industry kept maintaining its industrial capacity while expanding it abroad.

4 Shinohara (1996) cites a questionnaire survey conducted by the Japan Export-Import Bank on the worldwide FDI of Japanese corporations. It showed that in 1995 the share of FDI of 342 Japanese corporations in machinery industry (including transport equipment and precision instruments) was over 57 per cent of the total.

5 Naughton (2000) notes that cross-border trade data are not collected even in such developed countries as the United States.

6 In 1998 more than 600 state-owned (SOE) loss-making factories were closed. This represented one-fifth of the total number of SOEs in textiles. By 1999, 9.4 million cotton spindles were eliminated, and by the end of 2000, 1.4 million additional textile workers were laid off (Lardy, 2002: 23). This restructuring and rationalization of the textile industry was designed to improve its efficiency and competitiveness since the industry was in the red in the 1990s.

8 China's possible response to global competition

1 In April 2000 the US Administration asked Congress to authorize $22 million as additional resources for China's trade compliance, to be used by the Departments of Agriculture, Commerce and State, and the Office of the US Trade Representative (Nolan, 2001a: 207).

2 Lardy (2002: 149) counters this argument by noting that in China in the 1990s several local governments allowed foreign retailers (e.g. Carrefour of France) to operate in their territories even though national regulations on foreign participation in retailing was not very liberal.

3 Reform of the judicial system and legislation may be major bottlenecks to law enforcement in general and the WTO Agreement in particular. The judicial review process continues to remain weak in China, particularly the review of administrative actions related to trade matters. OECD (2002: 378) notes: 'Application and enforcement of China's laws and other regulations have lagged behind the establishment of national policy reforms, imposing unnecessary costs and uncertainties on the market...'. Poor and unpredictable enforcement results from such structural factors as multiple layers of administration, protectionism by local authorities, inadequate checks and balances and absence of tenure for judges who are usually appointed on political and party considerations rather than on merit.

4 Since late 1997, the black market rate of exchange in China hovered around 8.7 yuan to the US dollar, which implied a 6 per cent devaluation. In Taishan (Guangdong province) the exchange rate even rose to 11 yuan to the dollar (Chang, 1998).

5 For an analysis of the Asian financial crisis and the stability of the Chinese currency in its wake, see Bergston (2000), Bhalla and Nachane (2001) and Chang (1998).

6 Although there is no capital account convertibility in China, some loopholes exist which allow capital flight out of the country. The B shares of stocks in the Shanghai and Shenzhen stock markets are in theory reserved only for foreign investors. However, in practice many Chinese citizens also own these stocks because of the loopholes and preferred customers of the Securities Companies. In principle, foreign investors can sell the stocks and repatriate proceeds out of China. However, since their ownership of B shares form only a small proportion of the total amount of shares, such sales cannot significantly affect the exchange rate (Chang, 1998).

7 In the long run, when the Chinese economy becomes more open, the pressures to devalue the yuan may grow. One important factor that may put such pressures on the Chinese currency is the position of the Hong Kong dollar. Unlike China, Hong Kong is a very open economy and its currency is exposed to external shocks. The

appreciation of the Hong Kong dollar against the US dollar since 1990 (because of a much higher inflation rate than in the US) led to a loss of its competitiveness and deterioration of its trade balance. Pressure to devalue the Hong Kong dollar to raise competitiveness may lead to similar pressures on the Chinese currency (Chang, 1998).

8 These ratios are based on value of exports taken from UNCTAD (2001) and population data from the ADB (2002).

Bibliography

Abbott, Frederick M. (1998) (ed.) *China in the World Trading System*, The Hague: Kluwer Law International.

Abrenica, Joy V. (1998) 'The Asian Automotive Industry: Assessing the Roles of State and Market in the Age of Global Competition', *Asian-Pacific Economic Literature*, 12, 1.

Ahuja, V. and Filmer, D. (1995) 'Educational Attainment in Developing Countries: New Estimates and Projections Disaggregated By Gender', *World Bank Policy Research Working Paper* 1489, Washington DC: World Bank.

Akamatsu, K. (1935) 'Wagakuni yomo kogyohin no susei' (Trend of Japan's Wooden Products industry), *Shogyo Keizai Ronso*, 13.

Akamatsu, K. (1962) 'Historical Pattern of Unbalanced Growth in Developing Countries' *Developing Economies*, 1.

Almanac of China's Textile Industry, Beijing: Textile Press of China.

Almstedt, K.W. and Norton, P.M. (2000) 'China's Antidumping Laws and the WTO Antidumping Agreement', *Journal of World Trade*, December.

Anderson, Kym (1997) 'On the Complexity of China's WTO Accession', *World Economy*, September.

Anderson, K., Dimaranan, B., Hertel, T. and Martin, W. (1997a) 'Asia Pacific Food Markets and Trade in 2005: A Global Economy-wide Perspective', *Australian Journal of Agricultural and Resource Economics*, 41.

—— (1997b) 'Economic Growth and Policy Reform in the APEC Region: Trade and Welfare Implications By 2005', *Asia-Pacific Economic Review*, 3, 1, April.

Anderson, K., Huang, J. and Ianchovichina, E. (2002) *Impact of China's WTO Accession on Rural–Urban Income Inequality*, paper for the 5th Conference on Global Economic Analysis, Taipei (Taiwan), 5–7 June.

Appleton, S., Knight, J., Song, L. and Xia, Q. (2002) 'Labor Retrenchment in China: Determinants and Consequences', *China Economic Review*, 13, 2 and 3.

Asian Development Bank (ADB) (2002) *Key Indicators 2002 – Population and Human Resources Trends and Challenges*, Manila: ADB.

Bach, C.F., Martin, W. and Stevens, J.A. (1996) 'China and the WTO: Tariff Offers, Exemptions and Welfare Implications', *Weltwertschaftliches Archiv*, 132, 3.

Balassa, Bela (1963) 'An Empirical Demonstration of Classical Comparative Cost Theory', *Review of Economics and Statistics*, August.

Balassa, Bela (1965) 'Trade Liberalisation and Revealed Comparative Advantage', *Manchester School*, May.

Balassa, Bela (1989) *Comparative Advantage, Trade Policy, and Economic Development*, London: Harvester Wheatsheaf.

Batisse, C. (2002) 'Dynamic Externalities and Local Growth: A Panel Data Analysis Applied to Chinese Provinces', *China Economic Review*, 13, 2–3.

Bergston, C.F. (2000) 'Globalization and Sino-American Economic Relations', *Working Paper Series* no. 100 (3/00) Centre for Asian Pacific Studies (CAPS), Hong Kong: Lingnan University, May.

Bernard, M. and Ravenhill, J. (1995) 'Beyond Product Cycles and Flying-Geese Regionalization, Hierarchy, and the Industrialization of East Asia', *World Politics*, 47.

Bhalla, A.S. (1998) 'Sino-Indian Liberalization: The Role of Trade and Foreign Investment', *Economics of Planning*, 31, 2–3.

—— (2001) *Market or Government Failures? An Asian Perspective*, London: Palgrave.

Bhalla, A.S. and Nachane, D.M. (2001) 'The Economic Impact of the Asian Crisis on India and China', in Chang, H-J., Palma, G. and Whittaker, D.H. (eds) *Financial Liberalization and the Asian Crisis*, London: Palgrave.

Bhattasali, D. and Kawai, M. (2001) *Implications of China's Accession to the World Trade Organization*, Paper presented at DIJ-FRI International Conference, 'Japan and China-Cooperation, Competition and Conflict', sponsored by the German Institute for Japan Studies and the Fijitsu Research Institute, Tokyo, 18–19 October.

Blumenthal, D.M. (1999) 'Applying GATT to Marketizing Economies: The Dilemma of WTO Accession to Reform China's State-Owned Enterprises (SOEs)', *Journal of International Economic Law*, 2, 1, March.

Bodmer, F. (2002) 'The Effect of Reforms on Employment Flexibility in Chinese SOEs, 1980–94', *Economics of Transition*, 10, 3.

Boltho, A. (1996) 'The Assessment: International Competitiveness', *Oxford Review of Economic Policy*, 12, 3.

Bramall, C. (2000) *Sources of Chinese Economic Growth, 1978–1996*, Oxford: Oxford University Press.

Broadman, H.G. (2000) *'China's Membership in the WTO and Enterprise Reform: The Challenges for Accession and Beyond'*, Washington DC: World Bank, May (mimeo).

—— (2001) 'The Business(es) of the Chinese State', *World Economy*, 24, 7 July.

Broadman, H.G. and Sun, X. (1997) 'The Distribution of Foreign Direct Investment in China', *World Economy*, 20, 3, May.

Brooks, D.H. and Queisser, M. (1999) *Financial Liberalization in Asia: Analysis and Prospects*, Paris and Manila: OECD Development Centre and the Asian Development Bank.

Brun, J.F., Combes, J.L. and Renard, M.F. (2002) 'Are There Spillover Effects Between Coastal and Non-coastal Regions?', *China Economic Review*, 13, 2–3.

Cai, Fang, Zhang, Che Wei and Dou, Yang (eds) (2002) *Employment in Rural and Urban China: Issues and Options*, Beijing: Social Sciences Documentation Publishing House.

Cai, K.G. (1999) 'Outward FDI: A Novel Dimension of China's Integration into the Regional and Global Economy', *China Quarterly*, 160, December.

Cai, Wenguo, Smith, Murray, G. and Xu Xianquan (1996) *China and the World Trade Organization: Requirements, Realities, and Resolution*, Ottawa: Centre for Trade Policy and Law.

Carter, C.A. (2001) 'China's Trade Integration and Impacts on Factor Markets', in *OECD China's Agriculture in the International Trading System*, Paris: OECD.

Carter, C. and Huang, J. (1998a) *'China's Agricultural Trade: Patterns and Prospects'*, University of California-Davis, processed.

Carter, C., Chen, J. and Rozelle, S. (1998b) *'China's State Trading in Grains: An Institutional Overview'*, University of California-Davis, processed.

Cauley, J. and Sandler, T. (2001) 'Agency Cost and the Crisis of China's SOEs', *China Economic Review*, 12, 4.

Caves, R.E., Frankel, J.A. and Jones, R.W. (1993) *World Trade and Payments: An Introduction*, 6th edition, New York: HarperCollins.

Chang, G.H. (1998) 'The Chinese Economy in the Asian Financial Crisis: The Prospect of Stability of RMB', *Harvard International Institute of Development (HIID) Development Discussion Paper* no. 669, Cambridge, MA, December.

Chen, Chien-Hsun (1996) 'Regional Determinants of FDI', *Journal of Economic Studies*, 23, 2.

Chen, Edward K.Y. (1992) 'Technology Development and Industrial Specialisation in the Asian Pacific Region', in Gupta, S.P. and Tambunlertchai, S. (eds) *The Asian Pacific Economies: A Challenge to South Asia*, Delhi: Macmillan.

Chen, G. *et al.* (1999) *Zhongguo dazhong chengshi laodongli shichang gongzi jiawei* (Market Wages of Labour in China's Large and Medium Cities), Beijing: Laodong he shehui baozhang chubanshe.

Chen, Yu and Démurger S. (2002) 'Croissance de la productivité dans l'industrie manufacturière chinoise: une evaluation du rôle de l'investissement direct étranger' *Economie Internationale*, 92.

Chen, Yuming (2000) *China Joining WTO – Analysis of Chinese Industries in the Post WTO Period*, Beijing: Economic Daily Publishing House.

China, Development Research Centre of State Council (DRC) (1998) *The Global and Domestic Impact of China Joining the World Trade Organization* (Washington: Center for China Studies and Development Research Centre, the State Council of People's Republic of China), December.

China, Ministry of Labour and Social Security (MLSS) (Department of Training and Employment) and Rural Social and Economic Survey Team of the National Bureau of Statistics (NBS) (1999) *The Situation of Rural Workers' Employment and Migration in China, 1997–98*, Beijing: MLSS.

China, State Economic and Trade Commission (SETC) (2000) *Assessment of China's Industry after the WTO Accession* (mimeo) (internal report).

Choi, E.K. (2000) *The Asian Crisis: Growth that Immiserizes the South and Benefits the North*, paper presented at the International Conference on the Asian Crisis II, University of Washington, Seattle, 4–5 January.

Chow, P.C.Y. and Kellman, M.H. (1993) *Trade: The Engine of Growth in East Asia*, New York: Oxford University Press.

Christiansen, Flemming (2002), 'Will WTO Accession Threaten China's Social Stability?' in Holbig, H. and Ash, R. (eds) *China's Accession to the World Trade Organization*, London: RoutledgeCurzon.

Cline, W.R. (1984) *Exports of Manufactures from Developing Countries: Performance and Prospects for Market Access*, Washington DC: Brookings.

Cooper, Caroline G. (2000) *'The Impact of China's Accession to the World Trade Organization: Implications for Korea and Japan'*, Seoul: Korea Economic Institute, (mimeo).

Cosgrove-Sacks, C. (1999) *The European Union and Developing Countries: The Challenges of Globalization*, London: Macmillan.

Coughlin, C.C. and Segev, E. (2000) 'FDI in China: A Spatial Econometric Study', *World Economy*, 23, 1, January.

Crook, F. (2001) 'Trade Integration and Impacts on Natural Resources', in OECD, *China's Agriculture in the International Trading System*, Paris: OECD.

Cushman, D.O. (1987) 'The Effects of Real Wages and Real Productivity on Foreign Direct Investment', *Southern Economic Journal*, 54, July.

Deardorff, A.V. (1984) 'Testing Trade Theories and Predicting Trade Flows', in Jones, R.W. and Kenen, P.B. (eds) *Handbook of International Economics*, vol. 1, Amsterdam: North-Holland.

DeWoskin, K.J. (2001) 'The WTO and the Telecommunications Sector in China', *China Quarterly*, 167, September.

Di, Yinqing and Zheng Gang (2000) 'What Does China's Joining the WTO Actually Imply with Regard to China's Long-term Interests?', *The Chinese Economy*, 33, 2, March–April.

Dowling, M. and Cheang, T.C. (2000) 'Shifting Comparative Advantage in Asia: New Tests of the "Flying Geese" Model', *Journal of Asian Economics*, 11, 4, Winter.

Drysdale, P., and Song, L. (2000) (eds) *China's Entry to the WTO: Strategic Issues and Quantitative Assessments*, London: Routledge.

The Economist London (1997) 'China and the Chaebol', 20 December.

The Economist London (1999) 'China and the WTO', 20 November.

The Economist London (2001) 'China and the WTO: Ready for the Competition?', 15 September.

The Economist London (2002) 'The Yen on the Slide', 5 January.

European Union (EU) (2000) *The Sino-EU Agreement on China's Accession to the WTO: Results of the Bilateral Negotiations* (http://europa.eu.int/comm/trade/bilateral/china/wro.htm).

Fan, G. and Woo, W.T. (1996) 'State Enterprise Reform as a Source of Macroeconomic Stability', *Asian Economic Journal*, 10, 3.

Fan, G., Lunati, M.R. and O'Connor, D. (1998) 'Labour Market Aspects of State Enterprise Reform in China', *OECD Development Centre Technical Paper, no. 141*, October.

Fan, Ming-tai and Zheng Yu-xin (2000) *'China's Trade Liberalization for WTO Accession and Its Effects on China – A Computable General Equilibrium Analysis'*, paper presented at the Third Annual Conference on Global Economic Analysis, Monash University, 28–30 June.

Fan, Yang (2000) *Joining WTO and the Chinese Industry*, Institute of Economic Research of Chinese Social Sciences, Beijing.

Fan, Zhai and Li, Shantong (2000) *'The Implications of Accession to WTO on China's Economy'*, paper presented at the Third Annual Conference on Global Economic Analysis, Monash University, 28–30 June.

Far Eastern Economic Review Hong Kong (2000) 'WTO Cost: 40 Million Jobs', 5 October.

Fernald, J., Edison, H. and Loungani, P. (1999) 'Was China the First Domino? Assessing Links Between China and Other Asian Economies', *Journal of International Money and Finance*, 18, 4, August.

Fewsmith, J. (2001a) 'The Political and Social Implications of China's Accession to the WTO', *China Quarterly*, 167, September.

—— (2001b) 'The Political Implications of WTO Agreement on Agriculture', in OECD, *China's Agriculture in the International Trading System*, Paris: OECD.

Finger, J.M., Ng, F. and Sonam, W. (2000) 'Anti-dumping as Safeguard Policy', paper presented to the Conference on US-Japan Trade Relations, Department of Economics, University of Michigan, Ann Arbor, 5–6 October.

Fourin (1996) *1996–97 Asian Automotive Industry* Nagoya City: Fourin, Inc.

Freeman, R.B. (1995) 'Are Your Wages Set in Beijing?', *Journal of Economic Perspectives*, 9, 3.

Fu, X. and Balasubramanyam, V.N. (2002) 'Trade, FDI, Limited Linkages and Regional Income Inequality in China', paper presented to the 13th Annual Conference of the Chinese Economic Association of the UK, Middlesex University Business School, Hendon, 25–26 March.

Fuentes, N.A.F., Alegria, T. Brannon, J.T., James D.D. and Lucker, G.W. (1993) 'Local Sourcing and Indirect Employment: Multinational Enterprises in Northern Mexico', in Bailey, P. Parisotto, A. and Renshaw, G. (eds) *Multinationals and Employment*, Geneva: ILO.

Fukasaku, K. (1992) 'Economic Regionalisation and Intra-Industry Trade: Pacific-Asian Perspectives', *OECD Development Centre Technical Paper* no. 53, February, Paris: OECD.

Fukasaku, K., and Lecomte, H.B.S. (1996) 'Transition économique et réforme de la politique commerciale en Chine', *Revue d'Economie du Développement*, June.

Garnaut, R. (1998) 'ASEAN and the Regionalisation and Globalisation of World Trade', *ASEAN Economic Bulletin*, March.

Garnaut, R. and Song, L. (2002) *China 2002: WTO Entry and World Recession*, Canberra: Asia Pacific Press at the Australian National University.

Ghose, A.K. (2000) 'Trade Liberalization and Manufacturing Employment, *International Labour Office (ILO) Employment Paper* 2000/3, Geneva: ILO.

Gilbert, J. and Wahl, T. (2002a) 'Applied General Equilibrium Assessments of Trade Liberalization in China', *World Economy*, 25, 5, May.

—— (2002b) *Labour Mobility and China's WTO Accession Package: An Applied General Equilibrium Assessment*, Department of Economics, Utah State University, mimeo.

Gill, B. (1999) 'Limited Engagement', *Foreign Affairs*, July–August.

Gilley, Bruce (2000) 'Integrity Test', *Far Eastern Economic Review*, 23 March.

Goad, G.P. (2000) 'Turning Point – WTO Entry Signals a Seminal Shift in Chinese Thinking About the Country's Economic Future', *Far Eastern Economic Review*, 31 August.

Goodkind, D.M. and West, L.A. (2001) *'China's Floating Population – Definitions, Estimates, and Implications for Urbanization'*, paper prepared for a Conference on Urbanization in China: Strategies for Growth and Development, Xiamen, China, 27–28 June.

Goodman, D. (ed.) (1997) *China's Provinces in Reform: Class, Community and Political Culture*, London: Routledge.

Groomridge, M.A., and Barfield, C.E. (1999) *Tiger by the Tail: China and the WTO*, Washington DC: American Enterprise Institute.

Gu, E.X. (1999) 'From Permanent Employment to Massive Lay-offs: The Political Economy of Transitional Unemployment in Urban China, *Economy and Society*, 28.

Guo, Yan (2000) 'WTO Entry: More Benefit or Detriment?', *Beijing Review*, 27 March.

Han, D. (2000) *Pengzhuang: quanqiuhua xianjing he zhongguo xianshi xuanze* (Globalization Trap and China's Realistic Choice), Beijing: Economic Management Press.

Hare, Paul (2000) 'WTO Entry and Impacts on Russia and Eastern Europe – Lessons for China', *Discussion Paper, School of Management*, Heriot-Watt University, Edinburgh, UK.

Harrold, P. (1995) 'China: Foreign Trade Reform: Now for the Hard Part', *Oxford Review of Economic Policy*, 11, 4, Winter.

Harwit, E. (1994) *China's Automobile Industry: Policies, Problems and Prospects*, London: M.E. Sharpe.

—— (2001) 'The Impact of WTO Membership on the Automobile Industry in China', *China Quarterly*, 167, September.

Hay, D. and Liu, G.S. (1997) 'The Efficiency of Firms: What Difference Does Competition Make?', *Economic Journal*, 107, 442, May.

Hay, D., Morris, D., Liu, G. and Yao, S. (1994) *Economic Reform and State-owned Enterprise in China*, 1979–1987, Oxford: Clarendon Press

He, L. (2002) 'The Banking and Securities Sector', in Holbig, H. and Ash, R. (eds) *China's Accession to the World Trade Organization*, London: RoutledgeCurzon.

Holbig, H. and Ash, R. (2002) (eds) *China's Accession to the World Trade Organization*, London: RoutledgeCurzon.

Holland, Tom (2000) 'The Day of the *Renminbi*', *Far Eastern Economic Review*, 30 November.

Hoong (2001) *New China Rising: A Social Economic Assessment of WTO Entry*, New York: Writer's Showcase.

Houben, H. (1999) 'China's Economic Reform and Integration Into the World Trading System', *Journal of World Trade*, June.

'How Far is China Behind the World in the Auto Industry?' (2000) *Beijing Review*, 14 August.

Hu, A. (1998) *Jiuye yu fazhan: Zhongguo shiye wenti yu jiuye zhanlue* (Employment and Development: China's Unemployment Problem and Employment Strategy), Shenyang: Liaoning renmin chubanshe.

—— (1999a) 'Current State, Short-Term Prospect and Long-Term Trend of Economic Growth in China', *Strategy and Management*, 3, 1999 (in Chinese).

—— (1999b) *The Biggest Challenge in the New Century: China Enters a Period of High Unemployment*, Beijing: Chinese Academy of Social Sciences (unpublished).

—— (2000) 'High Unemployment in China: Estimates and Policies', a paper presented at the *International Conference on Centre-Periphery Relations in China: Integration, Disintegration or Reshaping of an Empire?*, The French Centre for Contemporary China and the Chinese University of Hong Kong, Hong Kong, 25 March 2000.

—— (2001) 'Creative Destruction of Restructuring: China's Urban Unemployment and Social Safety', in Lee, K.T., Lin, J.Y. and Kim, S.J. (eds) *China's Integration with the World Economy: Repercussions of China's Accession to the WTO*, Seoul: Korea Institute for International Economic Policy.

Hua, Sheng Bao (2000) *China's Floating Population Will Increase by Five Million Each Year*, Shanghai Jiefang Ribao internet version translated in FBIS Document No. CPP20000928000018.

Huang, J. and Chen, C. (1999) *Effects of Trade Liberalization on Agriculture in China: Institutional and Structural Aspects*, UNESCAP/CGPRT Centre, Bogor, Indonesia.

Huang, J. and Rozelle, S. (1999) '*Reform, Trade Liberalization and their Impacts on China's Agriculture*', paper presented at the Symposium on China's Agricultural Trade Policy: Issues, Analysis and Global Consequences, San Francisco, 25–26 June.

—— (2002) '*Distortion at the Border: Integration Inland: Assessing the Effect of the WTO Accession on China's Agriculture*', paper presented at the World Bank meeting on the Impact of Accession into WTO on China, July.

Huang, Yasheng (2003) *Selling China: Foreign Direct Investment During the Reform Era*, New York: Cambridge University Press.

Huang, Y., Woo, W.T. and Duncan, R. (1999) 'Understanding the Decline of China's State Sector', *MOCT-MOST Economic Policy in Transitional Economies*, 9, 1.

Hufbauer, G.C. and Rosen, D.H. (2000) 'Permanent National Trading Relations with China', *International Economics Policy Briefs* no. 00–3, Washington DC: Institute for International Economics, April.

Ianchovichina, E., Martin, W. and Fukase, E. (2000) *Assessing the Implications of Merchandise Trade Liberalization in China's Accession to WTO*, paper for presentation to the Roundtable on China's Accession to the WTO sponsored by the Chinese Economic Society and the World Bank, July 8, 2000, Pudong, Shanghai and for the World Bank Institute Training Seminar in Beijing, July 10–11.

International Institute for Management Development (IMD) (2000) *World Competitiveness Yearbook*, Lausanne: IMD.

International Monetary Fund (IMF) (2000) *World Economic Outlook*, Washington DC: IMF, October.

Jacobson, H.K. and Oksenberg, M. (1990) *China's Participation in the IMF, the World Bank and GATT*, Seattle: University of Washington Press.

Jefferson, G.H. and Rawski, T.G. (1994) 'Enterprise Reform in Chinese Industry', *Journal of Economic Perspectives*, 8, 2.

Jefferson, G.H. and Rawski, T.G. (1995) 'How Industrial Reform Worked in China: The Role of Innovation, Competition, and Property Rights', *Proceedings of the World Bank Annual Conference on Development Economics 1994*, Washington DC: World Bank.

Jefferson, G.H. and Singh, I.J. (eds) (1999) *Enterprise Reform in China: Ownership, Transition and Performance*, New York: Oxford University Press.

Jefferson, G.H., Rawski, T.G. and Zheng, Y. (1994) 'Institutional Change and Industrial Innovation in Transitional Economies', *Journal of Asian Economics*, 5, 4.

Jiang, Tingsong (2002) 'WTO Accession and Regional Incomes', in Garnaut, R. and Song, L., *China 2002: WTO Entry and World Recession*, Canberra: Asia Pacific Press at the Australian National University.

Jiao, J. (2000) *WTO and the Future of China's Financial Industry,* Beijing: China Financial Publishing House.

Johnston, F. and Li, H. (2002) 'Estimating China's Urban Unemployment Rate: Background, Mechanics and an Alternative', *Journal of Contemporary China*, 111, 31, May.

Jones, R.W. and Kenen, P.B. (eds) (1984) *Handbook of International Economics*, vol. 1, Amsterdam: North-Holland.

Kojima. K (1973) 'Reorganisation of North-South Trade: Japan's Foreign Economic Policy for the 1970s', *Hitotsubashi Journal of Economics*, 13, 2, February.

—— (1985) 'Japanese and American Direct Investment in Asia: A Comparative Analysis', *Hitotsubashi Journal of Economics*, 26, June.

—— (2000) 'The "Flying Geese" Model of Asian Economic Development: Origin, Theoretical Extensions, and Regional Policy Implications', *Journal of Asian Economics*, 11, 4, Winter.

Kong, Qingjiang (2000) 'China's WTO Accession: Commitments and Implications', *Journal of International Economic Law*, December.

Krueger, A.O. (1984) 'Trade Policies in Developing Countries', in Jones, R.W. and Kenen P.B., (eds) *Handbook of International Economics*, vol. 1, Amsterdam: North-Holland.

Krueger, A.O., Lary, H.B., Monson, T.D., and Akrasanee, N. (eds) (1981) *Trade and Employment in Developing Countries,* vol. I: *Individual Studies,* Chicago: University of Chicago Press.

Krugman, P. (1994) 'Competitiveness: A Dangerous Obsession', *Foreign Affairs*, 73, 4, March–April.

—— (1996) 'Making Sense of the Competitiveness Debate', *Oxford Review of Economic Policy*, 12, 3.

Krugman, P. and Lawrence, R. (1994) 'Trade, Jobs and Wages', *Scientific American*, April.

Kueh, Y.Y. (1996) 'Foreign Investment and Economic Change in China', in Ash, R.F. and Kueh, Y.Y. (eds) *The Chinese Economy Under Deng Xiaoping*, Oxford: Clarendon Press.

Lai, Hongyi Harry (2001) 'Behind China's World Trade Organization Agreement with the USA', *Third World Quarterly*, 22, 2, April.

Lall, S. (2001a) *Competitiveness, Technology and Skills*, Cheltenham: Edward Elgar.

—— (2001b) 'Competitiveness Indices and Developing Countries: An Economic Evaluation of the Global Competitiveness Report', *World Development*, 29, 9.

Langlois, J.D., Jr. (2001) 'The WTO and China's Financial System', *China Quarterly*, 167, September.

Lardy, N.R. (1992) *Foreign Trade and Economic Reform in China, 1978–1990*, Cambridge: Cambridge University Press.

—— (1994) *China in the World Economy*, Washington DC: Institute for International Economics.

—— (1996) 'China's Foreign Trade', in Ash, R.F. and Kueh, Y.Y. (eds) *The Chinese Economy under Deng Xiaoping*, Oxford: Clarendon Press.

—— (1998) *China's Unfinished Economic Revolution*, Washington DC: Brookings.

—— (1999) 'China's WTO Membership', *Policy Brief no. 47*, Washington DC: Brookings, April.

—— (2000) 'Permanent Normal Trade Relations for China', *Policy Brief no. 58*, Washington DC: Brookings, May.

—— (2002) *Integrating China into the Global Economy*, Washington DC: Brookings.

Laurenceson, James and Chai, J.C.H. (2000) 'The Economic Performance of China's State-owned Industrial Enterprises', *Journal of Contemporary China*, 9, 23, March.

Lee, Hong Yung (2000) '*Xiagang*, the Chinese Style of Laying off Workers', *Asian Survey'*, XL (6), November–December.

Leggett, K. (1998) 'China's State Banks Fortify Control on the Yuan Market', *Wall Street Journal*, Asia Section, 11 September.

Leonard, Sean (1998) *The Dragon Awakens: China's Long March to Geneva,* London: Cameron, May.

Leung, M-K. (1997) 'Foreign Banks in the People's Republic of China', *Journal of Contemporary China*, 6, 15.

Li, D.D. and Liang, M. (1998) 'Causes of the Soft Budget Constraint: Evidence on Three Explanations', *Journal of Comparative Economics*, March.

Li, Shaomin, Li, Shuhe, and Zhang, Weiying (1999) 'Cross-regional Competition and Privatization in China', *MOCT-MOST Economic Policy in Transitional Economies*, 9, 1.

—— (2000) 'The Road to Capitalism: Competition and Institutional Change in China', *Journal of Comparative Economics*, 28, 2, June.

Liang, Yanfen (2000) 'The Impact on China's Enterprises of Joining the WTO', *The Chinese Economy*, Special Issue on China and the WTO, Part II, 33, 2, March–April.

Lim, L.L., Sziraczki, G. and Zhang, X. (1996) 'Economic Performance, Labour Surplus and Enterprise Responses: Results From the Chinese Enterprise Survey', *ILO Labour Market Papers* no. 13, Geneva: Employment Department.

Lin, J.Y. (2000a) 'WTO Accession and China's Agriculture', *China Economic Review*, 11, 4.

—— (2001b) 'WTO Accession and Financial Market Reform in China', *Cato Journal*, 21, 1, Spring-Summer.

—— (2001c) 'WTO Accession and China's SOE Reform', in Lee, K.T., Lin, J.Y. and Kim, S.J. (eds) *China's Integration with the World Economy: Repercussions of China's Accession to the WTO*, Seoul: Korea Institute for International Economic Policy.

Lin, J.Y., Cai, F. and Li, Zhou (1996) *The China Miracle: Development Strategy and Economic Reform*, Hong Kong: Chinese University Press.

Liu, Guy (1996) 'Price Changes in Economic Transition', *Discussion Paper*, School of Economics, Middlesex University, London.

—— (1998) *The Pricing Behaviour of Chinese State Enterprises 1980–91, Theory and Evidence*, D. Phil Dissertation, University of Oxford.

—— (1999) *'Privatisation or Competition? A Lesson Learnt from Chinese Enterprise Reform'*, Economics Department, Brunel University, Draft.

—— (2001) 'China's WTO Accession and the Impact on its Large Manufacturing Enterprises', *East Asia Institute Occasional Papers/Contemporary China Series no. 30*, World Scientific Publishing Co. and Singapore University Press.

Liu, G.S. and Garino, G. (2001) 'Privatization or Competition: A Lesson Learnt from the Chinese Enterprise Reform', *Economics of Planning*, 34, 1–2, Autumn.

Liu, G.S. and Woo, W.T. (2001) 'How Will Ownership in China's Industrial Sector Evolve with WTO Accession', *China Economic Review*, 12, 2–3.

Liu, G.S. and Zhao, X. (2000) 'Developing an Efficient Exit System for Failed Enterprises in the Economy: A Key Issue of Enterprise Reform in China', *Journal of Modern Enterprise Herald*, Centre for Development Research of the State Council, China, February.

Lo, D. (1996) *Market and Institutional Regulation in Chinese Industrialization, 1978–94*, London: Macmillan.

Lo, D. and Chan, T.M.H. (1996) 'Machinery and China's Growth-Exports Nexus', *School of Oriental and African Studies (SOAS) Department of Economics, Working Paper Series* no. 64, London: SOAS.

Long, Yongtu (2000a) 'On Question of Our Joining the WTO', *The Chinese Economy*, Special Issue on China and the WTO, Part 1, 33, 1, January–February.

—— (2000b) 'On the Question of Economic Globalization', *The Chinese Economy*, Special Issue on China and the WTO, Part 1, 33, 1, January–February.

—— (ed.) (2002) *Rushi Yu Nongchan Pin Shichang Kai Fang* (WTO Accession and Liberalization of Agricultural Markets), Beijing: China Foreign Economic and Trade Press.

Lu, Ding (2000) 'Beefing Up For Competition: China's Telecom Industry on the Eve of WTO Entry', *EAI Working Paper no. 63*, Singapore, 24 November.

Lutz, J.M. and Kihl, Y.W. (1990) 'The NICs, Shifting Comparative Advantage, and the Product Cycle', *Journal of World Trade*, 24.

Lydall, H. (1975) *Trade and Employment*, Geneva: ILO.

Ma, Xiaohe and Lan, Haitao (2002) 'Research on Agricultural Subsidy After WTO Accession', *Guide to Agricultural Economics*, 10.

Ma, Jun and Wang, Zhi (2001) 'Winners and Losers of China's WTO Entry', *China Business Review*, March–April.

MacDougall, G.D.A. (1951) 'British and American Exports: A Study Suggested by the Theory of Comparative Costs', Part I, *Economic Journal*, LXI, December.

Maddison, A. (1998) *Chinese Economic Performance in the Long Run*, Paris: OECD Development Centre.

Mai, Yinhua (2000) 'China's WTO Entry: The Impact on the SOE Sector', *EAI Working Paper no. 54*, Singapore, September.

Martin, W. (2002) 'Implication of Reform and WTO Accession for China's Agricultural Policies', *Economies in Transition* (forthcoming).

Martin, W., Dimaranana, B. and Hertel, T. (2000) *Trade Policy, Structural Change and China's Trade Growth*, World Bank and Purdue University, processed.

Martin, W. and Ianchovichina, E. (2001) 'Implications of China's Accession to the World Trade Organisation for China and the WTO', *World Economy*, 24, 9, September.

Marukawa, T. (1995) 'Industrial Groups and Divisions of Labour in China's Automobile Industry', *Developing Economies*, 23, 3.

Mastel, Greg (1997) *The Rise of the Chinese Economy: The Middle Kingdom Emerges*, Armonk, NY: Sharpe.

Mazumdar, D. (1993) 'Labour Markets and Adjustment in Open Asian Economies: The Republic of Korea and Malaysia', *World Bank Economic Review*, 7, 1.

Mazumdar, D. and Basu, P. (1997) 'Macroeconomic Policies, Growth and Employment: The East and South-East Asian Experience', in Khan, A.R. and Muqtada, M. (eds) *Employment Expansion and Macroeconomic Stability under Increasing Globalization*, London: Macmillan.

McDonnell, J.E.D. (1987) 'China's Move to Rejoin the GATT System: An Epic Transition', *World Economy*, 10, 3, September.

McKibbin, W.J. and Tang, K.K. (2000) 'Trade and Financial Reform in China: Impacts on the World Economy', *World Economy*, August.

McMichael, P. (2000) 'A Global Interpretation of the Rise of the East Asian Food Import Complex', *World Development*, March.

McMillan, J. and Naughton, B. (1993) 'How to Reform a Planned Economy: Lessons from China', *Oxford Review of Economic Policy*, 8, 1, Spring.

Miner, W. (1996) 'China and the GATT/WTO: Agriculture', in Cai, Wenguo, Smith, Murray and Xu Xianquan, *China and its World Trade Organization: Requirement, Realities, and Resolution*, Ottawa: Centre for Trade Policy and Law.

Miner, W. (1998) 'China in the World Trading System: Agriculture and Agricultural Trade', in Abbott, F.M. (ed.) *China in the World Trading System*, The Hague: Kluwer Law International.

Miyanori, Yoshika (2001) 'Deepening Trade Relations Between Japan and China', *Asia Monthly*, August.

Mo, T. (1999) *Jiaru Shimao Yiwei Zhe Shenme? (What Does it Mean after WTO Accession?)*, Beijing: Chinese City Publishing House, in Chinese.

Mody, A. and Wheeler, D. (1990) *Automation and World Competition*, London: Macmillan.

Moreno, R. and Trehan, B. (1997) 'Location and the Growth of Nations', *Journal of Economic Growth*, 2.

Nakagane, K. (1999) 'The Workings of Unemployment in China', *Perspectives Chinois*, September–October.

Naughton, Barry (2000) 'How Much Can Regional Integration Do to Unify China's Markets?', *Working Paper no. 58*, Centre for Research on Economic Development and Policy Reform, Stanford University, August.

—— (2001) 'Provincial Economic Growth in China: Causes and Consequences of Regional Differentiation', in Renard, M.F. (ed.) *China and Its Regions: Economic Growth and Reform in Chinese Provinces*, Cheltenham: Edward Elgar.

Ng, F. and Yeats, A. (1999) 'Production Sharing in East Asia: Who Does What For Whom, and Why? *World Bank Policy Research Working Paper no. 2197*, Washington DC: World Bank.

Niu, R. (1999) *Kuoda Jiuye shi Shehui Jingji Fazhan zhongde Dawenti* (Increase in Employment is a Big Issue in Social Economic Development), *People's Daily*, 26 January (in Chinese).

Nolan, P. (2001a) *China and the Global Economy*, London: Palgrave.

—— (2001b) *China and the Global Business Revolution*, London: Palgrave.

—— (2002) 'China and the WTO: The Challenge for China's Large-scale Industry', in Holbig, H. and Ash, R. (eds) *China's Accession to the World Trade Organization*, London: RoutledgeCurzon.

OECD (2001) *China's Agriculture in the International Trading System*: Proceedings of a Workshop, Paris: OECD.

—— (2002) *China in the World Economy: the Domestic Policy Challenges*, Paris: OECD.

Ozawa, T. (1996) 'Professor Kojima's Trade Augmentation Principle and Flying-Geese Paradigm of Tandem Growth', *Surugadai Economic Studies*, 5.

—— (2000) 'The Flying-Geese Paradigm: Toward a Co-Evolutionary Theory of MNC-assisted Growth', in Fatemi, K. (ed.) *The New World Order: Internationalism, Regionalism, and the Multinational Corporations*, Amsterdam: Pergamon.

—— (2001) 'The 'Hidden Side of the 'Flying-Geese' Catch-Up Model: Japan's Dirigiste Institutional Set-up and a Deepening Financial Morass, *Journal of Asian Economics*, 12, 4, January.

Panagariya, A. (1993) 'Unravelling the Mysteries of China's Foreign Trade Regime', *World Economy*, 16, 1, January.

Panchamukhi, V.R. (1992) 'South-South Cooperation in South, South-East and East Asia: A Perspective', *Research and Information System for the Non-aligned and Other Developing Countries (RIS) Discussion Paper*, New Delhi, June.

Park, Albert (2001) 'Trade Integration and the Prospects for Rural Enterprise Development in China', in OECD, *China's Agriculture in the International Trading System,* Paris: OECD.

People's Daily (Beijing) (in Chinese), various issues.

Perkins, D.H. and Syrquin, M. (1989) 'Large Countries: The Influence of Size', in Chenery, H.B. and Srinivasan, T.N. (eds) *Handbook of Development Economics*, vol. II, Amsterdam: North-Holland.

Perkins, F.C. (1999) 'The Costs of China's Stateowned Enterprises', *MOCT-MOST Economic Policy in Transitional Economies*, 9, 1.

Petri, P. A. (1997) 'AFTA and the Global Track', *ASEAN Economic Bulletin*', November.

Pilat, D. (1997) 'Regulation and Performance in the Distribution Sector', *OECD Economics Department Working Papers* no. 180, Paris: OECD.

Poncet, S. (2002a) 'L'évolution de l'intégration interne et internationale des provinces chinoises', *Revue Economique*, 53, 3, May.

—— (2002b) 'Fragmented China: Measure and Determinants of Chinese Domestic Market Disintegration', *Working Paper, Centre d'Etudes et de Recherches sur le Développement International* (CERDI), Clermond-Ferrand, France.

Porter, M.E. (ed.) (1986) *Competition in Global Industries*, Boston: Harvard Business School Press.

—— (1990) *The Competitive Advantage of Nations*, London: Macmillan.

—— (2000) 'The Current Competitiveness Index: Measuring the Microeconomic Foundations of Prosperity', in World Economic Forum (WEF) and Porter, M., Sachs, J., Warner, D., Cornelius, A.M., Levinson, P.K. and Schwab, K. (eds) *The Global Competitiveness Report 2000*, New York: Oxford University Press.

Porter, M.E. and Stern, S. (1999) *The New Challenge to America's Prosperity: Findings from the Innovation Index*, Washington DC: Council on Competitiveness.

Posth, Martin (2002) 'The Automobile Sector', in Holbig and Ash, op. cit.

Powell, B. (2001) 'China's Great Step Forward', *Fortune*, September.

Probst, Hans-Jörg (2002) 'The Insurance Sector', in Holbig H. and Ash, R. (eds) *China's Accession to the World Trade Organization*, London: RoutledgeCurzon.

Rana, P.B. (1990) 'Shifting Comparative Advantage among Asian and Pacific Countries', *International Trade Journal*, 4.

Rao, V.L. and Das, R.U. (1995) 'Comparative Advantage and Pattern of Trade in Asia', in Panchamukhi, V.R. and Sobhan, R. (eds) *Towards an Asian Economic Area*, New Delhi: Macmillan.

Rawski, T.G. (1999) 'China: Prospects for Full Employment', *ILO Employment and Training Papers* No. 47, Geneva: ILO.

—— (2002) *'Recent Developments in China's Labour Economy'*, Department of Economics, University of Pittsburgh, mimeo.

Rawski, T.G. and R. Mead (1998) 'On the Trail of China's Phantom Farmers', *World Development*, 26, 5.

Rosen, Daniel H. (1999a) *Behind the Open Door: Foreign Enterprises in the Chinese Marketplace*, Washington DC: Institute for International Economics.

—— (1999b) 'China and the World Trade Organization: An Economic Balance Sheet', *International Economics Policy Briefs* no. 99–6, Washington DC: Institute for International Economics, June.

Rowthorn, R. (1996) 'East Asian Development: The Flying-Geese Paradigm Reconsidered', *Study No. 8 of East Asian Development: Lessons for a New Global Environment,* Geneva: UNCTAD.

Sachs, J. and Woo, W.T. (1994) 'Reform in China and Russia', *Economic Policy*, 18, April.

Satchit, B. (1999) 'China's Long March to the WTO', *Journal of East-West Business*, 4, 4.

Sauvé, P. (2000) 'Developing Countries and the GATS 2000 Round', *Journal of World Trade*, April.

Saywell, T. and Yan, Z. (2000) 'Ready for the Deluge', *Far Eastern Economic Review*, 23 March.

Schéller, Margot (2002) 'The Impact of China's WTO Accession on International Trade and Capital Flows', in Holbig H. and Ash, R. (eds) *China's Accession to the World Trade Organization*, London: RoutledgeCurzon.

Shafaeddin, M. (2002) 'The Impact of China's Accession to WTO on the Exports of Developing Countries', *UNCTAD Discussion Paper no. 160,* Geneva: UNCTAD.

Shen, Yiming (2000) 'China's Insurance Market: Opportunity, Competition and Market Trends', *Geneva Papers on Risk and Insurance*, 25, 3, July.

Shi, Yizhi (2001) *WTO Yu Zhongguo Fangzhi Gongye* (*WTO and China's Textile Industry*), Beijing: China's Textile Industry Publishing House, in Chinese.

Shinohara, M. (1996) 'The Flying Geese Model Revisited: Foreign Direct Investment, Trade in Machinery and the Boomerang Effect', *Journal of the Asia Pacific Economy*, 1.

Smith, P.J. (1999) 'Are Weak Patent Rights a Barrier to U.S. Exports?', *Journal of International Economics*, June.

Smith, S. (1993) 'Review of Michael E. Porter's "Competitive Advantage of Nations"', *Journal of Development Economics*, 40, 2, April.

Solinger, D. (1999) *Contesting Citizenship in Urban China*, Berkeley: University of California Press.

—— (2001) 'Why We Cannot Count the Unemployed', *China Quarterly*, 167.

Spinanger, D. (1984) 'Objectives and Impact of Economic Activity Zones: Some Evidence from Asia', *Weltwirtschaftliches Archiv*, 20, 1.

State Economic and Trade Commission (China) (SETC) (1999) *Jiaru WTO dui Woguo Gongmao Lingyu Zhuyao Hangye de Yingxiang yu Duice Yanjiu.* (Research on the Impact of the WTO Accession on Our Countries' Major Industries in Industrial and Trade Areas and Measures to be Taken) (mimeo). (Internal Report) (in Chinese).

State Economic and Trade Commission (China) (SETC) (2000) *Rushi hou de Zhongguo Gongye.* (*Assessment of China's Industry After WTO Accession*) (mimeo). (Internal Report) (in Chinese).

Sun, H. (1998) *Foreign Investment and Economic Development in China*, Aldershot: Ashgate.

Sun, H. and Parikh, A. (2001) 'Exports, Inward Foreign Direct Investment and Regional Economic Growth in China', *Regional Studies*, 35, 3.

Sun, Zhenyuan (2000) 'The Challenges that China Will Face with Regard to Its Agricultural Policies after Joining the WTO', *The Chinese Economy*, Special Issue on China and the WTO, Part II, 33, 2.

Thun, E. (1999) *Changing Lanes in China: Industrial Development in a Transitional Economy*, Ph.D. Dissertation, Department of Government, Harvard University.

Tuan, F.C. and Cheng, G. (1999) '*A Review of China's Agricultural Trade Policy*', paper presented at the IATRC Summer Meeting on China's Agricultural Trade and Policy: Issues, Analysis, and Global Consequences, San Francisco, 25–26 June (http://aic.ucdavis.edu/research).

UNCTAD (1994) *World Investment Report – Transnational Corporations, Employment and the Workplace*, Geneva: UNCTAD.

—— (2000) *Trade and Development Report 2000*, Geneva: UNCTAD.

—— (2001*) Handbook of Statistics*, Geneva: UNCTAD.

—— (2002) *Trade and Development Report 2002 – Developing Countries in World Trade*, Geneva: UNCTAD.

United States International Trade Commission (1999) *Assessment of the Economic Effects on the United States of China's Accession to the WTO*, Publication no. 3229, Washington DC: USITC.

Vernon, R. (1966) 'International Investment and International Trade in Product Cycle', *Quarterly Journal of Economics*, 80.

Voon, Jan P. (1998) 'Export Competitiveness of China and ASEAN in the US Market', *ASEAN Economic Bulletin*, March.

Wall, D. and Yin, X. (1997) 'Technology Development and Export Performance: is China a Frog or a Goose?', in Feinstein, C. and Howe, C. (eds), *Chinese Technology Transfer in the 1990s: Current Experience, Historical Problems and International Perspectives*, Cheltenham: Edward Elgar.

Walmsley, T.L. and Hertel, T.W. (2001) 'China's Accession to the WTO: Timing is Everything', *World Economy*, 24.

Wang, Luolin (2000) 'If China's Services Industry Is to Be Successful in Opening Up to the Outside World, It Must First Succeed in Handling Several Relationships Correctly', *The Chinese Economy*, Special Issue on China and the WTO, Part II, 33, 2.

Wang, Shaoguang (2000) 'The Social and Political Implications of China's WTO Membership', *Journal of Contemporary China*, 9.

Wang, Shaoguang and Hu, Angang (1999) *The Political Economy of Uneven Development: The Case of China,* Armonk, NY: M.E. Sharpe.

Wang, Xiaolu (2002) 'The WTO Challenge to Agriculture', in Garnaut, R. and Song, L., *China 2002: WTO Entry and World Recession*, Canberra: Asia Pacific Press at the Australian National University.

Wang, Zhi (1999) 'The Impact of China's WTO Entry on the World Labour-intensive Export Market: A Recursive Dynamic CGE Analysis', *World Economy*, 22, 3, May.

Wang Zhi and Zhai Fan (1998) 'Tariff Reduction, Tax Replacement, and Implications for Income Distribution in China', *Journal of Comparative Economics*, 26.

Wang, Zhi and Jun Ma (2000) *The Economic Impact of China's WTO Accession on the World Economy*, Hong Kong: Deutsche Bank.

Warr, P.G. (1994) 'Comparative and Competitive Advantage', *Asian-Pacific Economic Literature*, 8, 2.

Watanabe, T. and Kajiwara, H. (1983) 'Pacific Manufactured Trade and Japan's Options', *Developing Economies*, 21.

Wei, Ge (2001) 'Financial Sector Restructuring and Capital Account Management in China – Some Lessons for Economic Integration', paper presented at an UNCTAD Workshop on Management of Capital Flows: Comparative Experiences and Implications for Africa, Geneva: UNCTAD.

Wen, Mei (2002) 'Competition, Ownership Diversification and Industrial Growth', in Garnaut, R. and Song, L., *China 2002: WTO Entry and World Recession*, Canberra: Asia Pacific Press at the Australian National University.

Wen, Tiejun (1999) 'Zhong-Mei WTO tanpan zhong nongye tiaokuan dui woguo de yingxiang' (The Impact that the Terms in WTO Negotiations between China and the United States Involving Agriculture Will Have on Our Country', *Nongcun jingji daokan*, 6, June.

—— (2000) *WTO yuanzhe dui woguo nongye ji qita fangmian di yingxiang* (The Impacts of the WTO Membership on our Agriculture), Beijing: Ministry of Agriculture, unpublished manuscript.

Wilson, P. and Wong, Y.M. (1999) 'The Export Competitiveness of ASEAN Economies, 1986–1995', *ASEAN Economic Bulletin*, August.

Wong, J. (2001) 'China's Banking Reform and Financial Liberalization', *Review of Asia and Pacific Studies*, 22 (December).

Wong, J. and Wong, C.K. (2003) 'China's Telecom Industry: Poised to Grow After WTO', in Yao, S. and Liu, X. (eds) *Sustaining China's Economic Growth in the Twenty-first Century,* London: RoutledgeCurzon.

Wonnacott, Paul (1996) 'The Automotive Industry in Southeast Asia: Can Protection Be Made Less Costly?', *World Economy*, 19, 1.

Woo, W.T. (2001) 'Recent Claims of China's Economic Exceptionalism: Reflections Inspired by WTO Accession', *China Economic Review*, 12, 2 and 3.

Woo, W.T. and Ren, R. (2002) 'Employment, Wages and Income Inequality in the Internationalization of China's Economy', *ILO Employment Papers no. 2002/39*, Geneva: ILO.

Wood, A. (1994) *North-South Trade, Employment and Inequality*, Oxford: Clarendon Press.

World Bank (1996) *The Chinese Economy: Fighting Inflation, Deepening Reforms*, Washington DC: World Bank.

World Bank (1997) *China 2020: China Engaged*, Integration with the Global Economy, Washington DC: World Bank.

World Economic Forum (WEF) (2000) Porter, M., Sachs, J. Warner, D. Cornelius, A.M., Levinson, P.K. and Schwab, K. (eds) *The Global Competitiveness Report 2000*, New York: Oxford University Press.

World Trade Organization (WTO) (2001a) *Working Party on the Accession of China – Draft Report of the Working Party on the Accession of China to the WTO*-Revision, 12 July (WT/ACC/SPEC/CHN/1/Rev.7), Geneva: WTO.

—— (2001b) *Protocol of Accession of the People's Republic of China, Decision of 10 November 2001* (available online at: http//www.moftec.gv.cn).

Wu, M. (2000) *Wo guo shangye yinhang ru shi hou mianlin de xingshi ji duice* (Form and Policies Faced by Our Country's Banks after Entrance to the WTO, *Guoyan*, 19 and 23 October.

Wu, Y. (ed.) (1999) *FDI and Economic Growth in China*, Aldershot: Edward Elgar.

Xie, Ping (2001) *Reforming Banking System and Perfecting Capital Market* (unpublished manuscript).

Xu, D. and Chang, G.H. (2000) 'The Impact of Tariff Reductions on Structural Unemployment in China: A Computable General Equilibrium Analysis', *Pacific Economic Review*, 5, 2, June.

Yamamoto, H. (2000) 'Marketization of the Chinese Economy and Reform of the Grain Distribution System', *Developing Economies*, March.

Yamazawa, I., Hirata, A., and Yokota, K. (1991) 'Evolving Pattern of Comparative Advantage in the Pacific Economies', in Ariff, M. (ed.), *The Pacific Economy: Growth and External Stability*, London: Allen and Unwin.

Yang, Dong (1999) *Rushi Dui Zhongguo Qiche Gongye de Yingxiang* (The Impact of the WTO Accession on China's Auto Industry), in *China's Auto Market Almanac 1999*, Beijing, in Chinese.

Yang, M. and Tam, C.H. (1999) '*Xiagang:* The Chinese Way of Reducing Labour Redundancy and Reforming State-owned Enterprises', *East Asia Institute (EAI) Background Brief*, no. 38, Singapore: East Asia Institute, 20 July.

Yang, Q. (2000) *Zhongguo Duiwai Maoyi yu Jingji Zengzhang* (China Foreign Trade and Economic Growth), Beijing: China Economic Publishing House, in Chinese.

Yang, Yiyong (1998) *Shiye Chongjibo: Zhongguo Jiuye Baogao* (The Impact of a Wave of Unemployment: Chinese Employment Development Report), Beijing: Jinri Publishing House, in Chinese.

Yang, Yongzheng (1996) 'China's WTO Membership: What is At Stake?', *World Economy*, 19, 6.

—— (1999) 'Completing the WTO Accession Negotiations: Issues and Challenges', *World Economy*, 22, 4, June.

—— (2000) 'China's WTO Accession: The Economics and Politics', *Journal of World Trade*, August.

Yang, Y. and Huang, Y. (1997) 'The Impact of Trade Liberalization on Income

Distribution in China', *Economics Division China Economy Working Paper 97/1*, Canberra: Research School of Pacific and Asian Studies, Australian National University.

Yang, Y. and Zhong, C. (1998) 'China's Textile and Clothing Exports in a Changing World Economy', *Developing Economies*, March.

Yang, Y. and Vines, D. (2000) 'The Fallacy of Composition and the Terms of Trade of Newly Industrializing Countries', paper presented at a Seminar in the Department of Economics, University of Oxford, 9 November.

Yildirim, T., Schmitz A. and Furtan, W.H. (eds) (1998) *World Agricultural Trade*, Boulder: Westview Press.

Yoo Jin-Seok (1999) 'China's WTO Accession and Its Impact', in *The Impact of China's WTO Accession on the Korean Economy*, Seoul: Samsung Economic Research Institute.

Yu, Donghui (1999) 'News Background: China's Bid for Resuming its WTO Membership for the Past 13 Years', *China News Service (Zhongguo Xinwenshe)*, 15 November (http://dailynews.sina.com).

Yu, L. and Yu, J. (2001) *Rushi Hou Hangye Zoushi ji Mingyun* (Chinese Industries and Their Future After WTO Accession), Beijing: Economic Daily Publishing House, in Chinese.

Yu, Y., Zheng, B. and Song, H. (2000) *Zhongguo Rushi Yanjiu Baogao: Jingru WTO de Zhongguo Changye* (Research Report on China's Entry into WTO: The Analysis of Chinese Industries), Beijing: Social Sciences Publishing House, in Chinese.

Yu, Z. (2000) *1999 Nian Zhongguo Zhuyao Jiadian Chanpin Chukou Fenxi* (Analysis of Chinese Exports of Major Household Appliances in 1999), *China Appliances*, 4, in Chinese.

Yuan, Zhigang (ed.) (2002) *Zhongguo Jiuye Baogao* (China Employment Report), Beijing: Economic Sciences Press.

Yue, C. and Hua, P. (2002) 'Does Comparative Advantage Explain Export Patterns in China?', *China Economic Review*, 13, 2–3.

Zhai, F. (2000) 'Forecasts of the Automobile Demand', *China Development Review*, 2, 1, Beijing: Development Research Centre of the State Council of People's Republic of China.

Zhai, F. and Li, S. (2000) 'Quantitative Analysis and Evaluation of the Impact of Entry to WTO on China's Economy', *China Development Review*, 3, 2, Beijing: Development Research Centre of the State Council of People's Republic of China.

Zhan, J. (1995) 'Transnationalization and Outward Investment: The Case of Chinese Firms', *Transnational Corporations*, 4, 3, December.

Zhang, Jialin (2000) 'Sino-US Trade Issues After the WTO Deal: a Chinese Perspective', *Journal of Contemporary China*, 9, 24, July.

Zhang, Q. and Felmingham, B. (2001) 'The Relationship Between Inward Direct Foreign Investment and China's Provincial Export Trade', *China Economic Review*, 12, 1.

—— (2002) 'The Role of FDI, Exports and Spillover Effects in the Regional Development of China', *Journal of Development Studies*, 38, 4, April.

Zhang, S., Zhang, Y. and Wan, Z. (1998) *Measuring the Costs of Protection in China*, Washington DC: Institute for International Economics.

Zhang, X. (2000) 'China's Entry to the WTO: a General Equilibrium Analysis of Recent Tariff reductions', in Drysdale, P. and Song, L. (eds) *China's Entry to the WTO: Strategic Issues and Quantitative Assessments*, London: Routledge.

Zhao, H. (1997) 'Foreign Trade in the People's Republic of China: Past Performance and Future Challenges', *Asian Development Review*, 15, 1.

Zhao, Yaohui and Sicular, Terry (2002) 'Effects of WTO Accession on China: Labour Market Responses', *Working Paper*, Centre for Chinese Economic Reform, Peking University, Beijing.

Zhao, Yumin (1996) 'China's GATT/WTO Membership: Implications for China's Textiles Trade', in Cai, Wenguo, Smith, Murray and Xu Xianquan, *China and its World Trade Organization: Requirement, Realities, and Resolution*, Ottawa: Centre for Trade Policy and Law.

Zheng, J., Liu, X. and Bigsten, A. (2001) '*Efficiency, Technical Progress, and Best Practice in Chinese State Enterprises*', Department of Economics, Goteborg University, February.

Zheng, Z. and Zhao, Y. (2002) 'China's Terms of Trade in Manufacturing', *UNCTAD Discussion Paper* no. 161, June, Geneva: UNCTAD.

Zhong, C. and Yang, Y. (2000) 'China's Textile and Clothing Exports in the Post Uruguay Round', in Drysdale, P. and Song, L., *China's Entry to the WTO: Strategic Issues and Quantitative Assessments*, London: Routledge.

Zhongguo Fangzhi Gongye Nianjian (Almanac of China's Textile Industry), Beijing: Textile Press of China, original in Chinese.

Zhongguo Qiche Gongye Nianjian (China Automotive Industry Yearbook), in Chinese.

Zhongguo Haiguan Tongji (China Customs Statistics), in Chinese.

Zhongguo Duiwai Jingji Tongji Nianjian (China Foreign Economic Statistical Yearbook) original in Chinese.

Zhongguo Laodong Tongji Nianjian (China Labour Statistical Yearbook), original in Chinese.

Zhongguo Qigongye Tongji Nianjian (China Light Industry Statistical Yearbook), in Chinese.

Zhongguo Jixie Gongye Nianjian (China Machinery Industry Yearbook), in Chinese.

Zhongguo Jiying Bao (China Business Weekly) (2001), 13 February.

Zhu, Qiwen (1998) 'Private Sector Well Sheltered', *China Daily*, 23 October.

Name index

Subject index